A Writing
Project

D0074435

THE
UNIVERSITY OF WINNIPEG
PORTAGE & BALMORAL
WINNIPEG, MAN. R3B 2E9
CANADA

PE
1404
.D36
1985

A WRITING PROJECT:

*Training
Teachers of
Composition from
Kindergarten
to College*

HARVEY DANIELS
and
STEVEN ZEMELMAN

*Heinemann
Educational
Books
Portsmouth*

HEINEMANN EDUCATIONAL BOOKS INC.
70 Court Street, Portsmouth, New Hampshire 03801
Offices and agents throughout the world

© 1985 by Harvey Daniels and Steven Zemelman. All rights reserved.

First published 1985

LIBRARY OF CONGRESS CATALOGING IN PUBLICATION DATA
Daniels, Harvey A.
  A writing project.

  Bibliography: p.
  Includes index.
  1. English language—Composition and exercises—
Study and teaching. 2. English language—Rhetoric—
Study and teaching. 3. English language—Teacher
training. I. Zemelman, Steven. II. Title.
PE1404.D36 1985   808′.042′07   85-896
ISBN 0-435-08216-7

Printed in the United States of America

Design by Wladislaw Finne
Cover photo by Jasmin Tann
Back cover photo by Bob Tanner

10 9 8 7 6 5 4 3

Contents

Acknowledgments

This book draws upon the energy, ideas, and spirit of the many special people who have given life to the Illinois Writing Project over the past eight years. When we first began as the fledgling Chicago Area Writing Project in 1977, our cofounder and colleague was Betty Jane Wagner of the National College of Education. Since many of our earliest and best ideas were developed in collaboration with B. J., we like to think that her creative and thoughtful influence is threaded throughout this book.

Carl Sears, Curriculum Director of Elmhurst School District 205, was the matchmaker who actually got all the interested parties together in the first place; we proudly claim him as our Godfather. Marilyn Wiencek and Sherrill Crivellone both paused in their teaching careers to work full time as codirectors of the Project; and they have contributed countless ideas to the workshop program described here. Michael Anania, our house poet, has given priceless moments of inspiration to all of us. Anne Malone Trout, our project researcher for four years, created the research design and gathered the fine data reported in chapter 6, something we humanities types could never have done alone.

The bibliography at the back of the book shows where much of our theoretical background comes from, though we'd also like to note our special appreciation for Marty Gliserman, Ed Rocklin, Bob Gundlach, and Greg Baldauf. Over the past year, we've been excited to discover the writings of Richard Bandler and John Grinder, which offer a new, more integrated vision of the work we're doing.

The Illinois Writing Project has enjoyed steady and generous funding over much of its life, allowing us to work and learn and grow without constant hysteria about our survival. For this support, we are indebted to Title IV-C of the Elementary and Secondary Education Act (later Chapter Two of the Educational Consolidation and Improvement Act) and the Illinois Humanities Council. More humanly, we have been fortunate to work with James Mendenhall and Paul Kren of the Illinois State Board of Education and Jane Hood of the Illinois Humanities Council.

Many individuals have offered some special service to the Writing Project or to the preparation of this book. Among these are Terry Shepherd, Don Blattner, Barb Dill, Bruce Bandy, Dagny Bloland, Nancy Sindelar, Rachel Faries, Mary Schneider, Mary Jean Dirksmeyer, Cara Keller, Pete LaForge, John Rohan, Gary Magruder, Carol Lounsbury, Judy Johnstone, Marge Kusterman, Barb Whalen, Mary Scherb, Betty Watkins, Brenda Owen, Walt Kirsch, Marie Bolchazy, Marie Bartolotta, Tom Daniels, Kathy Daniels, and Rick Lane.

The spouses and families of authors are always due condolences for the time lost, opportunities missed, and chores undone as writers go about their endless work. Susan, Elaine, Mark, Daniel, Nicky, and Marny haven't exactly suffered in silence, but that would be out of character. They *have* given us love, encouragement, time, ideas, and samples of their own writing—and they've always agreed, even when they've felt cheated, that the Writing Project is important work. Thanks.

Our single greatest debt is to the hundreds of teachers and school administrators we've worked with over the past seven years. Running the Writing Project has been a constant and powerful reminder that, contrary to ill-informed outbursts in the popular press, American education retains a huge corps of bright, energetic, creative, dedicated teachers who deeply care about children.

Finally, we'd like to thank each other for being such good partners. Too many coauthored books end in collapsed friendship. Happily, this collaboration has brought us closer together, much as the Writing Project workshops nurture caring relationships among teachers. We've had a lot of fun writing this book.

Anyone who'd like to correspond with us can write care of the Illinois Writing Project at Roosevelt University, 430 South Michigan Avenue, Chicago, Illinois 60605.

Chapter

1

Introduction

As we write this book, American schools are in the middle—or, if we turn out to be lucky, toward the end—of something customarily called a "crisis" in literacy. The popular media, many members of the teaching profession, and hordes of disaffected taxpayers seem convinced that today's elementary, secondary, and college students cannot adequately handle the English language, especially as it is written. Without assessing the accuracy of this judgment or reviewing the long history of problems with student literacy, we recognize that this alleged literacy crisis has already spawned a whole array of responses to the perceived weaknesses in students' writing skills.

One of the most constructive of these developments has been the writing project movement. This approach to improving instruction in writing, which was begun in 1973 in Berkeley, concentrated from the beginning on retraining classroom teachers. The founders of the Bay Area Writing Project believed that teachers who were given the opportunity to write, to share their work with colleagues, to study recent composition theory and research, to reexamine their own classroom practice, and to develop their own plans for improved instruction would become more effective writing teachers. This simple and sensible notion turned out to be entirely correct, and with major funding from the National Endowment for the Humanities, BAWP grew apace.

BAWP quickly propagated itself around the country, using modest grants to seed new projects. At the same time, other groups of people began their own writing projects with support from Title IV-C of the Elementary and Secondary Education Act, from state resources, from colleges and universities, or from participating school districts. The authors of this book started one of the Title IV-C groups—the Illinois Writing Project—in 1977 and have been leading its programs since that time. As we write this book—a decade after the writing project movement began—there are more than 100 affiliated sites in what we now call the National Writing Project network; tens of thousands of teachers have been trained and more than four million students have benefited from the work of writing projects.

All of these assorted projects have shared certain common assumptions about writing and about teacher education—though each group has retained a strong local flavor, administrative autonomy, and plenty of charming quirks. It is the purpose of this book to illuminate the common beliefs and procedures of writing projects by offering a detailed description of one program.

The readers of this book, we imagine, will be quite a diverse group. Curriculum directors, English or language arts chairpeople, in-service training coordinators, and other school administrators may find the book useful as they consider departmental or schoolwide efforts to improve writing. Workshop leaders and teacher-trainers—happily, a growing number—may find assistance here as they prepare to train their colleagues. Methods instructors in colleges and universities can use this book with their preservice teachers of English, language arts, and writing. Individual working teachers who have not had the chance to participate in a real-life writing project workshop may give themselves a kind of private, surrogate training with this volume. And even other writing project people may find some amusement here and may enjoy comparing their experiences and methods with ours.

In calling the book *A Writing Project,* we have given ourselves, and perhaps our readers, a couple of problems. First of all, we are implicitly making the unfulfillable promise of capturing the spirit of more than 100 other writing projects spread all over the country. While we obviously can't do justice to each of the worthy idiosyncrasies of our colleagues, we can surely try to provide a true representation of the core values which writing project people share. We think the book is faithful to this more general aim; it tries to reveal the heart of the larger movement as it is manifested in one typical program.

The other problem we've created is to appear guilty of considerable hubris. Any people who write a book about the marvels of their own program are, and ought to be, open to skeptical scrutiny. All we can do about this problem is to deny any intention of sanctifying our own project. We'd be ill-advised to make such an attempt anyway, considering how many people have witnessed our countless errors, shortfalls, slip-ups, miscalculations, embarrassments, cost overruns, and administrative snafus over the past seven years. We also recognize, though unwillingly sometimes, that scores of other writing projects have worked the same magic that we have with teachers and kids.

Still, what we know best is what we have done—and we do know that, despite our own ample margin for error, a gratifying percentage of our teacher-participants have significantly improved their classroom teaching skills and their students have become measurably better writers. Just as importantly, all of the people involved in our training sessions—both the facilitators and the teachers—have enjoyed priceless interludes of caring, trust, support, and renewal. We are excited to have helped several thousand students become better writers. We are even more proud to have helped some individual teachers recommit themselves to a profession which demands so much and rewards so sparingly.

The spread of writing projects around the country has now slowed. National funding has diminished considerably, not just because of the generally adverse economic climate in education, but also because writing projects are no longer sufficiently "new" and "innovative" to entice the support of publicity-conscious funding agencies. However, because writing projects often arouse intense enthusiasm and commitment among their participants, many projects are finding ways to endure and even grow through this difficult passage by relying more heavily on volunteer staff, by affiliating with other institutions, or by charging fees for their services. We like to think this book is part of that growth and renewal process; that in describing one writing project's program it acts both as a summary of what the larger movement has accomplished in the past decade, and as a reminder of how much work remains to be done.

It has often been remarked that American educators are extremely susceptible to fads, quick to embrace any passing panacea, pedagogical or technological. It has less often been noted that we are just as fickle as we are promiscuous; educational innovations, both the insubstantial gimmicks and the ideas of deep significance, are typically abandoned in favor of something fresher and more alluring, often before they've even been adequately tested. The most embarrassing trait of American schools is not their attraction to the new, but their persistent unwillingness to stick with any idea long enough to see whether it works—and if it does, to enjoy its full benefits. Whatever the next wave of change brings to our schools, we should not allow it to sweep away the writing project network, which is a national asset, or to erase our commitment to making all kids writers.

Most books are designed to be read from the front to the back. This time-honored procedure usually saves everyone a lot of trouble, but it may not work for this book.

As you can see, we have decided to present our rationale first, opening with a fairly intricate discussion of our assumptions, beliefs, and purposes for the work that we do. Next comes a detailed, step-by-step description of the activities in our training program for writing teachers. Finally, we present some material which confirms the effectiveness of the program and, by implication, the soundness of the philosophy.

This sequence, it seems to us, observes the standard academic regulations for presenting an innovative program. One begins by describing the context, arguing the need for a change, challenging old assumptions, offering some substitutes, pointing toward a new sort of practice, and promising certain glorious outcomes if the new program is adopted. After all this groundwork has been laid, the innovator next presents the new program in all its splendor, giving a full account of its methods, materials, procedures, and demands upon instructor and instructed alike. Finally, the proposer must adduce some evidence that all this will actually work—proof, ideally, in the form of statistically significant results obtained from a sound experimental research design. Each of these expectations we have tried to fulfill here, and in the prescribed order, but not without some misgivings.

When we lead actual courses, as you will see, we observe quite a different sequence. We find it essential, for example, that participants experience writing activities first and draw conclusions later, rather than receiving lengthy prior explanations about what an activity is supposed to mean or how it confirms some philosophical principle. Even those people we train to be leaders must experience the workshops before studying the philosophy and methodology of workshop-leading; they need to live out the process in order to understand it deeply.

All of which is to say that the reader can attack this book in a number of different ways, depending upon what she needs. If you have been leading workshops on writing, or if you are familiar with recent theory and research on composition, you will probably want to read the philosophy chapter first, so that you can compare your assumptions with ours. If you are someone who's trying to learn about the writing project idea for the first time, or who wants to use the book for surrogate workshop training, you should start with the descriptions of the sessions in Chapter 4. If you are dubious about the whole business, you might want to begin at the end, studying the statistical and anecdotal results of one writing project.

Wherever you start, you will probably find that even the advice we've just given is slightly misleading. The philosophy chapter has a lot of practical material in it, the workshop descriptions often turn philosophical, and even the statistical tables provide some diversion. Our case, our explanation, our narrative develops on many levels, and we have not always tried to compartmentalize it. This book, we realize, is not just a how-to, a research report, or a philosophy, but a record of our own learning. As such, it will never be neat.

Chapter

3

*Assumptions
About Teaching
Writing and
Teaching
Teachers*

I would certainly have boys practice composition and be constantly employed in that exercise. . . . In boys we cannot demand or even hope for finished eloquence; yet there is more virtue in a rich endowment and noble aspirations and a spirit which in its inexperience yearns to reach the unattainable. . . . Let this age then be bold oft-times, inventive too and prone to delight in its own inventions, though they may still be lacking in exactness and clear-cut outline. It is easy to correct exuberance, but barrenness no toil can overcome. . . . This point too is worthwhile to urge, that youthful minds sometimes give way beneath the weight of correction excessively severe, for they become despondent and grieve and in the end conceive a hatred for their studies and, what is worst of all, in their fear of blundering everywhere, attempt nothing.

—Marcus Fabius Quintillian, 91 A.D.

There is no great mystery about teaching writing. If we observe the practice of successful teachers, if we review the ample testimony of professional writers, if we study the empirical and theoretical research on composition done in the past decade, even if we look back to some of the rhetoricians of antiquity, we get the same fundamental advice about instruction in writing. This recurrent set of ideas is sufficiently short and simple to set out in a few lines:

- You learn to write by writing. Practice is essential. Fluency is a worthy goal. Mistakes are inevitable, and evidence learning in progress.
- Writers must begin with what they know and care about, using language close and comfortable to the self. More formal and public modes of prose may be developed out of this expressive base.
- Writers need real audiences and genuine purposes. Writing is communication, not drill.
- Writing is a process, a variable series of steps or stages which moves, with conscious and unconscious recursions, from conception to planning to drafting to revision.
- Writing involves the personal risk of self-disclosure and self-discovery. Teaching writing carries these risks as well.
- Constructive evaluation of writing responds to the author and the message, as well as to the form.
- Writing is important. It is a highly practical and useful skill; more important, it enriches and empowers individual human beings.
- Writing is magic. It partakes of the primitive, deeply felt human need to make and share stories. Writing always holds the opportunity for joy.

13

Instructors who understand, and in some sense practice, all of these ideas invariably make good writing teachers. Those who practice *half* of these ideas usually make fine teachers too. The craft is neither so complex nor so exacting that wholesale adherence to the above list is required. In fact, enacting just the first idea—providing students with much writing practice—is, by itself, an enormously important step toward effective composition teaching.

The above list, then, is the "curriculum" of the Illinois Writing Project, and of the wider writing project movement. Our job, in in-service courses and summer institutes, is to bring these ideas to the attention of teachers who can then incorporate some of them into their work with students. For any reader who has doubts or questions about these essential principles, we will not debate with her or give philosophical arguments here. Rather, we urge such a reader to go directly to the workshop activities, try them out (preferably in the company of a group of interested teachers), and reconsider the ideas for herself.

Resistance and Change

If this composition curriculum is so simple, so effective, so ancient, and so obvious, then why hasn't it been universally adopted by teachers? To begin with, we have to admit that this question is a good one. Statistics from the National Assessment of Educational Progress suggest that only 7 percent of American high school students are receiving the sort of composition instruction which the above model implies—even after the schools' intensified emphasis on writing skills over the past several years. Clearly there are forces operating in schools which contradict or oppose the kinds of teaching which are crucial to learning to write. We don't wish to be discouraging, but anyone interested in serious change in a complex system must understand the forces with which he or she is contending.

In the first place, the list above (project teachers often call it the "process model" of writing instruction) implies that students learn by doing, practicing, and being coached by their instructors. The customary relation between teachers and pupils in American schools, however, is much more didactic: the teacher tells, instructs, gives rules, and the student listens, absorbs, and complies. This habitual role relationship, in other words, is ill-suited to the sort of collaborative effort that efficient writing instruction requires. The customary ruler-subject relationship, of course, has a long history and is firmly rooted in some of the other fundamental purposes of schools—socializing the young, instilling precepts of good citizenship, preparing workers for the labor force, and so forth. But without at this time debating the legitimacy of these latter functions of schooling, we must recognize that their usually authoritarian tone undercuts the more individualistic and humanistic goals of schools and teachers.

English and language arts teachers are, of course, influenced by these general institutional patterns and habits of mind, just as all teachers are. But they also have some special professional traditions and conflicts which further compromise sound instruction in writing. Though outsiders find it strange to discover this, most English and language arts teachers have relatively little training in writing or how to teach it. Composition has long been the stepchild of the "three Rs," a fact that is reflected in teacher-training just as it is in school curricula. Most practicing English teachers took only one or two writing courses during their own college careers—and almost none ever took a course in the methods of teaching writing. Given this gap in their training, teachers naturally emphasize what they *do* know about: elementary teachers concentrate on reading and high school teachers stress the interpretation of literature. Writing, when it does occur, is often harnessed to other tasks, such as testing the students' comprehension or interpretation of their reading. Instruction in writing does not follow the time-consuming, student-centered, largely inductive, teacher-as-coach process which works best, but much more likely, consists of delivering grammatical terminology and rhetorical regulations.

Still more deeply embedded in the context is the nature of the literary study that forms the basic training for most high school English teachers. It has long been dominated by the New Criticism (now far from new) which asserts that interpreting a text depends primarily on structures and patterns in the text itself, not in the reader's mind ("the pathetic fallacy") and not in the author's mind ("the intentional fallacy"). The writer's intentions and methods, in other words, cannot logically be connected to the final text, which may turn out to be something different than the author him/herself perceives. This is an understandable, if limiting, point of view when one is reading finished literary texts. But it is not a very useful perspective when one is *writing* a text, or helping others to do so. Treating the composition process as essentially unknowable simply cuts off all discussion. Unfortunately, this view dominates the thinking of many who teach English and has lent strength to the movement for teaching literature—much more than writing—in schools.

One might expect that teachers hindered by these obstacles would welcome any help in removing them; in reality, thankfulness is indeed the predominant greeting, although suspicion and resentment are also expressed by some teachers. There are altogether logical and predictable reasons why teachers sometimes react skeptically to such new ideas. First, of course, we must acknowledge the universal human reluctance to change. Teachers, like most other people, find change threatening, especially when it touches upon basic habits, attitudes, and behaviors. Even unsatisfying ways of being can become part of an individual's self-definition, and even the most promising changes can still be viewed as threats to the self. Everyone who works in the helping professions discovers, and must respect, these facts of human nature; anyone who works with teachers must recognize that, since teaching is an activity which calls deep personal beliefs into play, resistance will be encountered early, often, and powerfully whenever teachers are asked to change.

Given this understanding of teacher-human nature, we realize how little can be learned from the standard models of teacher retraining presently in use. Most attempts at educational reform in America involve telling teachers to do something differently. Anyone can *tell* teachers what new ideas to try—principals do it all the time, and so do department chairpersons, parents, taxpayers, colleagues, friends, students, and even high-priced out-of-town consultants— usually with no noticeable effect. It is only when teachers themselves, for some reason, *believe* in the change they are asked to make, that real shifts in classroom practice do occur. This is merely another way of reminding ourselves that teaching really is a profession, at least in the classic definition of its being an essentially intellectual enterprise. Teachers are people whose work is guided by ideas, by a philosophy or set of beliefs which, though it may only be semiconscious, nevertheless provides a foundation for everyday practice. If a teacher's behavior in the classroom is to change, then her philosophy—her beliefs, attitudes, and assumptions about the craft—will have to change, probably first.

Much too often, we treat teaching as though it were a simpler, more mechanical job than it is. We imagine that we can merely hand teachers a new tool, much as we would distribute a new kind of wrench to the workers on an assembly line, and teachers, being basically creatures of good will—or at least obedient employees—will give our new wrench a try in the classroom. But in the absence of the teachers' personal commitment to making the innovation work, the experiment is usually doomed. Their lack of enthusiasm communicates itself in countless ways to the students—in the ways assignments are given, in the shadings of emphasis, in the tone of voice used. Noticeable contradictions may develop between what dutiful teachers do to test out the new wrench, and what they feel about the whole process. The experiment is thus undermined, and everyone involved concludes that the ideas just weren't "viable" in the first place. At the end of this intricate process of change-avoidance echoes the refrain all teacher-trainers have heard a thousand times: "We tried that years ago, and it doesn't work!"

In the area of writing instruction, we've seen teacher ambivalence quietly subvert change any number of times. One example: a high school teacher became interested in peer critiquing and developed a guide-sheet for students to use in responding to each other's work. Now, one of the major functions of peer editing groups is to create a wider audience for students' writing, so that the work acquires more communicative purpose. True, the groups can also be used to encourage correctness, to increase practice in proofreading, and to make copyediting feel constructive. But this teacher's guide-sheet listed *only* mechanical and grammatical features of the writing, implying to students that communication with a wider audience was in fact not a valued goal in the class. Needless to say, the omission of any content-centered response categories from the guide-sheet quite accurately reflected the teacher's ambivalence about peer critiquing itself, as well as about the "process model" of writing instruction in general.

Teachers' attitudes, in other words, will largely determine whether any particular classroom method works or not. We have repeatedly found that teachers who really aren't interested in what students have to say will inevitably, even if only implicitly, communicate this to their students, and thus discourage any real engagement with writing. Teachers who consider their students unable to learn, or who identify a culprit like television and pronounce themselves helpless before it, or those who focus on punishing errors, rather than on helping students to develop meaning—such teachers will contradict the more constructive messages sent by any new teaching methods they may try.

On the other hand, a teacher who *does* care what students have to say may also be very demanding about grammar, spelling, and mechanics and achieve real success in improving students' writing. The mechanical aspects can, in other words, be fitted into a larger context of support, encouragement and real communication in the writing. What all this adds up to, then, is the recognition that trying to change the way teachers handle writing instruction means seeking changes in philosophy and attitudes.

So far we have only spoken about resistance in a rather general sense—of the understandable human reluctance of teachers to try something new, of the ways in which schools are bound to sometimes counterproductive tradition. But in an actual, specific writing workshop, with twenty-five or thirty flesh-and-blood teachers and one would-be facilitator, the idea of resistance takes on a much deeper and more particular significance. In this setting, one of the leader's most vital and challenging tasks is to cope constructively with many manifestations of the teachers' genuine and well-earned resistance to change.

At the start of a new in-service course on writing, teachers will display a wide variety of reactions. Many will plunge enthusiastically into the writing and the discussions, while others hold back. Some will remain silent and unreadable, not participating actively, but not attacking either. A few will be philosophically opposed and will argue their position. A couple of teachers may even be overtly hostile to the workshop, its leader, and any ideas it seems to be promoting.

Teachers may initially display this uninspiring assortment of attitudes because they come to in-service programs with genuine problems and reasonable doubts. Though they may not immediately articulate their concerns, the teachers usually would like to shout out things like: "You should see all the material I am required to cover in my course. An English teacher doesn't just teach writing, you know. In one short semester I am supposed to teach literature, spelling, vocabulary, speech, and grammar as well as writing." An elementary teacher might want to say: "When will I have time for writing? I've got to cover reading, spelling, handwriting, science, health, social studies, math, and all of the arts. I'm swamped as it is." Another doubtful teacher might note: "You're talking about using writing across the curriculum. How am I supposed to do that? There's no way I will get social science or biology teachers interested in this stuff. They're too busy getting students ready for the standardized tests or for advanced placement exams. Besides, they have no idea how much work we have to do grading 150 papers every time we give a writing assignment to all our classes. As far as they're concerned, writing is our job, not theirs." Another might argue: "Our administration has had to cut back on the amount of professional released time available to our department, so I have no time to think about any new ideas." Or: "When they close our building in two years, I'm likely to get fired, so why should I go to all this extra trouble?"

There are other concerns less likely to be aired aloud, but perhaps even more prevalent. Most teachers' experience with in-service training itself has been less than inspiring. Many feel they could better spend their time grading papers or researching a class presentation or preparing some materials for their room. Understandably, they don't always arrive bright-eyed and energetic at in-service programs. If they have been around awhile, they have seen new teaching fads come and go. Visiting presenters may have been more interested in advancing their own careers on the crest of the latest wave of clever solutions than attending to the real needs and problems of teachers. Workshop leaders need to recognize, in short, that teachers have a perfect and hard-earned right to be suspicious of in-service programs. Such skepticism is not necessarily a sign of laziness, lack of intelligence, pigheadedness, or inability to grow. Rather, it may be one of the survival skills teachers have developed in response to difficult working conditions.

Helping Teachers Learn

Teachers do not change their beliefs or methods merely because some certified expert presents them with the latest university-approved truths. As Carl Rogers has explained, adults undergo significant learning only when they are deeply, personally invested in the process. Deep personal investment hardly describes the customary orientation of teachers toward whatever in-service program their principal may have rustled up for them on any given Thursday afternoon. Rogers also reminds us that anything you can *tell* a learner, anything you can "teach" to him, will probably turn out to be either trivial or harmful; most truly powerful and constructive insights are learned, not taught. Thus, any effort to help people reexamine personal beliefs and cherished professional practices must begin with the establishment of a climate: creating an environment in which the learner feels free, safe, accepted, supported, and encouraged to explore real issues with peers. Teachers need a genuine chance to learn, not to be told, how to improve their teaching.

One of the best ways of establishing such a climate is for the program to be led by a peer or colleague, rather than by an outside "expert." Indeed, this peer leadership has become one of the key features of National Writing Project workshops all around the country. There is something very special and appropriate about teachers leading their own colleagues in the discovery of new materials and methods; at its best, such peer teaching offers an example of what a genuinely effective "master teacher" program—so widely and glibly recommended by critics of education—might look like. However, this does not mean that any useful workshop for teachers must be led by a local peer. An outside person, a person from some other level of education, can make a perfectly effective leader of an in-service program on writing if that person has faced and is facing analogous challenges in her own teaching—if she is actively addressing problems with writing and with students herself. Such an outsider, of course, needs to make a special effort to learn about the context in which the workshop participants are operating, to share with the group some examples of her own teaching work, and to demonstrate ways in which she sees her own problems as related to theirs.

One of the main differences between our writing project and most of the others around the country is that we insist on having one person—whether inside peer or outside facilitator—conduct the entire thirty-hour program. Elsewhere it is common for one person to serve as a master of ceremonies for a number of different workshop leaders who visit the group, each presenting a teaching idea he or she has developed. One of the benefits of this latter model is that it strongly demonstrates that teachers—all kinds of teachers—can become experts, leaders, and resources for their colleagues.

But we've found that this way of delivering an in-service program has some serious drawbacks as well. When you use a series of, say, ten teacher-consultants, you are compelled to use each of them for the specialty she has previously developed; each person comes in, shows her idea (often an extremely valuable and replicable one), and then leaves. On the other hand, if you want a program that has an order or sequence, that develops from beginning to end, you must have continuity of leadership: the same person needs to be responsible for the development of the group, for assessing people's needs, for observing their reactions, for remembering their ideas and worries, for keeping track of the group's achievements, and for offering a continuous and consistent example of facilitative teaching behavior. We are not claiming that our approach to leadership is inherently better than other structures; since the goals are different, the results are not comparable. But we *do* believe that our ability to document measurable improvement in the writing of our participants' students is related to the way our program is structured and how it is led.

Our institutes and courses for teachers employ inductive learning processes wherever possible, encouraging participants to draw upon their own experience, their personal writing, their students' written work, their related readings, as well as the resources of the leader, in reconstructing their own theories of what writing is and how it can best be taught. There is very little emphasis on presenting "new material" in the courses because there are few ideas which teachers haven't already heard. Instead, our goal is to get a fresh hearing for some old ideas which many teachers have long since, often repeatedly, rejected. In a learning experience like this one, there is no hope—and no need—that every teacher will end up with the same revised philosophy, the same understanding of writing, or the same plans for the classroom. What is important is that each teacher will have genuinely opened himself up to the possibility of learning, honestly examined his own beliefs and practices, seriously entertained some alternative ideas, and willingly committed himself to make whatever changes he believes in and is excited about.

The demands on the leader in such a program are extraordinarily complicated. As our reliance upon Carl Rogers's theories implies, the fundamental role of the leader in our writing workshops is that of *facilitator*—a genuine, accepting, empathic figure who provides experiences and materials from which the teacher-participants may derive personally significant learning. There are times, however, when the leader must in fact lead, must become an unabashed *instructor*. This need to employ a more traditional, directive approach derives both from the leader's personal desire to be honest and direct, and from the fact that once a self-directed learning style has been established, the group can occasionally benefit from direct teaching without sinking into passivity or uncritical acceptance. A third role which the workshop leader plays—in fact, plays constantly and simultaneously as she shifts between facilitator and instructor—is a *model* of teaching behavior. The teacher-students in the program tend to view everything done by the leader, from the content of her lessons to the nature of her demeanor, as exemplifying the preferred outcomes of the workshop itself. As the program advances, this expectation becomes less literal, but the participants continue to measure the behavior of the leader against their own teaching style. A fourth role, which supports the other three, is that of *observer*. After all, the leader can only determine which role is appropriate for a given situation by observing the participants and judging their needs and states of mind as carefully and sensitively as possible.

The first obligation of the leader in the role of facilitator is to nurture a humanistic climate, to follow Carl Rogers's prescription for an atmosphere of genuineness, acceptance, and empathy. What the leader is striving for, in order to have real issues and real change seriously considered, is that participants feel free to reveal themselves deeply both through their writing and in discussions. Members of the group need to accept and respect each other as individuals, regardless of differences in their views on writing, students, or life in general. Both the leader and the participants should be quick to offer sympathetic attention to problems raised by any member of the group. Affective matters—concerns with morale, energy, and friendship—must be accorded as much attention as content issues. The workshop leader has two main ways of establishing this sort of learning climate: one is by demonstrating its component attitudes in his own handling of the program; the other is by making a persistent, explicit effort to become acquainted with each individual within the group, to find some basis for personal connection and warmth.

In the handling of the program, a facilitator's main educational duty can be described as arranging opportunities for participants to learn from certain experiences, materials, or other people. At the very start of the IWP writing program, for example, just this sort of facilitation is necessary to lead people through the writing experiences which introduce the issues central to the rest of the course. The leader's main job during these first eight hours of the program (beyond maintaining the positive learning climate) is to present learners with the sequence of writing tasks; to help them prepare, draft, and revise each one; to set up ways in which the resulting writing may be "published" within the group; and to assist the participants in drawing the widest possible range of conclusions and implications from these experiences. While coordinating these activities, the facilitator also acts as a co-learner within the group, doing all of the writing assignments with the others and sharing her own writing when appropriate. As all this implies, the facilitator does not "teach" *anything* during this phase of the course; in fact, she will probably duck any attempts by participants to cast her in a more didactic role. The "teaching" is done by the experiences themselves, by the personal writing tasks which the participants undertake. These activities are so inherently powerful, involving, and replete with implications for both theory and methodology that the teachers are strongly, almost automatically drawn into a self-directed, inductive learning process, a mode of operation characterized by serious commitment to individual inquiry and active concern for the progress of the group.

These writing activities and the learning processes they initiate go a long way toward dealing with the many layers of resistance which members of the group may feel. Yet an effective facilitator is more than an arranger of opportunities; he must also take active steps to meet and channel resistance, to help participants work through the doubts, frustrations, conflicts, and blockages which inevitably occur as the planned activities unfold. The facilitator's first move in dealing with such resistance is to make it a part of the group's work, rather than ruling it out of bounds. If teachers become upset or confused by what is happening in the group, even if they complain about the general discouragements and frustrations they face back in their own classrooms, the facilitator must recognize these feelings as legitimate and must allow time for the group to work them through. Sometimes the leader may even feel that tangential issues (the influence of television, unsympathetic administrators) are being raised as a subconscious attempt to deflect the group from more immediate obligations or to test the leader's own commitment to the plan. Yet, whatever their origins, the facilitator accepts that the expressed concerns of the group members must be taken seriously, attended to, and in some sense conquered before the teachers can address the workshop's core issues.

It is much easier to recommend this unflappable, open-minded attitude than to enact it. In reality, resistance usually manifests itself in one of two quite discomforting ways: (1) as an open challenge to the authority and credibility of the leader, to her ideas, to the material she is presenting, or to the immediate activity the group is being asked to carry out; or (2) as a more passive resistance, a lukewarm participation, perhaps with complaints voiced only to other participants outside workshop sessions, or even total nonparticipation, with accompanying body signals indicating boredom, hostility, and disconfirmation of the leader.

The open kind of confrontation usually turns out to be a critical incident in the development of the group. Participants often report afterward that the showdown provided an important turning point for them. If the facilitator can refrain from reacting defensively, can tell himself that this challenge is not really about *his* competence as a leader, *or* about the resistor's *incompetence*—then the leader can avoid trying to answer or argue. He can respond more openly along the lines, ''It sounds as if you have real concerns here, and these may be very important for the whole group to understand. Could you explain some more of what you are thinking?''

Several things almost inevitably happen when a leader meets dissatisfaction in this empathic way. First, the challenger is usually surprised to find himself taken seriously, instead of being either rebuked or lured into an endless no-win debate. Second, other participants feel encouraged to join in, and a discussion may ensue during which the leader can remain mostly silent, while simultaneously learning a good deal about the range of views that actually exists within the group. In this setting, workshop participants receive a hearing for ideas which, if presented by the leader, would be met with much more skepticism. Participants earn credibility by working in the classroom every day, alongside others in the group, and they do not usually have the same vested interest in ''ideas about writing'' as someone who has organized a workshop. The participant is more like a skeptical consumer free to examine, test out, adopt, or reject any given method or suggestion. Some of the best teaching will be done by such people in the group.

A third result of the nondefensive response is that the group begins to permit the voicing of real objections without having them ridiculed, punished, or ignored. This habit of openness is essential for avoiding more passive resistance later on, when new disagreements arise, and it helps the group adopt a process of real inductive learning—searching through difficult problems honestly, rather than leaving all the work to the leader while taking mental or verbal potshots at her. In our own experience, we have gone from fearing such confrontations to worrying if one does not occur.

Dealing with more passive resistance involves the same essential mindset for the group leader, but she will probably have to seek the resistor(s) out and invite the challenge individually—''Something seems to be on your mind and I'm wondering what it is.'' Sometimes this direct, individual expression of interest in the teacher-learner activates his or her participation quite promptly; with other individuals, no amount of group or private attention seems to alter the nature of their passivity. Yet a very common recollection of experienced group leaders concerns the individual who remains quiet, passive, and seemingly uninvolved throughout most of the program and who, inexplicably, like a time bomb going off, explodes with activity, excitement, and affirmation at the very end of the program. Though these cases of passive resistance do not always have happy endings, the efforts of the facilitator clearly influence the out-come—and the leader must make the effort to lure every individual into the work of the group.

Though the facilitator role is clearly the predominant one taken by the proj-ect workshop leader, there are times when he or she needs to be more direc-tive, to take charge, to serve as the instructor. Of course, this obligation does not come as a total surprise to anyone; the Rogerian facilitator role can never be entirely pure. From the start of the workshop, it is the leader who introduces activities, who says when work should begin and end, who distributes mate-rials, who writes on the board, who moderates discussions, who checks the level in the coffee pot, and who exhibits scores of other behaviors unmistaka-bly associated with power and control. None of these details is lost on the par-ticipants, who will want the workshop leader to function as much more of a boss and expert than she actually does. And although the success of the pro-gram does depend in large measure upon minimizing and delaying these shifts from facilitator to instructor, the leader will have to satisfy these demands for authority on some occasions.

How does the leader know when to switch roles, when to become more dominant? Some of the most important cues come from the contours of the program itself. Though we tend to describe our whole program—the complete sequence of forty workshops described later in this book—as a set of inductive learning experiences, the fact is that the activities vary in inductiveness. Some, like the sessions covering the first eight hours of the program, raise questions, bring out feelings, illustrate problems, and highlight contradictions without pro-viding any answers or explanations. Other workshops, however, *do* give an-swers: the session on assignment-making and the one on charting student me-chanical problems, to give just two examples, offer the participants very specific teaching suggestions. Even in these sessions we do not try to foist off prepackaged answers, but rather to demonstrate structures teachers can use to generate their own methods and materials. Nevertheless, sessions like these are certainly not inductive and self-directed in the same sense as the personal writ-ing workshops. These later activities do have something to teach. Given this range in inductiveness, the leader obviously has to adjust his style to the activi-ties at hand. Just as it would be a mistake for the leader to turn "instructorly" during the sharing of memoirs, so too would it be disingenuous for him to pre-tend neutrality during workshops which offer concrete suggestions.

The contour of the program is not governed only by patterns in the work-shop plans. Very often it will be the people, the teacher-participants, whose needs pressure the leader to take on a more dominant role. Frequently, groups of teachers (or their volunteer spokesperson) will ask an in-service leader quite formally and forthrightly to reveal "the right answers." In one sense at least, this is a reasonable request. Teachers have a right to expect that anyone con-ducting a workshop and taking up their time should know a good deal about the subject at hand. The leader of a writing workshop *should* know what he's talking about, should be experienced with many teaching techniques, should be familiar with much of the recent theory and research on writing, should have given serious thought to his own philosophy of writing and teaching, and should be able to give useful and interesting presentations on a number of issues involved in composition instruction. But none of this means that the leader should necessarily demonstrate any of these skills, should become a traditional information-giving instructor, whenever his students ask him to do so. His first responsibility, instead, is to evaluate the origins of any request for authority, to determine whether the teachers are trying to bypass the difficulties of exploring ideas on their own, are testing the leader's resolve to stick with the plan, or whether they are genuinely in need of some expert material with which they will engage both actively and critically. When this latter condition exists, obviously it will be fine and appropriate for the leader to instruct, to teach, to offer both information and opinion to the group.

One surprisingly problematic function within the instructor role involves giving writing assignments and topics to the participants. This seemingly routine procedure is actually a matter of great controversy among composition people. The complications require some explanation here. Many experienced writing leaders share the belief, most powerfully argued by Donald Graves, that teachers who give their students writing assignments rob them of their opportunity to develop their own subjects, their own motivation, their own voice. Instead, in the ideal writing classroom, as Donald Graves describes it:

> Writing is not delayed. No more than five minutes into any class, whether of 6 or ten-year-olds, everyone is writing, including the teacher. There are no stories, sentence starters, long discussions of what writing is all about, or exactly what to do on a page.
>
> —Donald Graves, *Writing: Teachers and Children at Work,* p. 19

Students get their topics from themselves, from other pupils, from the literature they've heard read, from watching the teacher write, from conferences. This means that sometimes kids will have trouble making these choices, that everyone will have occasional dry spells, that pupils will often get stuck on a single topic, and that at any given time only about one-fifth of the students will be writing on a "hot topic"—a fully engaged, deeply meaningful piece of writing. The priceless benefit of this freedom is that students take ownership of their work and learn early on to see writing as a genuine opportunity to make meaning for real audiences and not as an additional teacher-aimed school exercise.

We've seen such classrooms work beautifully and yet we don't follow their model—we go right ahead and assign particular writing topics to our teacher-writers. Why? A comment by Graves in *Writing: Teacher's and Children at Work,* begins to explain our special circumstances,

The exercise of judgment in choosing topics takes time. At first, children may write about last night's stale TV plot, or the same topic for six successive writings. This is where it begins, but not where it ends. For some children it may take six months or more to learn to trust their own judgments. Six months is a very short time when we consider that a majority of college freshmen panic at the thought of choosing their subjects, or stumble when trying to limit a topic intelligently.

—Graves, p. 31

In an in-service workshop, we are not dealing with elementary school children who know they can write; we are dealing with grown-up adult teachers who, as often as not, believe they *can't*. As Graves suggests, as people get older, they seem to accumulate more fears about writing and more reasons for avoiding it. Teachers are often especially skittish and insecure because they feel that being a skillful writer is an expected professional credential—a credential they somehow lack. Given a roomful of colleagues for an audience and an open choice of topics, many teachers (not all, but many) freeze up, resist, feel terribly uncomfortable, and might need days or weeks to thaw out, take some honest chances, and find an authentic voice in their work.

In a thirty-hour workshop course, we don't have that kind of time, and we certainly don't have the six months Graves mentions. So instead, we have developed a series of assignments explicitly aimed at short-circuiting much of the fear and resistance while offering people genuine opportunities for personally significant choice and the use of their own authentic voices.

Such assignments must be thoroughly explained so that the leader balances topic suggestions with the explicit indication that wide choices are available. Balance is required, too, between encouraging self-revelation and communicating that whatever level of openness the writer chooses will be respected and accepted by the leader.

These balances between assignment and choice can help wean adults (and older children) from the need for directions and authority, a need most have highly developed over the years. Even Carl Rogers, the prime advocate of self-directed growth and nonauthoritarian roles for teachers and therapists, has recognized that adopting a nondirective mode may involve a gradual process in the classroom. In *Freedom to Learn,* Rogers praises the work of an elementary school teacher who divides her class into those who wish to work independently and those who find they aren't yet ready to. She then concentrates on helping the more dependent children gain confidence so they can move to the independent group. In writing project workshops, too, the leader can encourage self-direction, while providing assignments in such a way as to lower anxiety and help those participants who insist on receiving direction to gradually accept freedoms.

We'll describe each of the writing tasks in turn later in the book. For now, we'll simply add that once we have used them with a group, we must all reflect back together on the ways in which these assignments have structured the experience—and may in fact have stolen some people's ownership of their work. For a number of reasons (to be considered later), we use assignments of our own devising far more than writer-generated topics. Unless the implications of this instructor role are explicitly critiqued, participants will understandably jump to the false conclusion that the project endorses assignment-giving as a central function of the effective writing instructor.

Another important use of the instructor role arises when the leader has to assert some control over the group; when individuals or the whole get trapped in repetitive, nonconstructive behavior. This problem can take several forms. Sometimes one or two participants cannot get synchronized with the rest, cause disruptions, lag behind, or conspicuously sabotage any attempt to move ahead. The leader may elect to approach these people privately, rather than confronting them in class sessions; but finally he or she may have to publicly assert the need for the group as a whole to progress in spite of their unwillingness.

More commonly, a whole group can get bogged down in directionless behavior, treading water, pursuing tangential and circular debates. In such circumstances, when gentle facilitation fails, it is appropriate for the leader to be arbitrary—to say, for example: "We have now spent one full hour on this topic. I really feel that the subject is of minor importance and that after another ten minutes or so we should move on."

If the needs of the group sometimes require the leader to change roles, it is only logical that the leader's own needs may also occasion such shifts. Though the predominant facilitator role generally obliges her to remain neutral and non-judgmental, the leader always retains the right to stand up for her own beliefs about writing, teaching, or students. If authenticity and openness are being cultivated within the group, it is only fair that the leader be issued the same license, even if she intends to use it sparingly. Honest assertiveness may be required of the leader when, for example, a participant exclaims hopelessly: "I tried that technique ten years ago and it didn't work." If no one else speaks up, the leader may have to respond: "Just because it didn't work for you at that time doesn't mean it won't work for anyone any time. In fact, I've seen this method used and used it myself. What we need to do is look at the idea further and try to figure out why it is so hard to implement, why it so often goes astray." Somewhat less common are occasions when the leader needs to oppose someone's evaluation not of a teaching method, but of teaching itself, or of students. The workshop leader is under no obligation to let bitter, cynical, or despairing statements circulate through the group unopposed.

The leader's third essential role, one played continuously and mostly unconsciously, is as a model. Anyone who leads a writing workshop quickly realizes that he is teaching into a mirror. The audience, after all, is composed of teachers—people who, though they will certainly participate, will also constantly ask themselves: "Why is the leader doing this?" Everything the leader does, every activity he promotes, every attitude he expresses will be viewed by many of the participants as embodying the attributes of the Perfect Writing Teacher. Though the personal idealization of the workshop leader is not a goal of the program (and is rarely an outcome of it), the behavior of the leader does indeed reflect both the IWP's and the leader's beliefs about teaching and writing. Some of the most important ideas which are modeled by the leader include: the preference for facilitation over instruction; the commitment to self-directed, inductive learning where possible; the consistent effort to know and understand each individual participant; the use of much class time for prewriting, drafting, and sharing in small groups; the balancing of individual, small-group, and large-group activities; the seasoning of discussions with humor and praise; the stress on personally supportive, content-centered evaluation of writing; the regular publication of students' work.

Perhaps as important as any of these, the leader writes, shares her writing, and thus takes the same risks as the participants. What *this* models is modeling itself. Teachers are always struck by this participation immediately, and begin to think—if they haven't already—about its impact in their own classrooms. What it demonstrates, perhaps beyond any of the roles we've named, is that writing for real communication in the classroom means that writing is a two-way affair, not just a student-for-teacher performance. If risk-taking is to be encouraged in students' or workshop participants' writing, it must be good enough for instructors, too.

The fourth role a leader takes on is that of observer. Much of what we've already said indicates the many points at which a leader must be aware of what participants are thinking and feeling, what questions or doubts they have, and what ideas they are ready to take on next. Such observation is perhaps one of the most important—and least discussed—of teaching skills. No *one* teaching method, no matter how valuable, how well backed by research, or how theoretically "correct" by anyone's standards, is appropriate *all* the time for *all* people. A leader can only judge what is needed by accurately observing the workshop participants, by discovering what they are thinking, and assessing their needs at each specific moment. A good leader is an expert reader of both verbal expression and body language. Eye movement, facial expression, body position, seating choice, how and when people laugh, how they go about various tasks as the leader gives assignments and organizes groups—all reveal as much or more than the words people speak.

This is why we prefer to team-teach workshops whenever possible, and it is one reason why we recommend teams of two or three for establishing programs and conducting training in school districts. Though this may seem a luxury, an important advantage of team teaching is that one person is always free to observe while the other is performing or leading a discussion. The nonperforming partner need never consider herself "off duty." The leader who is on stage must attend to so many things at once—especially if the discussion is heated—that close observation of a group of twenty or thirty people simply cannot be thorough; and in addition, the active leader has more need *not* to see disturbing or discouraging signals that might dampen the enthusiasm he wants to project. Because the observer sitting on the sidelines needn't feel these pressures, he can perform vital functions for the workshop, spotting participants' signaled needs and problems and either putting in a helpful word right away, talking to someone after the session, or planning to attend to the concern in the next session. We find that a great proportion of our planning time between sessions is devoted to talking over the state of mind of each participant.

All of these roles, when taken together, define the larger spirit of the program. As she leads participants through the program, as she assumes the duties and roles which promise the most support for the learners at any given point, the leader models something more than a way of improving writing instruction; she demonstrates how a teacher can help her students do what human beings do best: learn.

Workshop Part I—Writing and Sharing

How does inductive teaching work when specifically applied to a course on teaching writing? It is important to understand that while we work to have teachers make their own discoveries, this does not mean "Do anything you want," or "Believe anything about writing that you choose to believe." We offer a structured set of experiences to workshop participants, and because human problems, needs, and abilities follow distinct patterns in life, the participants consistently come to some basic, similar conclusions on their own.

Our subject—writing—is admirably adaptable to this approach. Teachers can *write*, and in so doing, they not only experience the activity they are trying to understand, but they communicate with each other *and* they can think on paper about the pedagogical concerns before them. Writing becomes the experienced, observed subject, a cement for group processes, and a tool for thinking about the issues under discussion.

We are not trying to *teach* writing, as if teachers don't know how to write well—though most participants do feel they have refreshed or sharpened their writing skills by the end of the program. More important in this context are the discoveries which each teacher makes about his or her own writing process. The focus is on using writing to communicate and think, and then to observe ourselves in the process of using writing, so as to understand what student writers experience. For the first eight hours of the workshop, the participants write on a special series of assignments and share the results with each other in certain structured ways. This phase of the program is highly crafted and systematic: the assignments move steadily from lighthearted, reassuring tasks toward more challenging and intimate topics. The sharing sessions promote mutual support and encourage self-disclosure. In many ways, the remainder of the course merely elaborates on the powerful discoveries which teachers make during this first segment of the workshop.

For example, by doing their own autobiographical and expository writing the participants discover (or rediscover) that composing is a process: that writing is a series of steps or stages which, though it varies greatly from person to person and task to task, moves with many recursions from prewriting to drafting to revision. This single realization can shed much light on some of the most prevalent and troublesome student writing problems, and offers abundant suggestions for new teaching practices. Working out the pedagogical implications of this one concept—writing as a process—can occupy many later hours of discussion, reflection, and planning. Similarly, by experiencing their own writing, teachers can make discoveries about other aspects of composing: about the relative importance of form and content; about the demands of different audiences, subjects, and purposes; about the sorts of writing assignments which facilitate meaningful, satisfying writing work; about the kinds of feedback that help writers to improve and grow; and on and on.

Except for actually doing the personal writing, the most significant experience for teachers in the workshop is sharing their own writing. At first many are fearful about other *teachers* seeing their work. They are relieved when their peers accept it and very naturally engage with the substance of the writing, rather than picking at the form. Usually, the activity deepens to become a social glue and a nourishment. As the sharing ranges, people benefit from it in varying ways: learning about each other, finding common bonds, empathizing, sharing practical curriculum ideas, recalling moments of success or disappointment in the classroom, finding philosophical issues to argue over. Teachers become spectators of their work, seeing it from different angles as they hear their own ideas restated in different ways by their readers. Writing itself becomes more and more a means by which the people in the workshop advance, getting to know one another personally and professionally, working through questions and problems, and forming a cohesive, supportive community.

It's surprising—though it shouldn't be—just how much good, moving, reflective, informative, and funny writing can be produced by a group of twenty-five people over a few weeks or months. The discovery of this fact by members of the group is exhilarating. Writing may be difficult, but its results really can be magical. And whatever else it does, the sharing of writing builds teachers' confidence in their own composing. Many reveal, in discussion, that they have drawers full of poetry and stories they've written but never shown to anyone except a spouse or close friend. Once they have shared their writing with others, they can see it as a powerful means for relating to other people, not just an artifact to be made perfect. Teachers discover that they needn't let perfectionism cut them off from an audience. Writing doesn't have to be perfect to be enjoyed, compared, and talked over. Writers may still want to polish their writing, but bringing it out into the world where it can have a real effect on other people becomes a great incentive for revising and for writing more.

The sharing of writing can be structured in a variety of ways, for a variety of purposes. We have found two particular formats to be most useful in our programs. Reading groups of three people are especially effective because they provide the intimacy and nonthreatening condition of a small, face-to-face audience, but at the same time make interesting comparisons of writing possible for the three people. Each writer gets the benefit of hearing two different reactions to the same paper. Variations in the responses can be explored so that the writer sees what elements, either in his writing or in the readers' thinking, affect the interpretive process. Teachers can consider what it means for their own teaching that two competent and sympathetic readers may have very different reactions to a piece.

Reading compositions aloud in the full workshop group is also important, though no individual participant is ever *compelled* to read in this situation. What generally happens when volunteers are sought in the large group is that some of the bravest members (and often, some of the most skilled writers) will offer to read—and their example usually encourages a few others to take the risk. *Some* large-group sharing is vital to the success of the first segment of the workshop: it gives dramatic evidence to everyone, simultaneously, of the risk of sharing, the power of words, and, often, the depth of shared feelings. There is something elemental about a group of *homo sapiens* sitting in a circle sharing stories: the intensity of such occasions seems to confirm the contention of novelist Reynold Price that the human need for storytelling is second only to the need for food—even more deeply rooted than the desire for shelter or love.

Because story-sharing is so elemental and instructive, we prefer to let response take its natural course, and then for people to ponder what their intuitive responses to colleagues imply about their handling of student writing. Obviously, one of the main things that teachers notice when they share their own writing aloud is that almost any natural response to another person's writing will emphasize content rather than form. Living this fact, experiencing it viscerally as an author, can be a very important lesson, rich with pedagogical implications. At the same time, we know of many other writing projects where the structuredness is reversed; where assignments are wide open but the writing is fed into closely controlled and guided mechanisms of response. Obviously, both approaches have their own lessons to teach, and perhaps even lead to the same place in the long run.

The experience of being an audience, as well as a writer, can have a strong and educative effect on participants. When a peer takes the risk of revealing something highly personal and significant, as in the memoir writing, appropriate responses invariably cluster around the experience itself and similar experiences among the hearers. Questions to the writer urge him to elaborate and expand, to give more details or explanations, to help others know even better what it was like for him. This gentle pressure of the group brings a new awareness of the importance of a sympathetic audience—other people who attend to meaning and who care about the writer.

Suddenly, it is not the imperfections of a particular piece that matter, but what the writer has said. Even teachers long habituated to copy-editing student writing find their red pens much less comfortable in the hand—and much less useful than they usually seem. To respond first to the writing's form or errors and not to its content seems trivial, even irresponsible. Readers sense that a piece of writing that comes out of personal experience is a gift to be sensitively appreciated. A grounding of trust develops quickly, and the closeness of the group becomes the soil in which further shared writing flourishes.

Occasionally, a teacher will actually pull out a red pen (or some oral equivalent) at the first session and proceed to savage a colleague's work. The pity and terror evoked by this act will provide a vivid lesson for the group and will usually be worth the momentary damage. Most victims find this "let's fix this sucker up" approach discouraging, if not heartbreaking, and once they have admitted these reactions, the stage is set for making some crucial comparisons between the way adult peers instinctively treat each other's writing and how teachers customarily react to student work. Complaining and proofreading—probably the two most widely practiced modes of teacher response to student writing—have turned out to be surprisingly unhelpful, sometimes even damaging, in the workshop's small and large groups. Given this discovery, teachers may have to reconsider the appropriateness of their habitual approach to their pupils' writing as well.

As writing, reading, and responding proceed, participants quickly begin to consider implications for the classroom—"Should we use these same assignments for our students? Do children's and adults' writing problems differ? How might I adjust these approaches to fit the grade I teach and the cultural setting my students come from?" Some enthusiastic teachers will go directly to their classes the next day to try out writing activities they did in the workshop the night before, and bring back reports of the outcome. Other people may begin to express their doubts—"This writing is fine for us adult teachers, but it won't work with my kids."

These responses are, of course, the very thing we want the writing tasks to provoke—teachers' honest thoughts, whether positive or negative, about writing in their classrooms. A great many of the best insights develop in the discussions following writing or other activities, and groups often discover their independence and strength at these times. A workshop leader can almost always count on participants "teaching" themselves and drawing plenty of worthwhile conclusions as they talk over what they have done.

However, not all the thinking-through needs to be done immediately after a writing activity. More skeptical groups, or whose who simply aren't aware of the implications needn't be rushed into long discussions of practical issues after the first or second writing and sharing activities. The thoughtful experiencing of a variety of writing tasks can convince doubters about the importance of expressive writing more effectively than any verbal argument a workshop leader or anyone else might present.

Furthermore, teachers can be so tyrannized by the pressure to find gimmicks for next Monday that they never have the opportunity to develop a coherent set of concepts to guide their work. The leader may therefore want to limit practical discussions during the first eight hours of the workshop, while giving assurance that the practical implications will be explored thoroughly once the group has had some writing experience and has thought through the concepts that emerge from it.

On the other hand, the implications *are* important. Teachers are practical-minded people, and their initiative needn't be discouraged. Perhaps the best advice we can give leaders, then, is to gently encourage the doubters and the impatient to wait until the practical sessions before drawing all their conclusions. But if someone clearly needs to voice a doubt, share a realization, or receive some help thinking about the significance of a writing activity, one can provide the opportunity they need. As in all the workshop activities, the leader's on-the-spot best judgment is more important than any lesson plan.

Workshop Part II—Theory and Practice

The remainder of the program shifts character noticeably. Once the essential initial experience—writing in several modes, sharing and understanding the process—is complete, the workshop can then turn to theoretical and practical issues in the teaching of composition. While there is some flexibility about coverage, depending on participants' interests and the levels they teach, the issues derive from the major research and theory of composition that has developed over the past decade. These include:

- Developmental Issues: stages of growth in the acquisition of writing; relationships with the learning of oral language, reading, other representational activities; cognitive models of writing.
- Students: strengths and weaknesses of student writers of different ages; relations between writing and other aspects of students' lives and development.
- Context: understanding the social, political, economic, and cultural issues underlying literacy instruction both in and out of schools; issues in the history of composition teaching.
- Writing Process: working out the pedagogical implications of a stage or step model of composing; supporting prewriting, drafting, revision in the classroom.
- Assignment-Making: subjects, instructions, and procedures used by, and available to, teachers in eliciting writing.
- Purpose: examining the effect of varying purposes in shaping discourse; reviewing classical and modern rhetorical principles.

- Audience: the writer's sense of audience and how it develops; ways of providing genuine, varied audiences for student writers.
- Language: reviewing those principles of linguistics central to the understanding of composition: standardization, usage, dialects, and related matters.
- Evaluation: responding to, evaluating, and/or grading students' written work: teacher-student conferences and peer editing; examining the choices and alternatives.
- Activities: developing specific teaching plans, projects, assignments, and activities that embody the teachers' understanding of the above ideas.

Most of these topics lead to one or more workshop sessions, and chapter 4 lays out one example of the sequence.

Whatever the order and emphasis of the topics, the workshops in the latter two-thirds of the program have a kind of inductive rhythm somewhat akin to the exploratory format of the first eight hours of the course. In other words, we like to begin each workshop session with some concrete experience, that embodies the issue being raised. This may be a writing activity, a simulation or role-playing, or an evaluation of sample student papers. After the concrete experience, we turn reflexive; sharing the writing or evaluations, reporting, analyzing what took place. This often occurs in small groups first and then is reported to the larger group. Finally, the implications for teaching emerge, and often participants are eager to conceive practical applications.

Writing itself continues to be a central activity in many workshops, and participants get chances to try a number of different modes: they imitate student writers, revise a child's story, compose with new grammar rules. The teachers begin to experience writing not just as a channel for communication, but as a source of pleasure and play, and as an extraordinary tool of thought. As their appreciation for writing deepens, so does their urge to teach it well.

We also use writing in supporting as well as starring roles in various workshops. For example, we tend to use many quick writing tasks of the two- to five-minute focusing type. Often, this "prewriting" can be handy prior to a whole-group discussion on a controversial issue. Rather than simply plunging into a free-for-all (or the even more dreaded nobody-will-start-things-off syndrome), it helps to have participants take two or three minutes to write on a few focusing questions. We tend to favor simple items like: "X makes me feel . . ." or "In my school, one thing you can never get away with is X," or "Three things I'd like to know about X are. . . ." Such brief exercises accomplish several things. First of all, everyone invariably comes up with something; no one is embarrassed to make private notes, though some are shy about speaking up in a group. The mere existence of some notes under a normally retiring participant's nose can encourage him to risk his first public comments. Similarly, if everyone has some notes, the leader can call upon a range of participants without seeming to threaten. The use of focusing questions can also help to keep a discussion on task, as well as offering the facilitator a built-in opportunity to shift topics when the time seems right ("Let's move on to the second question now . . ."). And finally, these short writing assignments are a nice demonstration of one way writing can be used as a tool for learning in any classroom.

A related topic is journal-keeping. Some workshop leaders encourage participants to keep a journal of their experiences in and reactions to the program. If such a journal is being kept, then the kinds of short assignments described above would naturally be done in the journal, along with other in-process and reflective jottings. The journal, of course, can reach beyond such short assignments, offering an opportunity for participants to write at length about issues of immediate concern—or matters more distant and speculative.

Workshop activities can also involve reading some of the essays that have so effectively changed many people's ideas about writing. When we present a longer version of this program for graduate courses or summer institutes, we assign a considerable amount of this literature, for it is important that teachers become well-read in a field they are committed to trying to understand. They discover they are part of a larger context of inquiry, and gain the confidence they will need when they must explain themselves to colleagues or administrators. A bibliography of important readings appears in the Appendix.

In the workshop plan presented here, however, reading plays a minor role. We have discovered—somewhat reluctantly—that when assigned during an *in-service* program, readings about writing are not very effective, and tend to be unpopular among participants. Teachers devoting thirty hours of their free time to a writing workshop justifiably see additional homework assignments as impositions, not opportunities. Even when enthusiasm builds, as it typically does, after the first few hours of writing and sharing, reading assignments are still likely to engender misunderstanding and complaint. Participants will often ask to do more writing instead of discussing "some irrelevant article." Luckily, other segments of the program introduce, illuminate, and reinforce the important concepts quite effectively, and so we need not moan too much about the modest role played by reading in our efforts. A few particular articles are still important, of course, and our ways of using them are explained in the commentaries on particular workshop sessions. For the rest, it is probably wise for the prospective in-service leader to accept the fact that reading is a supplement, not the foundation, or even a load-bearing support, to the structure of the workshop.

During the last few hours of the workshop, there is a distinct emphasis on practical problem-solving, on transforming the insights of the previous workshops into effective classroom practices. This doesn't just mean cooking up catchy-sounding writing assignments, but involves working along the whole range of pedagogical issues: thinking about how to create a supportive and purposeful climate in the writing class, how to enact the stages of the writing process in class activities, how to provide sharing and publication opportunities for students, how to stimulate school-wide writing activities across the curriculum, how to implement appropriate and constructive evaluation systems in the classroom, how to enlist parental support and assistance with writing programs, and many other concerns. By this stage in the program, the confidence and energy of the group usually makes such practical planning a pleasure. The group now recognizes that it can move from theory to practice on its own: it can generate 100 valuable new writing activities in ten minutes; it can think of dozens of new audiences for student writing; it can recast one writing assignment into scores of others; it can think of countless roles a teacher can take in evaluating students' writing. The group members realize, in short, that they need no expert to bring them ideas about teaching writing. They have rediscovered, through the whole series of workshops, that every teacher is a theorist whose text is her own experience—and that every teacher is a practitioner whose performance may be profoundly enriched by growth in her own self-constructed theory of teaching and writing.

Practical Matters

The rest of this chapter works at a different level of abstraction from everything that has come before—so different, in fact, that from here on we will be addressing the reader directly. You may find some of the brief comments in this section to be quite mechanical and logistical in nature. While this is true in a sense (and explains why they have been segregated in this backwater of chapter 3), these matters still have a philosophical dimension. The way in which a workshop leader handles the seemingly superficial or administrative aspects of a program reflects his or her philosophy of learning, and can significantly affect the climate which develops among the members of the group.

1. **Elementary and Secondary Teachers:** Where possible, we always try to have a widely mixed group of teachers—elementary and secondary; English and other subjects; people from different buildings, neighborhoods, or districts. We've found that the inevitable exchange of ideas and viewpoints is a wonderful corrective for our teacherly tendency to cast blame at the people in the grades above or below us. It's easy to blame last year's teacher for the shortcomings of this year's classes. It's another thing altogether to meet that person firsthand and learn what she's up against—and what she's like.

    Accordingly, all elements of the program—the workshop activities, the writing samples, the selections of student writing, the classroom teaching ideas—are appropriate for K–12 groups. There's balance; everyone gets their turn, but everyone is also exposed to the work and the problems of other grade levels. This means that people have to adopt a patient and open attitude, and that they have to be able to translate ideas to their own grade level. The leader should not underestimate the challenge that this translation process presents for some participants; it is difficult to generalize from one teaching level to another, and some individuals or subgroups may occasionally feel neglected. We've found that if widespread grade-level tensions of this sort do develop, it is helpful to break the participants into age-based task groups (K–3, 4–6, 7–9, 10–12) more frequently than called for in the basic plan—not to separate the groups, but to produce classroom-applicable results for everyone.

Needless to say, where the leader is working with a segregated group (all high school English teachers, for example), the emphasis of the program can be adjusted appropriately. But the elementary-related materials here should *not* be deleted or skipped over. Even if there aren't any flesh-and-blood elementary teachers in the group, this is still probably the only chance these high school teachers will ever get to review and think seriously about what younger writers and their teachers actually do.

2. **Strangers and Colleagues:** There is a big difference between bringing new views of writing to teachers in another county and trying to sell the same bill of goods to the folks you've known for a decade or two as your daily coworkers. In your own school, you have preexisting relationships which prevent others from seeing you afresh—and which encourage colleagues to think that they know exactly what to expect from you. It is even remotely possible that there will be some other teachers in your own school along with whom you cannot get.

These are just some more of the reasons why the IWP program takes the inductive, student-centered, process-oriented approach. You don't have to teach your colleagues anything; you simply have to create a climate in which they may learn. It is still a big job, but there *is* a difference between telling and showing. They do not have to accept (or yield to) your ideas—they merely have to participate in the activities you have organized. They will learn from the doing, and not from your pounding. Still, it is wise to be prepared for the expectations of your colleagues—and above all, perhaps, to promptly shy away from partisan debates and "Let's-hear-the-right-answer" traps, especially when working in your own building.

3. **Participant Responsibility:** One discovery we have made in leading groups: where individual members and self-appointed committees organize things, group vitality is high. If you have people who want to plan some special event, bring in something, give a demonstration, make dinner, whatever—encourage them. In its most academic form, this urge might result in presentations of articles, research findings, or personal teaching experiences by individual members. Again, given the nature and demands of this workshop, such extra work cannot be required, and when it develops spontaneously, it demonstrates a high degree of involvement.

Of course, the leader can do subtle things to encourage such spontaneity. We sometimes ask for volunteers to keep a log of each session—rather like the minutes of a meeting. The volunteer is supposed to prepare the log (we always encourage an original, comic, or idiosyncratic approach) and then distribute it at the start of the next session. This document always attracts much attention as the teachers file in for the next meeting—and then another log-taker is drafted. By the end of the workshop, a comprehensive, multi-authored docudrama will have been produced.

A related practice is to designate a workshop bulletin board—a place where anyone can post their own poems, newspaper clippings on literacy, or other items of interest for everyone to share. You don't need a real corkboard—just use a piece of posterboard or the room's bare door. Put your stuff up fifteen minutes before the session if need be, and take it down when you leave. People will browse around the board during breaks, discuss its features, and perhaps bring something of their own next session. (This project introduces perhaps the lowest-level logistical matter imaginable, but consider this: What goes in a workshop leader's briefcase? Answer: Masking tape, scotch tape, thick magic markers, paper clips, plenty of pens [teachers pull that trick, too], blank paper or pads, scissors.) One last idea which is rarely applicable but fun when appropriate: giving the group a name. This has been useful where two or more groups are working side by side. Past winners: Ruby and the Romantics, Skywriters, and The Cursive Crew.

4. **Digressions and Free-for-Alls:** Teachers like to debate—some would say argue—about any number of topics. The all-time favorite, if our experience is any guide, is the impact of television on the youth of today. This subject, like the financial crunch, the shenanigans of the NEA, and the riffings in District #999, is an important issue, and deserves some attention in a writing workshop if people want to talk about it. We recognize, we *embrace* the fact that we are really doing teacher morale workshops as well as workshops on writing. However, there is a point beyond which discussion of issues distant from writing becomes counterproductive. We have occasionally had to do two things in response to persistent requests to deal with some semirelevant issue: first, to formally and officially set aside some time to work on it; and second, to assert the need to move ahead once this special session has been completed. If an interested contingent still wishes to pursue the issue further, the leader can help them to arrange meetings before or after sessions, during meal breaks, or whenever the members are free.

5. **Nominations:** The sharing of writing among teachers is enormously important, and in the ideal workshop series, every participant reads several pieces aloud in small groups and at least one to the whole group. This risk-taking experience

often helps the teacher to make an empathic connection with his students that he can never entirely forget—and which not infrequently becomes the catalyst of real changes in his classroom behavior. We strongly hope, in other words, that this sharing will occur.

On the other hand, the leader shouldn't compel, threaten, or shame people into reading unwillingly. We do not want to overstretch anyone's capacity for self-disclosure. At the same time, we know that many participants *want* to share their accident or their memoir, but are perched, fearful and indecisive, on the brink of volunteering. The best way around these problems is to introduce early in the workshop (during Prepositional Poetry or the first Accident sharing session) the idea of *nominations*. Any participant may nominate another person to read aloud, either because the nominator has heard and appreciated the piece in a small group, or simply because he wonders what that person did with the topic. The nominee must always be free to decline. In our experience, however, only about one of ten nominations ends in a declination; most teachers really do want to share their writing and a nomination is just what they need to get launched.

6. **Printing and Publishing:** To facilitate the widest possible exchange of the participants' writing, it is helpful to be able to make photocopies for circulation in the group. If this is not permitted by whatever creature guards the copier in your building, it should still be possible to type up a story on ditto masters. Writing workshops always generate a lot of paper, both original and borrowed, and much of it deserves circulation.

Whatever your reproductive capabilities, it is always a good idea to keep final copies of each teacher's writing in a file folder. The contents of this file make an important souvenir of the course, and a potential exhibit for the teacher's own students. At the end of the series, each person can review and select his or her favorite work to contribute to a book of writings, to be copied (somehow!) and bound for distribution among the group. Publishing teachers' writing is not only a way of celebrating the prodigious work they have done, but also provides another illustration of the role of audience in motivating and guiding the writing process.

7. **Scheduling:** We have tried almost every conceivable arrangement of the IWP thirty-hour program, from fifteen weekly two-hour sessions to the two-weekend, full-speed crash course. With some qualifications, we've found that quicker is better. The only advantage we've ever discovered to the two-hours-a-week-until-hell-freezes-over approach is in its appliedness, if there is such a thing. Even though the elongation of the program drains most of the energy and potential for intimacy, it does provide multiple opportunities for participants to test out teaching ideas in their classrooms between sessions, reporting back successes

THE
UNIVERSITY OF WINNIPEG
PORTAGE & BALMORAL
WINNIPEG, MAN.   R3B 2E9
CANADA

39   *Assumptions about Teaching Writing and Teaching Teachers*

and failures. Heaven help the workshop leader who is distributing ineffective teaching methods to a group on this schedule. Talk about accountability.

Whatever else happens, the program should never be delivered in chunks smaller than two hours—and the whole course should never stretch over more than two months. Some of the arrangements which have seemed most productive have included:

- Four consecutive Saturdays, seven and a half hours each.
- One whole day (an in-service day, often eight hours); five sessions of three hours each; another whole day to conclude (only seven hours this time).
- Thursday evening, Friday evening, all day Saturday—twice, two weeks apart (this is now our standard, and most popular schedule, believe it or not).

Most of these schedules will be greeted with horror by prospective participants—in fact, almost any workshop series which demands a thirty-hour commitment will earn groans, whatever its topic. When the time comes, however, the energy and enjoyment inherent in writing, sharing, and discussing carries the group through any difficult schedule. But again: the more intense and concentrated the course is, the more energy is likely to be generated and sustained through the program.

8. **Room and Equipment:** The IWP program has been conducted in settings ranging from a dank basement with 5'10" headroom to velvet-draped *salles* in fancy-schmantzy hotels. It doesn't seem to make much difference how opulent the surroundings are as long as a few basic needs are met, such as:

- Enough room for the people in the group to sit comfortably without crowding each other.
- Enough extra room for participants to re-form into various small groupings. Even better is another room or two (or other area) where individual writers or small groups seeking privacy can work.
- Movable furniture (obviously) so that this dividing and regrouping can occur without the use of tools for removing desks bolted to the floor. While we're on furniture, tables seem to be better than desks, and we generally find ourselves rearranging the furniture quite a lot, whatever it is.
- The project demands no audiovisual innovations, just a blackboard or a flip chart. The latter is slightly better (though less ecologically sound) because completed pages can be hung up around the room as reminders, souvenirs, and evidence of the amount of work accomplished.

9. **Food:** Doughnuts and coffee, potluck suppers, carry-out pizza and cheap wine—these are the fuels on which many a workshop runs. A snack is critical for

THE
UNIVERSITY OF WINNIPEG
WRITING & BALANCE.
WINNIPEG, MAN.   R3B 2E9

teachers who come to in-service sessions at the end of a long working day, tired and in need of inspiration and good humor. Elevating the blood sugar level is a place to start. Some groups prefer fresh fruit, granola, and herb teas; others like cheetos, cokes, and cookies. Whatever the repast, food supports the flow of talk and the building of personal as well as professional relationships. The bare-bones minimum, at any hour, is hot water, instant coffee, and tea bags. In many groups, participants will promptly devise their own food-bringing assignments, circulating sign-up lists and debating menus. Needless to say, such activity deserves hearty support from the leader, and not just because he will benefit personally from such projects. Participants often make conscious connections between the food and drink shared in the group and the intellectual sustenance of the program itself. In the written evaluations distributed at the end of the program, an astounding number of people describe their experience of the workshops in terms of nourishment and refreshment—often explicitly pointing out the symbolic importance which the snacks have had for them.

Chapter

4

The Writing
Project Program

The sequence of sessions which follows is *one* version of the basic writing project plan. Every in-service program has been, and will always be, different in many ways from its predecessors and successors. This is as it should be.

On the other hand, the course outlined here isn't exactly random either. It is perhaps something on the order of "IWP's standard program," a sequence of sessions and clusters of sessions which have been special and powerful in the past. If you choose to follow this plan step-by-step, it will probably serve you very well. If you elect to modify it substantially to suit your own personality and your group's peculiar needs, that will probably work fine too. But some parts of the plan are more modifiable than others. You switch things around in the first eight hours at your own peril; if people don't write and share and feel some risk in doing it, what happens later will be pale and shallow. The middle and late parts of the course are much more flexible—all sorts of rearrangements seem possible and are tolerated well by everyone involved.

As you have already discovered, we always have a hard time describing our activities without commenting on their philosophical underpinnings, introducing alternative approaches, forecasting teachers' varying reactions, and so forth. In order to tame these expansive tendencies and to keep the sequence of activities clear, we've laid out the following session plans methodically. First, for every workshop we outline the basic activities of the session, delivered in the form of instructions to a prospective leader. After each description, we've added whatever materials seem useful. Some sessions use *handouts,* and we've included the crucial ones. For each workshop that yields written results, we offer one or two *examples* of teachers' writing. If we have *variations* for a workshop, we outline them briefly. If we find we must offer our own insights and opinions about a session, we segregate them as *comments* or *digressions.*

Generally speaking, the program is overplanned. The discussions which spontaneously arise in any group, the extra sharing time, the reports of classroom experiments, the digressions, the logistics, and so forth usually guarantee that you will not get to everything on this agenda. For example, in one thirty-hour course that we recently taught, only twenty of the forty sessions were actually used—the first nine in sequence, followed by eleven other sessions that seemed appropriate and important for that particular group.

We're serious when we talk about the need for flexibility and adjustment on the part of the leader. But just because the program really is overplanned, and because each group will find its own spots to slow down and spend extra time, doesn't mean that you cannot be caught short of material during any one session. The time estimates offered here will sometimes give you uncannily precise predictions of how long an activity will take, and other times will miss by a factor of 200 or 300 percent. Beware!

IN-SERVICE WORKSHOP TIMETABLE

session		typical session length	running time (hour no.)	page number
1	Introductions	15 min.	1	49
2	Agenda Building	30 min.		50
3	Overview of Program	15 min.		52
4	Interviewing	30 min.	2	53
5	Prepositional Poetry	30 min.		55
	Do	(15)		
	Share	(15)		
6	Accident	1 hr. 30 min.		60
	Prewrite	(10)	3	
	Write	(30)		
	Share in 3s	(10)		
	Share with Whole	(20)	4	
	Discuss	(20)		
7	Memoir of a Person	2 hrs.		67
	Prewrite	(20)		
	Writing Time	(45)	5	
	Share in 3s	(15)		
	Share with Whole	(30)		
	Discuss	(10)	6	
8	Transactional Writing	1 hr. 15 min.		73
	Prewrite	(10)		
	Write	(40)		
	Share with Whole	(15)	7	
	Discuss	(10)		
9	Modeling the Process	45 min.	8	78
	Overflow Time	35 min.		
10	Process Model Handout Review	15 min.	9	81
11	Bad Student Writing	45 min.		83
	Write	(10)		
	Share with Whole	(10)		
	List Problems	(15)		
	Discuss	(10)		

session	typical session length	running time (hour no.)	page number
12 Developmental Issues	1 hr. 40 min.		91
Review Materials	(30)	10	
Task Groups	(40)	11	
Discussion & Listing	(30)		
13 Leader Presentation— Development	20 min.		99
14 Key Concepts Agenda	20 min.	12	103
15 Assignment-Making	1 hr.		105
Village Voice	(20)		
Cereal Box	(20)		
Remaking	(20)	13	
16 Purpose	40 min.		117
Brainstorm Purposes	(15)		
Reconcile	(25)		
17 Audience Shift	30 min.		119
Write to Friend	(10)	14	
To Parents	(10)		
Discuss	(10)		
18 Revising a Child's Story	40 min.		122
Write	(10)		
Share	(10)		
Discuss	(20)	15	
19 Forty Audiences Plus	30 min.		124
Review List	(15)		
Add More	(15)		
20 Leader Presentation— Prewriting Activities	20 min.		127
21 Drafting: "How I Write"	1 hr.		130
Write	(15)	16	
Share	(15)		
Implications.	(30)		
22 Content vs. Correctness	1 hr.		135
Read/Evaluate	(15)	17	
Whole Group Discuss	(45)		

session	typical session length	running time (hour no.)	page number
23 Guk-Bo	40 min.		141
"Lecture"	(10)	18	
Write	(10)		
Share	(10)		
Discuss	(10)		
24 Leader Presentation— Grammar/Dialects	20 min.		144
25 Revising Own Writing	1 hr. 30 min.		148
Confer	(30)	19	
Rework	(20)		
Reconfer	(20)	20	
Discuss, List Ideas	(20)		
26 Evaluation Expectations	50 min.		152
List	(15)		
Small Groups	(15)		
Discuss, Summarize	(20)	21	
27 Response Roles	50 min.		155
Brainstorm	(15)		
Respond to Paper	(15)		
Discuss	(20)	22	
28 Conferencing	1 hr.	23	161
29 Peer Editing	50 min.		164
30 Proofreading	30 min.	24	171
31 Dealing with Grading Pressures	30 min.		174
32 Toward Expository Writing	45 min.		179
Potato-Game—Write	(15)	25	
Find Potato	(15)		
Discuss	(15)		
33 Want Ad for a Teacher	1 hr.		181
Write	(15)		
Share	(15)	26	
Discuss	(10)		
Develop Assignments	(20)		

	session	typical session length	running time (hour no.)	page number
34	Leader Presentation—Expository Writing	15 min.		182
35	Curriculum Fair—Participants' Sharing	1 hr. 20 min.	27	184
36	Curriculum Fair—Leader's Ideas	40 min.	28	186
37	Owning Activity	30 min.	29	187
38	Appreciation—Enjoyment	30 min.		189
39	Evaluation	30 min.	30	191
40	Summary and Celebration	30 min.		193

Introductions

1 There is only one thing about the first session of a writing workshop which is *always* the same, in every school, and at all grade levels: it starts late. Teachers, who may spend much of their classroom time enforcing rules of punctuality, are rarely on time themselves. So be it. This explains why the fifteen minutes devoted to introductions here (see workshop timetable) may seem unnecessarily long; in reality, you may find yourself slipping behind schedule once the tardiness and the introductions have been accommodated.

You will probably want to personalize your way of getting acquainted with the group. The point is simply to get each person to identify him- or herself and say a few things out loud to the group. There are other ice-breaking activities ahead, so this session does not have to strip people down to their bare souls. One version we like is simply to go around the circle (they *should* be in a circle) and have each person tell her name, grade level or subject, and one strange (funny, odd, unexpected) thing about herself. This usually results in a few creative, amusing answers, which the leader is certainly free to play off of. Another approach is to ask each person to add to his or her identification something about "What I did last summer" (handle with heavy irony), "on my last trip," "last night," etc. Whatever terms you set up, remember that *you* have to follow them as well.

Agenda Building

2 It is important to demonstrate at the outset that the members of the workshop can guide the work of the group—that you have not arrived to force some prearranged doctrine down the collective throat. Obviously, this openness can be demonstrated by asking the participants to list their concerns about teaching writing and their objectives for the workshop. You can frame the issues quite directly:

We have planned for thirty hours of work together here. Of course I have a number of things which I think are useful and valuable and interesting which I can share with you at some point. But I also need to know what your situation is, what your needs and concerns are in the area of writing. If you can give me some ideas about what you'd like for us to take up in these workshops, I will try to blend them together with mine and come up with a schedule. So—when you read your students' writing, or watch them at work writing, what are your concerns? What things interest you or worry you or make you curious?*

Usually a prompt like this is plenty to get a discussion started. It is important that you conspicuously copy down what is being said either on the board or a flip chart. After a good deal of sharing and suggesting, you should review the list, informally pointing out patterns or categories of overlapping problems raised.

The leader should hand out a simple, straightforward schedule of topics at the *next* meeting, whenever it occurs. Your printed schedule should lean toward making the participants' contributions explicit: use the group's own terminology where possible. Undoubtedly, most of the issues they raise will be the same as those you intended to take up—and identical with those in this

---

*These italicized word-for-word instructions to be delivered by the leader—and the verbatim leader "quotes" that appear in many sessions—may at first seem rather over-specific. After all, if we can't even trust prospective workshop leaders to utter their own sentences during a workshop, how can we claim that our program is replicable and usable by others? However, we really don't wish to be as dictatorial as these suggested monologues may imply. Rather, our aim is to present a concrete picture of what *we've* done, to let the reader hear some of the actual discourse that our leaders have gradually developed for certain key moments in the program. Instead of trying to describe the nature of this communication in narrative form, we want to let the prospective leader gauge for herself the vocabulary, affective tone shadings, level of formality and degree of directiveness. We have also found that in certain situations, the specific words a leader uses *do* make a difference in how people respond to a given activity. In session 9, for example, the omission of just four words ("Put down your pencils") completely changes the response of a group to the whole activity. So what we're saying by presenting these quotations is that we've developed some fairly specific ways of explaining some elements of the program. Other words may produce interesting and different results, and good workshop leaders will certainly learn by experimenting with variations. It is important, though, to become sensitive to just how much difference the leader's choice of words can make.

plan. And it is important to be honest about saying that *you* have an agenda too—and so the first third of the course, which the participants probably have *not* requested, stands legitimately as your pet segment of the plan.

EXAMPLE CONCERNS LISTED BY TEACHERS AT BRENDONWOOD SCHOOL

1 Dispelling fear . . . students' and own.
2 Mechanics vs. content.
3 Giving writing a purpose (to students).
4 Peer editing.
5 Mechanics through real writing.
6 Relationship of oral and written.
7 Journals . . . making them work.
8 Prewriting.
9 How to help other teachers (in brief time).
10 Getting support from other teachers.
11 Across curriculum.
12 Changing audiences.
13 What research says.
14 Interesting vocabulary . . . sentence variety.
15 Kid's own initiative.
16 Evaluating without discouraging.
17 Evaluating for grades . . . alternate evaluation.
18 Revising . . . serious revising.
19 Why write???
20 Commitment
    interest
    voice
    reader
    student's own initiative.
21 Writing as fun—not drudgery . . . student's own topics.
22 Development/stages (school purposes).
23 Publishing/sharing.
24 Shaping the official curriculum.
25 Writing to critique subject matter.
26 Writing as self-discovery.
27 Spelling.
28 Paper load.
29 Grammar (place, purpose).
30 Articulation.

3

If you have just finished soliciting the group's advice, you may not want to sound too certain about the future direction of the course. The syllabus is indeed forthcoming and will achieve a synthesis of their ideas and yours. What you can—and should—tell them at this point is that the course is divided into three main parts: the first composed mainly of their doing some writing and looking at it in various ways; a second section in which teachers review some of the research and theory on writing which has recently been done, as well as doing some research on their own students and their writing; and the third part in which they apply what they have learned earlier to develop new, practical classroom activities. You might also need to say here that whatever else happens, the group *will* at least spend some time talking about _____ and _____ (here, fill in whatever seemed to be the most pressing concerns in the agenda-building session—often these include evaluation, grammar, motivation, expository vs. creative forms, parent pressures, etc.).

Interviewing

4 The purpose of this activity is for each member of the group to get to know one other person and have the experience of addressing the whole group with a report. The aim is the sharing of some energetic, good-natured talk. It is important to understand this objective, because you may know of some other activity which, in about the same amount of time, can just as effectively help people get acquainted and begin sharing with a larger group. If so, use your own version if you wish.

One reliable activity is the interview-switch game. The leader asks the group to form in twos. In each pair, one person interviews the other for five minutes, finding out as much basic and interesting information as she can. We usually announce beforehand that odd, off-the-wall questions often reveal more about a person than the more standard queries. We define off-the-wall as: "Who would you like to be marooned on a desert island with?" "What's the worst book you ever read?" "What should your tombstone say?" "What household appliance do you identify with most?" After five minutes, the pairs switch roles. When the interviews have been completed, go around the circle asking each participant to introduce the person they have interviewed by name and tell the *two or three* most interesting things about this person. Enforce this last rule or suffer the consequences, which may include a fourteen-hour "getting acquainted" session. No matter how assertive your discipline, this session does have a tendency to get out of control time-wise, even with the limits, so try to be genially tough in enforcing the highlights-only clause.

When this session works well, it really helps establish the tone and the habit of sharing—that's why we keep doing it even though it is sometimes hard to control. Note that if you are working with a group of people who know each other well to begin with, then you should instruct interviewers to find out things they *do not already know*—and which other people in the group do not already know. These can be trivial things, but the self-disclosure is vital; later, people will thank you for "helping me to find out things about my colleagues which I never knew before."

VARIATION Instead of leaving the interview questions wide open, you can focus the whole workshop on a single subject: people's names, for example. Have people get into pairs and work their way through the seven questions below, with one person taking the other through the whole list, and then switch roles. People should be encouraged to digress, to feel free and comfortable following any line of conversation that develops during the interview. This exercise is an excellent way of helping the members of a new group learn each others' names—and it also models the importance of teachers and students taking the time necessary to learn about each other. Interestingly, this workshop also works very nicely with groups of people who already know each other well; these somewhat probing questions about names invariably put familiar people into a fresh, new light. The questions:

1   What is the history, origin, or definition of your name?
2   How and why did your parents choose the name they gave you?
3   What nicknames have you had?
4   What attitudes do people display toward your name?
5   What influences has your name had on your life? Advantages or disadvantages?
6   Would you prefer another name? If you were forced to adopt another name, what would you call yourself?
7   What would you (or did you) name your own children?*

VARIATION   Our friend Bob Gundlach has responded to workshop participants' strong desire to learn each other's backgrounds at length by turning the task into a full-blown essay. To capitalize on this interest, you may wish to use the material gathered during this exercise as the basis for the transactional writing assignment in workshop #8. If so, you should stress note-taking here, so that people will have some tangible, as well as experiential data to return to later.

*Adapted from Louis Thayer, Ed. *Fifty Strategies for Experiential Learning, Book One* (San Diego: University Associates, 1976).

Prepositional Poetry

5

The instruction for this initial writing activity is simple enough: *Write a poem using only prepositional phrases.* After allowing a few seconds for the shock to register, you can restate the task. Normally, people will turn to the job fairly promptly, if only because it seems too ludicrous to bother arguing about. We usually try to supply people with a list of prepositions, either by merely handing one out (they are *so* happy to see it) or by doing a brief brainstorm at the blackboard in which people call out prepositions until a good-sized list has been developed. Allow about ten minutes for the writing, or until most (90 percent) seem done. If they start passing their poems to each other before you declare the writing time ended, you will know you've got a live bunch.

Ask for volunteers to read their poems aloud to the whole group. Sometimes you'll need to deprecate the assignment for a moment to lower the pressure and give people time to screw up their courage. Yet generally, the assignment seems so silly that several people volunteer without violent prodding. When someone reads, the leader must show appreciation of the sharing itself and also praise something about the content or form of the poem. Your job is to demonstrate to everyone else what pleasant rewards are available to those people who share their work with this group. Read your poem too when a lull arrives or when you're asked. This may be a good time to introduce the "nomination" procedure (see pages 37–38).

The main thing to discuss when the reading is done is simply how good the writing was—especially considering the strangeness of the assignment. Usually, you will be able to comment with genuine enthusiasm about (1) the general quality, (2) the range of subjects, (3) the number of spectacular individual word choices and poetic turns, and (4) the enjoyment the group found in this—what a magical activity writing can be. You may want to ask the group whether the arbitrariness of the assignment actually liberated them; whether the alternative assignment, "Write a poem," would have resulted in such fine verses. This discussion is not vital: if all the time is expended in sharing of poems, fine. The message is there in the experience.

EXAMPLES

THOUGHTS

In the forest
Under the tree
Near the lake
On my knees

Of faith
In earnest
Without doubt
To God

Betty Riebock

DEAR CUSTOMER:

Unless your payment is received
At our office
By noon on Friday
On you go
In accordance with established procedures
To our Adjustment Department
For collection.

In the morning, dunning letters
At work, chats with your supervisor
At night, annoying phone calls.

Around you, beside you, behind you
Everywhere
After your money
On your case
Without mercy
Until you pay.
                    Have a nice day.

Col Cutler

THE JOURNEY
(a poem of prepositions)

In spite of time and the river
Between the chasm of hope
and
despair
with grave misgivings
and
faltering
courage

valley
lush green
narrow
the
Up   through
a
c
h
a
o
t.
i
c
DARKNESS INTO

a veiled and secret place
down
a
tumultuous
tortuous
path

IN

a lighted chamber, broad and dry and high—
ACROSS
intervening oceanic miles
El Greco's 'grazia'
a beauty and grace of spirit
haunts
me.

Pat McGuiness

VARIATION The diamante is another poetic form that lends itself to this moment in the workshop—mostly because its rules are so rigid. The diamante takes this structure:

<pre>
                           NOUN
             ADJECTIVE   ADJECTIVE
          VERB   VERB   VERB
  PARTICIPLE   PARTICIPLE   PARTICIPLE   PARTICIPLE
          VERB   VERB   VERB
             ADJECTIVE   ADJECTIVE
                           NOUN
</pre>

Put this model up on the board, explain it, and give people about ten minutes to concoct their own. If people are fearful about beginning, suggest that they fill in the top box with "something you'd never find in a poem." You can also suggest that they work toward some movement or relationship (e.g., opposites) between the top word and the bottom word.

EXAMPLES

<pre>
                        Orkin
               efficient   effective
             spray   kill   destroy
     gasping   panting   kicking   dying
             sneak   hide   wait
               clever   forever
                    cockroaches
</pre>

<pre>
                     English
                 Alive   Vital
          Reading   Writing   Discussing
       Talk   Think   Debate   Listen
          Lecturing   Drilling   Testing
                 Numb   Hazy
                     Sleep
</pre>

VARIATION   Chicago poet Michael Anania has shown us another structured poetry exercise which works well at this early stage of a workshop—particularly if the group is mostly made up of high school English teachers. This procedure, which traces back to the Surrealist movement, is sometimes called the "Exquisite Cadaver," emphasizing its often fortuitous juxtapositions. The instructions:

1 *Write down two words which are opposites (hot/cold, left/right, war/peace, clean/dirty) at the top of a sheet of paper, one word on the left side and one word on the right. Now direct your attention to the left-hand word, and write under it the first word which comes to mind when you think about the stimulus word. Write down this association directly underneath the original word. Now, ignoring the top word, derive a quick association from the second word and write it underneath. The principle here is to develop a string of free associations, each one drawn only from the previous entry. It helps to stretch, to feel free, to enter off-the-wall associations. Continue until you have a list of fifteen words under the original one.*

2 *Now, using the right-hand word of your opposing pair, derive another association chain, using the same procedure—but this time list just ten words.*

3 *Now you have a total of twenty-seven words on your page: the two opposites, fifteen words on the left and ten on the right. Your job is to take exactly twenty-five of these words and make them into a poem. You may rearrange them into any order you wish, and you may verbalize them ("purple" may be changed to "purples" or "purpling") but no other words may be added. No articles, auxiliaries, nothing extra—just use twenty-five of these twenty-seven words.*

4 The leader allows about ten minutes of work time, and then checks to see if people are finished. Then she announces that everyone must remove five words from their poem. After the groaning has died down, the leader allows another five minutes or so for this revision. Next, the leader demands another revision: *Take out three more words.* What often happens at this point is that the participants will balk at changing their poem any further: some may even get angry, while others quietly break the rules, neglecting to follow the deletion instructions. The participants have suddenly taken ownership of their poems and are protecting them. People who fifteen minutes before probably wouldn't have said they could write a poem worth defending are now ready to defy an instructor who would tamper with their creation.

5 People who wish to read their poems to the group are encouraged to do so. Without fail, some remarkable images will be revealed.

6 Discussion can now center on questions similar to those following the Prepositional Poetry exercise.

Accident

You can move quite directly from Prepositional Poetry into this session—it seems fine to praise the virtues of people's poems and then to suggest that the group move on to something bigger.

Here's a step-by-step plan for the Accident session:

1 *I'd like you to think of an accident which you can recall. Everyone's been in an accident at one time or another—or they've seen one or been affected by one. Most accidents involve injuries, of course; sometimes they happen in cars, but not always. There are other kinds of accidents too, and there are even happy accidents. We meet people by accident or stumble upon something good by accident.* This loose, somewhat circular talk is meant to give people some time to search their memories for the accident they want to work with.

2 Look around the room at faces, closely. *Do you have an accident you'd like to write about? Have you got it clearly in mind?* Ask several participants to tell in just a *few* words what accident they've picked. If anyone fails to come up with an accident, then you must work with him or her. Offer suggestions: *Have you ever been hurt, broken a bone, had stitches, fallen?* Offer to lend them an accident of your own (it gets a laugh, anyway). You cannot go on until everyone says (sincerely) that they have an accident in mind.

3 You must give your next instruction confidently and matter-of-factly: *Now put down your pencils and close your eyes. I'm going to take you back to a time just one minute before your accident happened. Try to take yourself back to that place and time in your mind. The clock is stopped at one minute before your accident.* Then pitch the following questions gently into the silence with long pauses between each.

- *Take a good, long, slow look around. Where are you? What do you see?*
- *Turn and look to your right. What do you see?*
- *Turn and look to your left. What do you see there?*
- *Turn all the way around and look behind you. What's there?*
- *Is there someone else with you? Who is it? How do you feel about this person, or these people?*
- *What are you doing?*
- *How do you feel?*
- *Now your accident is about to happen. The clock is running. Your accident is now beginning. Let it happen.* (Long pause here, and give the next instruction *very* softly.)
- *All right. Now you can open your eyes. I'd like you to quickly make a list of*

what you have just seen and felt: words, phrases, images, colors, feelings, memories—include anything you've recalled. Just make a list—no need for sentences or for organizing the entries.

4 Allow participants to list for a full five minutes, longer if they are still working. Announce that their job is simply to write an account (a rough draft, actually) of their accident, taking any approach they wish. The notes can be used in any way they assist the writer. Tell them that they will be asked to read the narrative aloud to two other people. Announce a particular time, about thirty minutes off, when the group will reassemble to share. Encourage people to find a quieter, more private place to work if they wish—as long as they come back on time. This is also a natural moment for an on-the-run coffee break. Be sure, of course, to use the time to write up your own accident.

5 When teachers reassemble, you must set them up in threes. Go ahead and tell them that the number three is magic, important, and necessary—while you're going around the circle threeing them off. Announce that they will have fifteen minutes in their groups, and that each person is to read her narrative aloud to the others. Encourage their getting physically apart from the noise and bustle of the larger group. (You should plan to go off with a group yourself, ideally one that's short a person.)

Say nothing, or say something opaque about the sort of response they're supposed to give (e.g., *Give each other some feedback on your stories, whatever seems appropriate.*) Some teachers who have been dutiful students themselves may ask for more detailed instructions about the response they are to give to one another's papers. If they do, stress that it is entirely up to individuals to decide, but that you will be glad to discuss the varieties of response later. (During the discussion in step 7, it will usually emerge that most responses were supportive and were focused on *content*—and most writers will agree that they were very happy their writing was treated this way. But now it is crucially important for the group to *discover* this natural tendency, and if they are *told* how to respond, they will not experience their own instinctive behavior.)

6 When teachers return to the whole group, ask for volunteers to read aloud. This may come as a semi-surprise, but usually a few will immediately offer to read. If you haven't introduced nominations before, this is a good time to do it. As people read, your job is to support their willingness to share, and to find elements of their stories which you can honestly, enthusiastically praise. After each reading, try to get comments from other listeners before *you* talk (inadvertently closing the case on what's good about the paper at hand). In general, the more reading the better—if everyone wants to read (as happens in some groups), then let it happen. This will eat up much time, but goes far in building group cohesiveness and teaches powerful lessons about the writing process.

7 After all volunteers and nominees have read, there are a few questions which need to be introduced and reviewed:

- How did you feel when you heard the assignment at first?
- Did the prewriting experience help you? How?
- What problems did you encounter in getting the piece written?
- How did it feel sharing your story with others?
- What kind of response did you want from your listeners?
- What response did you actually get?
- How did you feel when you acted as an audience?

Each of these is fairly open—there are no right answers to be teased out. Perhaps the most important item, though, is the one about sharing and feeling vulnerable as a writer—above all, this experience is supposed to foster empathy with students.

Do not feel rushed to discuss practical classroom implications of the exercise. Many participants will be quietly thinking about them, which is, of course, one thing you want to happen. If group members have practical ideas they wish to bring up, encourage them within the limits of the time available. If people are uncertain or doubtful about the teaching implications, you can assure them that there will be plenty of practical suggestions later, and that the first step is just to do and appreciate the writing so that the group can have a meaningful set of experiences to reflect upon. After all, if teachers can't concentrate for a while on writing itself, how can they expect their students to do so? However, if a really good, serious discussion springs up, don't squelch it. Use your own judgment; the mental processing of the writing experience is important. But it may be a waste of energy for the group to try working out *all* the implications before some of the basic concepts about writing have been made explicit. As a final note in the discussion, you will probably want to stress again the wonderful quality and diversity of the writing done.

COMMENT While this writing activity models prewriting, drafting, and sharing techniques, it does *not* have a formal revision stage. Neither does the Memoir assignment coming up next. Why not? Our goal in this part of the workshop is to move teachers quickly through a series of assignments that will energize them, excite them, show them the considerable extent of their own powers as writers, and put them intimately in touch with the other people in the group. With these purposes in mind, we have chosen writing assignments that tend to lead to very strong first drafts. People get such quick-developing, "publishable" results because these assignments make use of prewired topics—important life events or ideas that the writers have previously thought about a good deal, told aloud as stories, and otherwise rehearsed.

Since revision *is* a vital part of the writing process, it is important to remind people during this phase of the program that they will have workshop time later to pick one or more of their pieces to develop further. Revising has been saved until later (Session 25) for several additional reasons. First, many in-service programs are scheduled to take place over two weekends, or over a period of a month or so. Delaying revision gives first drafts the rest that many writers find necessary in order to approach their material afresh. It also allows people to build up a backlog of written pieces, so they can work on one they most want to improve. Finally, it creates an opportunity to return to serious writing during the more practical portion of the series, providing fresh data about activities and teacher responses that encourage good revision.

In spite of this carefully thought-out plan, however, some eager or compulsive people, or those who find it difficult to write on demand in the workshop sessions, will revise at home just after a writing activity has been completed—valuable testimony to how much the writing process varies from one individual to another. You can point out that people are free to rewrite pieces out of class and bring the new versions back for a reading. While there isn't time in the workshop to rework each piece, you can always find a little extra time to be an audience for folks who revise on their own.

COMMENT   We've stressed that the leader should write and read his own writing along with others in the group. Sometimes, when leaderly tasks intervene, or when individual participants need special attention, you may not be able to complete the task. It's no fair looking for an easy excuse, but if the distraction is unavoidable, or if you need to confer with a troubled participant, you may want to have on hand a previously written draft for the assignment. While this sacrifices the direct modeling shown when you sit and bite your pen along with the others, it does retain the essential risk-taking involved in reading an expressive piece to the group.

EXAMPLE   DIGITAL INPUT

I'm smoking hard, my pipe heating up this big Ford wagon beyond the 90° air temperature, and I am driving hard to get home after a bad day. My pulse rate is up in the rush-hour competition, and my stomach feels full of paper. My hands slide on a film of sweat as I turn into my neighborhood of little houses—deserted. Sixty-seven little kids have been called in to dinner, and I am clear to coast down Nordica Avenue, roll up the asphalt drive past the old tree, and fall safely through the front door.

Brake!

Right there in the driveway is a tricycle. Goddammit! There is a little red three-wheel vehicle left dead in the driveway and I can't roll smoothly and effortlessly up to the front door.

Right here in my path someone has carelessly, negligently, possibly maliciously, placed a kiddy bike between me and the gin!

I squeeze the slimy steering wheel with both hands and jam my hot foot on the brake pedal, wrenching squeals and hiccups from the old car.

I am not angry; I am beyond that in self-righteous ire. I am injured in my soul that at this point in this day, so near to succor, I should be stopped.

I am roaring with rage as I pivot in the seat; the door handle is hot in my hand, and the afternoon sun is full in my eyes. Right knee over the left thigh I burst from the car to grab the trike that I will throw over the house and into orbit forever.

(I must slam the door, of course. To do this you grasp the trailing edge of the door with thumb to the outside, four fingers inside, and you put your body behind the muscle group in your shoulder, gaining full leverage on your thumb, pulling the door across the front of your body so that as it swings closed you can stride dramatically past it to the attack.)

The door is swinging and I know, clearly, coldly, certainly, what is going to happen. There is no defense. The door is shutting inexorably, and I cannot react fast enough.

I can only wait helplessly.

The car door has not clanged shut—it has thunked.

My finger is in the door.

I do not feel pain. I am silent now. I am sick with dread.

Dick Nugent

VARIATION The tone of this writing experience can be significantly shifted if, instead of asking participants to describe an "accident," the leader instructs them to tell about a time they "got hurt." This change obviously invites emotional as well as physical hurts. In running through suggestions and helping people find their own topic, the leader need not lean upon the spiritual hurts; if people have had their hearts broken they won't need any prompting to remember it. Most of the prewriting remains exactly the same whether you use "accident" or "hurt," though the focusing on an individual moment works less well for the spiritual injuries—which, needless to say, are as often gradual and cumulative as they are sudden "crashes."

EXAMPLE At the second mail call that day I got a letter from Evelyn. In the morning I had received a box of chocolate chip cookies that Evelyn had made. I walked to my two-man tent spiked into the Texas dirt, slipped into the opening and flopped on my belly and opened the letter. "Dear Pete"—that should have been my first clue, for every day before that it had been "Dearest Pete." There was only one paragraph and I remember only one sentence: "My heart belongs to Billy." I suppose I was stunned, but I don't recall being so. I ripped the letter into small pieces and let them fly out of the tent opening. "That's that," I said.

Perhaps where I was and what I was doing rendered even this terrible rejection less tragic. Behind us a sluggish river steamed on. In it, we had been warned, slithered thousands of cottonmouth moccasins. That morning on the :45 range above the silhouettes two vultures watched us kill imaginary enemies at close range. It was an appropriate spot for death, a spot where a "Dear John" letter seemed remote, even trivial.

Two months later, after I had been ill, after my records had been lost, after all of my friends had shipped out, after a month of KP and guard duty, I sat on the edge of my bed on a Sunday afternoon, remembered, and I wept.

Pete LaForge

VARIATION   One of the nice things about the accident assignment is that it invites people to write about their own lives while retaining complete control over the degree of self-revelation they offer. They can write about significant, life-changing occurrences, or about passing, minor bumps and scrapes. Still another topic that invites a wide and deep range of responses is "a loss." Writers can choose between losses of insignificant objects, losses of faith, or losses of loved ones—all of which clearly fulfill the assignment. Again, the prewriting for this assignment is much like the activities used with accidents. But like the hurt, not everyone's loss will be as sudden and as definite as accidents usually are, so you'll have to ask people to pick a moment when they discovered their loss, or most acutely felt their loss, or even the moment that is most memorable about their loss—rather than having them focus on the instant when the loss actually happened.

Before you get into the self-hypnosis, you can help everyone review the losses they've experienced and select one they wish to think and write about. We've found it helpful to have people jot down notes as the leader quietly goes through these three sets of questions and examples: *(1) What are some things you've lost? As a child, did you ever lose a toy, a ball, a tooth, your mittens, a book? Did you ever drop something down the drain, into the snow, behind a radiator? Have you ever lost your coat, wallet, glasses, credit cards, your car in a large parking lot, your car keys, watch, socks, contact lenses . . . ? (2) What ideas or feelings or beliefs have you lost? Childhood myths and legends—Santa Claus, the Easter Bunny, the Tooth Fairy? Belief in the omnipotence, perfection of your parents? Lost innocence, trust, illusions? Have you ever lost your confidence? Lost your cool or composure? Lost your temper? Have you ever lost sleep? Have you lost faith in someone or something? Ever feel that you'd lost your mind? Lost yourself? Of all these things you've lost, what are some that you'd like to regain? Which ones are you better off without? (3) What people have you lost in your life? When people grow up, change, become different, we sometimes lose them. People sometimes move* away. *You can lose track of people, lose contact with them. Have you ever lost a friend because of a dispute or misunderstanding—perhaps someone you loved? Did you ever lose a child in a store or somewhere else? Ever lose someone who died?*

After you've taken people through this series of categories, have them select the one loss they'd like to think and write about. Get them to identify the key moment in their loss, focus on that—and then take them into an internal research activity based on the model of the Accident prewrite.

Memoir of a Person

7 This assignment can directly follow the discussion session at the end of the Accident workshop. You might insert a break in between if people are getting tired—but have no fear about doing all this personal writing in one day, if that's what your schedule requires. The all-at-once approach builds much energy and group solidarity.

The Memoir session is often an experience which brings the group to an emotional peak. When people share in threes and in the large group, feelings tend to run high, since subjects of considerable personal importance have been addressed in the writing. One subtle job of the workshop leader is to nurture this open, expressive attitude right from the start of the exercise. This may come out in the leader's tone of voice, in the examples she elects to give, and in the use of certain cues which seem to prompt intimate recollections. The following step-by-step plan is laden with implicit hints that the assignment calls for a very personal approach.

1 *I'd like you to think of a person who has been important in your life; someone you'd like to think about and write about today.* Notice the leader uses *has been,* opening the way for both past and present relationships to be explored, or for participants to write about lost loved ones. Often this initial description of the topic needs to be repeated softly, perhaps slightly rephrased, as people ponder.

2 *Write this person's name down at the top of a sheet of paper. Don't worry—this may be tentative. You may change your mind and decide to write about someone else. But just put down that first name that comes to mind.* In this assignment you do not ask people to tell out loud who they've picked; but you do have to monitor expressions to make sure everyone has picked a person.

3 *Now I want you to think back over your relationship with this person and remember some of the things you did together, some of the times you shared, some of the events that stand out. I want you to simply make a list of as many specific incidents involving you and this person as you can remember. Just list the incidents; no need to describe them now. Express them in the fewest words possible to identify them, like 'Christmas of 1974,' or 'the car crash,' 'fishing on Lake Michigan,' or 'the hospital visit.'* Allow about five minutes for the listing—shorter or longer (as always) depending on how people are doing.

4 *Now I'm going to give you a few questions to help you remember more. After each question, you can just jot down notes, words, details, ideas that come to mind. I'll pause between questions so you can make your notes. First: How would you describe this person to someone who did not know* *him/her? (Pause.) What places were you together with this person? (Pause.) Do you associate this person with any special things—objects, pictures, songs, books, movies, holidays, etc.? (Pause.) What feelings do you have when you think about this person? (Pause.)*

5   *Now go back to your original list of incidents. Find the one event that seems the richest, the most interesting, the most meaningful to you and circle it—or, if you've just remembered such an incident, write it down now. You are looking for the incident that most fully reveals your relationship with this person, or perhaps when the feelings between the two of you were at a peak.*

6   *Now go through your other lists and circle or check each item which pertains to the incident you've chosen.* Pause and allow about two or three minutes for this. When you see people starting on bits of prose, you'll know things are rolling.

7   *Using your lists however they help you most, write a memoir of this special person, focusing on the incident you've chosen. Try to reveal what your relationship was like, why indeed this person has been important in your life. You'll get to share your memoir with two other people—and with the whole group if you wish. We'll reassemble back here in forty minutes.*

8   Sharing in threes should take about fiteen to twenty minutes, and again, give no specific guidance about the kind of response group members should offer to each other.

9   Reassemble in the large group and seek volunteers as with the accident session. You may have to endure some longish silences between volunteerings or nominations—but it is usually worth the wait. When the sharing is completed, you will very likely have a timely opportunity to point out the power, the personal significance of the written word. This above all should be clear by the end of the reading time, for the memoirs are always deeply felt, highly communicative writing, and the sharing of them is recognized by all as an unusual and important experience.

10   After you have completed the preceding step, the group should discuss the same questions which followed the Accident readings:

- How did you feel when you heard the assignment at first?
- Did the prewriting experience help you? How?
- What problems did you encounter in getting the piece written?
- How did it feel sharing your story with others?
- What kind of response did you want from your listeners?
- What response did you actually get?
- How did you feel when you acted as an audience?
- Does this experience suggest any immediate implications for your own classroom or your students?

Select the questions most appropriate to the tone and interests of your group, as well as to how the memoirs developed. Usually you will again want to stress their own discoveries about the importance of a personally supportive content-centered response.

MRS. DAVIS

Mrs. Davis was my teacher. She taught me about fascinating compound words like breakfast (breaking the fast), about authors like John Steinbeck, and above all, how to kiss. She was my teacher, and I owned her in 1967. I planned her going away party in room 11, was given the honor of recording grades in her grade book, and got to go with her to pick up her mysterious husband at the airport. I sat awed in the back seat of her car, a color and make I am surprisingly unable to recall, and drove with her to an unfamiliar yet enchanting destination where we would meet a man called Joe. Eventually, a tall thin man, outlined in a black beard walked briskly up to our awaiting car and opened the passenger's door. I prepared to watch every move that each would make.

"Hello," he said.

"Hi, honey." She then turned to me, a goggle-eyed twelve-year-old in the back seat and said, "Joe this is Robin, the student that I was telling you about." Immediately, I was relieved by assuming she must have told him everything. Surely she described the weather board and my land maps of Asia, and above all, my oral report on *Death Be Not Proud*.

"Hello, Robin."

"Hi."

The passenger's door was still open and his right leg hung outside of the car. Their profiles in front of me again, I quietly waited for what seemed like hours until they finally kissed. But it was a quick kiss, too much like my father's hello and goodbye kisses to my mother, and I was desperately disappointed. Simultaneously, they got out of their seats and met the porter at the rear of the car where Mrs. Davis leaned her body into this strange man, and I peered through a foggy window pane at their paired lips.

So, in 1967, after twelve years of fighting with my mother to leave my hair at a length that varied somewhere between the center of my back and the top of my hips, I cut those once treasured locks to a rather unfeminine bob that resembled Mrs. Davis's. That also was the year that I wanted crooked teeth and large calves, both of which were only two of her most fascinating features. In private, I practiced her laugh which was merely a rhythmic breathing and twinkle in her eye until it exploded into a gush of giggles that always seduced those around her to join. I read *The Pearl* and did a visual explanation of the word minutemen, consisting of two huge clocks with cardboard legs and arms. In social studies, Marcy Cantor and I studied the Lewis and Clark Expedition and actually constructed a brown canoe out of the endless sheets of construction paper which we then pasted on several chairs. In this, we rowed across the classroom while the rest of the class cringed at their desks.

It was also during that mythical year between sixth grade Barbie doll houses and eighth grade kissing parties that I learned what a "Catholic" was because Mrs. Davis couldn't eat meat when she came to my house for lunch one day over Christmas vacation. Years later, still teaching me beyond her awareness, she wrote and told me that Joe was Jewish and that she had since converted. Joseph Michael was his full name, she explained, a beautiful name I thought, and later, her sons were Jonathan, Jason, and Joshua.

Unfortunately, like every other teacher that I had from the time I was in kindergarten until I graduated from the eighth grade at South Grammar School, Mrs. Davis got pregnant and had to leave in the middle of the semester. On her last day, the day that Norman Goldberg chose for his pantomime project to imitate a dog urinating by a tree, on the day she nicknamed smart alec Joey Katz "omno" explaining that it meant all-knowing in Latin, on that awful day in the middle of May, we gave her a grand party. Unlike Mrs. Halvorsen, Mrs. Rossi, Mrs. Shapiro or any other of the pregnant teachers I had given parties for, since I was usually the party organizer, Mrs. Davis did not cry. She never threw up in her waste paper basket the way Mrs. Wallace did, nor did she get nauseous headaches on Fridays the way Mrs. Stephanini did. Not Mrs. Davis. She had a regal sense of dignity. When she smiled, her upper lip caught the edge of her crooked tooth and I became so conditioned to that funny gesture that nothing she did thrilled me more. She had a calmness about her, and when I spilled the orange punch across the table and onto her lap, she blotted her skirt and smiled reassuringly. That was it. Amidst new breasts, awkward conversations with boys, and hysterical fights with mothers, she was reassuring. Even when she gave you a D or wrote "sloppy" across your map, there was a promise of improvement.

And that is how I remember her. Sitting sideways at her desk with her sleek calves crossed, pen in hand signing yearbooks during a hot day in May. That is why at the end of a long day, I often like to lock my classroom door for just a minute, imagine that the chaos just outside my room is really miles away, and sit at my desk with my legs crossed while feeling the serenity that her image recalls descend upon me.

Robin Kacel

COMMENT   For many groups, this session provides an emotional turning point. The intensity of the feelings evoked marks a deepening of intimacy that can never be lost. Because this experience can be so significant to the future of the group, it is vital for the leader to nurture it—to encourage fearful readers, to allow plenty of thinking time between readings, to offer warm support to anyone who shares. We have found, in fact, that if this session is rushed, or if somehow those writers with the most intimate subjects aren't enticed to read, the group may later have to backtrack to build the sense of connection which this session usually establishes.

It may not be easy to learn about this experience from a book or to imagine it, if you have not been through it. The directions may seem manipulative, playing upon people's emotions. However, such assignments *are* open-ended. Participants who wish to write about less risky or revealing topics will do so. And for those who do risk, the feelings as well as the ideas are real and important. We embrace the fact that these workshops carry an element of teacher renewal, an attempt to reintegrate personal values and the work of teaching—two areas that sometimes get separated as teachers struggle to survive, day to day.

In addition, we've discovered that the topics participants write about are not just "emotional," though they do call upon the emotions. The memoirs almost always deal with basic values and preoccupations—childhood memories focused on abiding sources of family identity, parents, death, cultural inheritances, people who served as models, realization of the pain and difficulty experienced by those we admired. In other words, reading memoirs aloud in the group is not just a sharing of feelings but a comparison of some shared, some varying backgrounds. This comparison has a strong effect on the reading of *other* kinds of writing later. It allows participants to trust one another's constructive intentions when comments on writing, suggestions, and differences of opinion are aired later. Sharing personal, expressive writing has a *transactional* effect on the group.

Once teachers realize this effect, this importance of climate, they begin to consider its significance for their own classes. However, high school teachers are often aware of their students' shyness about vulnerable feelings and beliefs, and may doubt that students will read expressive writing aloud in class. Back in the classroom, this fear is just one of the factors that leads to the abrupt collection of student essays so that only the teacher sees all the results, making each student's writing a sort of secret communication, a private channel between teacher and student. Experienced teachers find they can break down the barriers to students' communication with peers by inviting a good deal of classroom *talk,* discussion of students' values and interests, verbal story-telling—beginning the enterprise at the oral level. It seems that *every* aspect of a classroom ultimately influences every other—and thus contributes to a climate for writing.

COMMENT   Every once in a while, one or more participants will find it extremely difficult to write on this or another topic, a situation which calls for immediate, sensitive attention from the leader. People may need individual conferences to talk over possibilities and overcome their anxiety, just as younger writers do. Some may find that the assignment, in asking for personal introspection, brings up overly disturbing memories, and they may need to redirect their thinking or identify another kind of topic of their own choosing. In such a situation, people can be helped to realize that the choice of topic is always their own, and that writing which provides meaningful expression for the writer is far more important than dutifully trying to follow directions which for some reason haven't proved helpful.

However, if a participant resists writing on the grounds that "this is a waste of time," or claims he "already knows how to write," you may need to take a different approach. Such unwillingness is one way to express the resistance described in Chapter 3, and it's especially troubling because it isn't open to the inductive process, which we count on to do much of the convincing in a workshop.

In this case, the leader can still show respect for the individual by probing to see if a particular issue is troubling him. Perhaps some administrator forced him to attend and he resents the coercion. Perhaps he has projected a particular stance upon the leader and is already arguing mentally. Uncovering such matters will often remove the obstacle. Beyond an honest dialogue, however, you may once in a while need to point out that if a person really chooses not to participate, he can insure that he'll get nothing out of the sessions. Occasionally such people attend workshops, and many of us as teachers feel we've failed if we haven't reached everyone. It's important to resist this perfectionism and go on to be one's most positive self for the other participants who want what the workshop has to offer.

Transactional Writing

After the personal writing participants have now done, it is vital for them to try an expository form so that they can make comparisons between modes. The task described here is a persuasive exercise obliging teachers to do "research," to find (for the first time in the workshop) material for writing from somewhere other than their own memories. This is a vital contrast, and we like to have it occur physically—for people to get up and prowl around, taking notes on something they cannot reconstruct from memory. Deviations from the basic assignment are welcome, but they should preserve the researching component, as well as the fundamentally expository, not expressive, purpose.

1 The assignment should ask people to write a partisan, persuasive report about the building in which they are meeting. An example: *You have been appointed the school design critic for* Today's Education *(hold up a copy of this, or* American School Board Journal, *or the like). This magazine is read every month by approximately 250,000 educational leaders; primarily school administrators, board members, professors of education, as well as some elementary and secondary teachers. For each issue, you will write a column in which you will review a particular school building—and for your first column you are going to do* this *building. Now, what sorts of factors or aspects of a building do you suppose a school design critic would have to take into account?* Here, work with the group to brainstorm a list on the board. It will likely include:

Functionality	Noise Control
Safety	Energy Efficiency
Aesthetics	Security
Structural Integrity	Floor Plan/Layout
Durability	Facilities
Decor	

Now in one short column you may not be able to touch on all these issues, but they are at least worth considering. One additional instruction: if you want to make a big splash with your first column, you will probably want to take a fairly strong position. No one really likes to read a critic who can't make up his mind, hedges, hems and haws—do they? You will have forty-five minutes to write your review—so if you go somewhere else, please be back here on time. As always, you'll get a chance to share your work with some other members of the group. If everything goes as usual, a number of people will immediately leave to do research, and others may ask you if they can work in teams, interview janitors, etc. Approve of everything: *Do whatever you need to do to get the review written.*

2 Upon reassembling, ask for direct sharing in the whole group. These reviews are sufficiently impersonal, and the group mature enough, that stopping off in threes isn't necessary for this assignment. You will probably get a range of reviews, from the humorous to the straight-faced—and, in any case, there will be much less intensity and depth than in earlier sessions. (Be prepared, however, for the occasional situation in which the teachers have strong feelings about their building—especially if it is threatened with closing.) Enjoy the writing of as many volunteers as come forward and then move into discussion.

3 The discussion needs to work through the following questions, roughly in this order:

- How did you feel when you first heard the assignment?
- How was this task different from the other ones we've done? (Here you want to stress that it wasn't personal or intimate—and that one had to get information from the real world, not from memory.)
- How did you get the piece written? What did you have to do?
  (Collect examples of how different participants got their material for writing. Some will have gone around observing and making notes; others will have interviewed staff members, if they could find them; some will have worked from memory, no matter how pale or inaccurate it might have been; still others may have simply made up the whole thing. Just get samples of the different approaches people have used.)

The leader should make some summary comments here, along the lines that this has been an expository, and not a personal, writing task—and that while there is some overlap between the two kinds of writing, many of the demands and procedures of the two types are different. Note that expository writing is the kind we increasingly expect kids to be able to produce in school as they get older. Yet expository writing, by and large, seems to be harder for most people—young and old—to do, perhaps because working with internal material often seems more important, and more mental processing of the topic has usually been done in advance. While the present task is designed primarily to help the group focus on their writing processes, you can promise them that later in the series you will devote time to methods for teaching expository writing.

VARIATION: A less purely transactional—and, frankly, much less predictable assignment, is to ask people to find a place somewhere near the meeting room that others in the group ought to know about. It might be a facility (bathrooms, a coke machine), something worth contemplating (a stained glass window, an odd cluster of pipes), a place to get some quiet work done, or some other point of interest. The actual writing assignment then requires that author to explain how this place he's discovered might be valuable *and* how to get there. When the pieces are completed, they are posted around the walls of the meeting room, and everyone circulates to read them. As you might expect, many people usually take a highly personal, creative approach to the assignment (what would you expect after the three previous personal writing assignments, after all?) so that the results won't necessarily parallel the official modes of expository writing. On the other hand, if you don't mind a little unpredictability, this assignment does have the advantage of being less artificial than the school design version.

EXAMPLE   A MODEST PROPOSAL

GENTLEMEN, I see there are no ladies present, so we can proceed. The building next to Edens Highway at Lawler and Old Orchard Road is ideal for our purposes. The access exits and entrances both north and south will provide excellent cover for our operational movements. Large parking lots both to the north and west of the building provide legitimate space to house and dispatch a large number of vehicles without raising suspicion. The football field and tennis courts to the south and west of the building are in a more discreet location and we can house and train the Tibetan tribesmen to withstand the rigors of a Chicago winter.

At the front entrance of the building is a large theater with four double access doors at the front and two on each side that can be secured while our indoctrination programs are being held. There are also large dressing rooms backstage that can be used to make up and disguise the Tibetan tribesmen before they emerge for calisthenics on the football field. We don't want to be accused of infiltrating the neighborhood.

Next to the theater are small practice rooms that are soundproof. These will be perfect interrogation and debriefing rooms. There are also larger band practice rooms that can be converted to demonstration centers for tactical nuclear weapons which we can use in the field. There are no windows, no outside access except through two doors and in case of accident the place can be sealed off immediately, with everyone inside of course.

In back of this wing is the auto and airplane repair section. We can dismantle and reconstruct an aircraft in fifty-six minutes flat with these facilities. License plates, fuselage repainting, engine stamping, serial numbers reworking; it can be done in one swift smooth operation. Those vehicles that are in excess of our needs can be sold down the street to Fergus Datsun as used cars. We can conceivably keep the whole operation running on profits from used cars.

Our main office can be concealed in what is now the LMC. Command can be secured as you enter the main doors and turn left. There are rooms without windows and visitors can be screened and debriefed as they enter each room. When they finally reach the back room, they can confront the Old Man—head of operations—H.C. himself.

Gentlemen, there is only one drawback to the building as I see it. This drawback is securing the numerous exits and entrances to the building. However, this can easily be solved by removing doors and building walls as they have done in the cafeteria. It's a fine example of a covert operation that is out in the open. We'll even make it half brick and half glass and tell the Tibetan tribesmen to wear their makeup at all times and to take off their boots!

Our decision is necessary today and I place before you the opportunity to purchase the property that can make us all secure—here in Skokie, Illinois, and in the world.

Pat McGuinness (Agent 008)

VARIATION   Here's a descriptive-informative task that employs the material gathered during the interviews in session #4. Instructions:

1 Have participants take their notes from the interview session. Explain that their job will be to write a two hundred-word description of the person whom they interviewed earlier. The purpose of these descriptions is to provide the fullest, deepest, most precise possible description of the person—a description which would help a stranger quickly come to know and appreciate the uniqueness of the person. The descriptions, when completed, will be dittoed and shared with everyone in the group, so that every participant will learn more about all the others.

2 Participants should go through these steps in preparing their description:

a   Spend a few minutes studying their notes, recollecting the interview, and preparing some new, pertinent questions to ask at a second interview.
b   Reinterview the person, shifting roles halfway through so each gets to ask questions.
c   Write a draft.
d   Read the draft aloud to the subject. Get his or her response, feedback, and suggestions for changes.
e   Revise.
f   Submit to the whole group, in writing and, if appropriate, aloud.

COMMENT   This Transactional workshop marks the end of the initial burst of writing and sharing. Participants will write more later, at various times, but not in such sustained and personal ways. Of course, the workshop sessions that follow include numerous writing tasks integral to particular activities. In addition, the workshop leader on her own initiative can use brief writing periods to help participants refocus, re-establish concentration after a coffee break or after a week of teaching has intervened between sessions, to help a discussion get started, or to let people record their thoughts at a significant moment before the flow of debate races on. The point, of course, is that writing is not just polished, completed performance, but also a tool for thinking and for advancing the work of an inquiring community.

Where it is possible, we have found it valuable to pause at this point and invite a professional writer to visit the group. If you can find a poet, fiction writer, or journalist who will read some of her own work and discuss its creation, you may wonderfully enrich your program. The teachers in such a session approach the "real" writer in a different way than they would have a few sessions before. They feel a much more informed admiration, respond as fellow writers, near-peers, and revel in the opportunity to learn more secrets of the craft.

Modeling the Process

This activity culminates the first third of the workshop. It is one of the main mechanisms by which participants formalize the discoveries they have made from their own writing experiences. Here is a lively way to get things started.

1 Give out a large (3' × 4') sheet of newsprint or flip-chart paper to every participant. Provide all the magic markers in all the colors that you can possibly get your hands on (a bribe to one's own or a friend's children usually does the trick). Review how the group has done several pieces of writing, from a quick and innocuous prepositional poem, through some important personal recollections, and into a bit of transactional writing about the building you are in. What is needed now is to make a model of the writing process, in order to reflect upon how the work has gotten done. Participants need a model that shows what comes first, what comes second, and so forth. To generate the data for this, each person should make a graphic model of his or her own process, drawing whatever diagrams, combinations of words, arrows, pictures, or flow-charts seem necessary to represent it. The task is serious, but try to encourage everyone to have a little fun.

2 After about fifteen minutes of drawing, tape all the charts onto the walls or chalkboards and invite everyone to browse through the gallery.

3 Once the jokes and laughter have died down (with any luck, you'll get a good cartoonist, class comedian, or nonverbal wisecrack artist or two, who will produce true works of art and entertainment), you can begin to collate the representations into a more verbal, analytical chart. Explain that it will help if the group can now develop a more general model, broad enough to fit different kinds of writing and different types of writers. It should be applicable to many writing situations and yet specific enough to say something helpful about the composing process. As a way to begin, ask how any piece of writing gets started: "What's the very first step?" A general comment: you are embarking here on an attempt to let people make their own model, while delaying and redirecting them when necessary. In other words, groups will usually come up with a decent model if you help them to be cautious enough to think of everything as they go along. There is no way to outline every contingency, but you want to end up with a structure that at least has prewriting, drafting, and revising (or their semantic equivalents) in the model, in that order. It is also vital to officially acknowledge recursiveness somewhere—if the people don't mention it, *you* should add it in as backward-reaching arrows.

Here is the process model produced by one recent workshop group:

WRITING PROCESS MODEL

Ruby and the Romantics Version

RECURSIVENESS

Prewriting
1 Motive for writing—an URGE
   an ASSIGNMENT
   an IDEA
2 Considering the topic—thinking the subject over
3 Finding an approach (may be tentative)
   —involves considering AUDIENCE, PURPOSE
   —deciding to be (e.g.) serious, sarcastic, scholarly, etc.
4 Gathering material (RECALL/RESEARCH)
5 Organizing material—selection, ordering, arranging

Writing
6 Writing a draft

Revising
7 Reviewing—Rereading
   —may involve letting it rest; finding someone to read it; reading it aloud to yourself, etc.
8 Revision—making changes in the CONTENT
9 Proofreading—editing for mechanics, spelling
10 Recopying
11 Publishing—Sending—Letting go—Turning in, etc.

This group decided on the steps listed 1 to 11 first, and noted the larger categories of prewriting, writing, and revising later.

The group called Ruby and the Romantics created its own unique model of the writing process, as every group should produce a different version. On the other hand, the Romantics originally wanted to list "organizing material" as step 1. They needed to be asked: "Is that step *really* the very beginning of the writing process, the absolute first thing that happens? Think about the writing you've just done. Did *you* start by organizing material?" And so forth. Often people will list a step (or use a term) that applies only to one sort of writing (e.g., getting the assignment) and then the leader must broaden the item to make sure that the entry can apply to all kinds of writing (e.g., a stimulus). As your group works through the model, you are trying to facilitate a full representation of the process, in a defensible order, with terminology broad enough to span all sorts of writing. The model above fits these requirements just fine—and so do many others.

Sometimes you will get through four or five or six steps and the group will become restless. People feel that the model is not representing their own writing process, and they lose confidence in it. Often, the root of this problem is that they recognize that their own writing process is constantly recursive, yet the official model hasn't yet accommodated this possibility. Tease this complaint out and incorporate it. You need to say at some point: *The model isn't perfect, is it? Because writing is not a straight-line, sequential process. Almost every writer moves in fits and starts—forward, then back, then forward again. We may find while doing a draft that we lack material and have to return to the gathering stage. Or, we may find while rereading a draft that (God help us) the whole thing is hopelessly boring, and we have to return to step 1. It is normal to have many of these recursions in any writing task. Often it seems that writing and revising are a single collaborative process. Still, we can recognize that writing does largely move in one, definable direction. You can't proofread a draft that doesn't exist; you can't organize material you haven't gathered; you can't publish a topic sentence. It is a sequence which, despite its necessary recursions, does move from Prewriting to Drafting to Revising.*

Once the group has worked up its model of the process, and accommodated as many of its internal disagreements as possible, it is time to reflect upon the significance of the model. Often, it helps to leap directly into the heart of the issue by asking the group: "What implications does this model have for teaching writing to your students?" This query usually generates a useful list of remarks concerning inexperience with expository writing, ignorance of researching and organizing skills, etc. You do not have to press too hard on the significances; they will emerge from future activities.

COMMENT   Some groups of teachers—often the most sophisticated ones—refuse to concoct a model at all. They see, perhaps before you even begin with step 1, that no one model can account for all writers or modes of writing. There are two ways to cope with such a response. One is simply to make a list of all the actions that go into any one writing task, irrespective of their order. Simply compile on the board, in other words, every element or ingredient of the writing process which the participants suggest. After this is done, you may ask whether anyone would like to propose divisions or categories within the larger list. In this way, the group may work itself back to a prewriting/writing/revising model after all.

The second alternative involves asking the group to play along with your model-making scheme for a while, in spite of the imperfections they can foresee it will contain. You can, of course, point out that a model is only a model, meant to help us think about the real thing but not necessarily explain *all* its varieties. If you inscribe the concept of recursiveness prominently on the model-in-the-making, acknowledging that any real writer's process will indeed shift back and forth through all stages in the model, that it may vary sharply for different writing tasks, and that different writers may stress or omit various parts of the process, people will probably allow you to complete the construct. When it is finished, it is important to talk about the extent to which it accurately reflects real stages in writing, and the extent to which it may mislead or oversimplify.

10

Process Model Handout Review

The group's handmade model of the writing process is a very important construct—and it deserves to be reviewed at the beginning of the following session if any significant time period has intervened. The natural opening for such a recapitulation is when you hand out photocopies of the model which you have copied off the board and had reproduced.

Why is this reviewing so important? Many participants in our workshops spontaneously start calling themselves "process" people, or identifying the staff as "process-oriented." We certainly don't insist that folks adopt such terminology, and like to think it simply reflects something they have learned. Also, the model itself has become the agenda for the rest of the course. You will be working through ideas and implications from both the participants' own writing and from research throughout the rest of the workshop—first issues relating to prewriting (assignment-making, purpose, audience, motivation), then drafting ("how I write," conditions for writing, teacher intervention), and later revision (response, evaluation, grammar, editing, grading). Finally, the model allows opportunities for you to discuss terminology (transactional, expressive, poetic, etc.) to the degree appropriate for your group. We've often been able to work the Aristotelian triangle into the discussion of early steps in the model. You will note that the timetable calls for the leader simply to distribute the copied model and conduct a discussion along the above lines for about fifteen minutes.

This session also provides a good moment for the leader to make an announcement that is very important for later work in the program: *About ten workshop hours from now, there will be an hour and a half set aside for each participant to work on revising one chosen piece of his or her own writing. At that time, each author can elect to further develop one of the four pieces started during the early phase of the workshop, or can work on some other piece of personally important writing. Many of us have some writing job that we really need to do, want to do, but that always seems to end up on our permanent back burner: a letter to a distant friend, a reminiscence that deserves to be written up, a resumé to be updated, a note to write to one of our children, a message of appreciation, a memo to the principal. This writing workshop offers everyone the chance to complete such an important personal piece of writing, whatever mode or style or audience it involves. People who want to take advantage of this opportunity should try to get something drafted in time to participate in the revising activities ten hours hence.* Sometimes (just to add another complication) the workshop leader will take a few minutes somewhere in the second third of the course to have everyone do some focused free writing on potential pieces of this type. That way, everyone gets a chance to see whether they'd like to pursue one of these, to retrieve something important from the back burner, or to work on their Accident, Memoir, or other workshop piece.

Bad Student Writing

11

During the first hour of the workshop, right after the introductions, your participants had a chance to announce their concerns about writing and students. Chances are that these discussions yielded some rather general complaints and agenda items for the group. Now, some eight hours later, we return to a discussion of students and their writing problems. The difference is that the teachers have spent most of the intervening time writing, sharing, and reflecting on the nature of the process. It is time to make some connections between what they have just experienced and their classroom situations.

One jolly way to initiate this connecting is to have participants mimic the flawed writing of one of their own students. Encourage them to think either of a particular kid with serious writing difficulties, or of an amalgam kid in their classes; either way, the idea is to impersonate an unskilled student writer. Naturally, if you want bad writing, it helps to have a bad assignment, and below is one in elementary and secondary versions. Adjust each to the age and style of the kids your people actually teach. If you have a lot of primary teachers, further simplify the language of the elementary version and say that it would be given orally, rather than in writing. For some elementary classes, a student with writing difficulties might write very little or not at all, and if this possibility is mentioned by participants, be ready to adjust—they are welcome to imitate "average" writers, rather than bad ones, if they wish. Don't deprecate the assignment until later, however—just act as if it is a swell task.

HANDOUT

Elementary

There have been many important inventions in the last one hundred years, including the car, television, and computers. These inventions have changed the way people live in their families, their neighborhoods, their jobs, and their schools.

But some people think that the *telephone* has been the most important invention of all—that it has changed our lives more than any other modern discovery.

How important do you think the telephone is? Do you agree that it is a more important invention than TV or cars or computers? Explain some of the ways that the telephone has changed life for people in their families, neighborhoods, jobs, and schools.

Secondary

It has often been noted that some modern inventions—like television, the automobile, and computers—have transformed (and in some ways degraded) our lives. But the telephone, which is probably the single most significant invention of the past century, has been consistently ignored. This device has caused more change in basic cultural arrangements, family relations, communication patterns, business practices, and other elements of life than any other technological creation of the modern era.

Agree or disagree with the above quotation, defending your position by drawing on your own reading, study, observation, and experience.

Allow about fifteen minutes for the assignment and the writing, and then have some examples read aloud to the whole group. Enjoy the laughs. Next, ask the teachers to identify the problems they were trying to imitate, while you list them on the board. Toward the end of the listing, encourage them to add other problems they have observed among their students. Then ask the group to distill the list (probably fifteen to twenty-five items) into related sets or categories (i.e., capitalization + comma splices + quotation marks = punctuation). This is likely to yield categories like: grammar, spelling, punctuation, disorganization, ignorance of the subject, not following the assignment, personalizing the assignment. Discussion should be focused on the latter issues: kids' ways of dealing with poor assignments, their tendency to use personal material in any context, their attitudes toward the demands of writing.

Very likely, the participants will have been pitching in with comments about the similarities between students' problems and their own recently experienced difficulties. If this has not been happening on its own, you will want to start prodding here: "What problems did you encounter back in the Accident or Memoir assignments that your students share?" "What audiences do your students have?" "How would your writing have been treated if you'd turned it in at school?" (Heavy-handed, that last one, eh?) You can rely on this session to surface some degree of teacher-student empathy, though it may not necessarily be dramatic, confessional ("My God, how wrong I've been!"), or unanimous. But often, this session leads to a very serious and important discussion of the fundamental relationship between teachers and students. (We've heard it start with disputes over the term "touchy-feely," for example.) If you sense things moving in this latter direction, by all means encourage it. If this workshop can give people a chance to think about why they became teachers in the first place, and about what teaching still does (or might) mean to them, nothing could be more appropriate.

EXAMPLES   Thats right. My dad says he's gonna yank ares right out of the wall. I think its because of my sister she's the worst. I never get to use it. I'd like to have my own phone and number to. When the phone rings at supper time dad won't let us answer it so mom says but it could be something important Jim. I'd like to have one where you can see people like a TV. I like the telephone alot.

Eleanor Henry Pierce

I think the telephone is a good invension because it brought people together over long distances and is a way to talk to people who live far away and who you dont get to see and would like to talk to. You can talk all the way to California for a little amount of money and New York costs the same and when my brother who calls from college in Arizona calls home to wish you a happy birthday or something like that my parents don't mind him calling but if he calls collect to ask for money then my mom says that it would be cheaper to write but then they really get mad when he calles his girlfriend who is also away at a different college and then charges the amount to our home phone then you should hear the screaming all the way to Mexico.

—Sharon Kociak

The telephone, which is probably the most significant invention of the past century, has been generally ignored. This device has caused more change in basic cultural arrangements, family relations, communication problems, business practices, and other elements of life than any other technological invention of the modern era.

First, this device has caused more change in basic cultural arrangements. In addition to causing more basic change in cultural arrangements it has caused more basic change in family relations. Besides change in family relations, it has created change in community problems. Fourth, it has created change in business practices and lastly it has created change in other elements of life.

It has often been noted that some modern inventions like tv, the auto, and computers have transformed and in some ways degraded our lives but the telephone should not be ignored.

—Herb Best

COMMENT This exercise, which was primarily designed to help teachers address a potentially difficult topic in a fresh and good-humored way, does offer some insight into the problems which student writers face. Many of these imitation essays show the "students' " lack of awareness that writing—at least of the expository or transactional variety usually required in school—is not a spontaneous, quasi-magical act, but a process requiring a series of steps or stages. Most of these impersonations are of writers who have no information about the subject at hand, have made no effort or had no opportunity to gather any material, or at the very least, have failed to shape whatever information they do have into some kind of whole. These are the essays of "students" who, given a writing task, seem to believe that the first (and last) stage is to write a draft.

But the lack of material with which to work, as these samples make clear, does not necessarily keep student writers from filling up a page. What students may often do is recast the task in a way which allows them to write *something* which may or may not be relevant. Some students essentially ignore the assignment and write recollections loosely gathered around the topic. Others slice off a manageable part of the assignment and deal only with that. Some use the instructions as a stimulus to producing a personal or "creative" response. Students who have mastered the art of padding may try to fake their way through. And, of course, many students will simply rewrite (or even reproduce) the assignment itself. All of these avoidance maneuvers seem to stem from the common problem of not knowing what to say—and more deeply, not understanding how to find something to say and then to organize its saying.

Our "student" writers also demonstrate another class of problems: their writing is full of mechanical faults: run-on sentences, spelling errors, usage flubs, failures of punctuation, diction, and grammar. The technical skills and conventions of written language, to say the least, are often not sufficiently attended to. These flaws in the surface of student writing, recently rediscovered by critics of education, have always been a concern and preoccupation of teachers, whose supply of red ink has never seemed to match the need for correction. But these samples may also point to a more productive way of viewing such errors. Just as student writers are often unaware of the opportunity for prewriting work (researching, talking, outlining), so too may they be unpracticed at the revising activities successful writers usually use. In fact, we cannot really tell from these samples (or from samples of real students' writing) exactly what the authors do and do not know about the conventions of writing. Spontaneous, unedited writing only tells us how good students are at one-shot tasks. Often, students have a passive command of many conventions of writing which they can use when convinced to actually revise and edit their work. In other words, our teaching of spelling, punctuation, and grammar has not necessarily been lost but is often not manifested because students lack familiarity with the process of beginning, developing, and finishing a piece of writing.

While this imitation writing exercise usually provides teachers with a hearty, albeit usually sympathetic, laugh at their students' expense, the joke is also on the assignment-giver. The bad writing elicited by this assignment is at least as much the product of its vague, abstract, and ill-conceived instructions as it is of students' incompetence. The telephone assignment *is* representative of many school writing tasks which present students with a rather hopeless set of alternatives. In the context of a study of modern inventions and their impact upon social life, it might be a defensible (but unpromisingly broad) assignment, but such writing tasks often are not even presented as a part of such study. All too often, we tell students to write on large, distant topics for unspecified audiences and for no clear-cut purpose other than the somewhat circular goal of fulfilling the assignment. The rhetorical emptiness of such assignments would daunt even the most skilled writer, who must have some investment in the process, understand his subject, know his audience, and have some purpose.

DIGRESSION Sometimes we have misgivings about using this workshop, because it comes perilously close to ridiculing students. We have learned never to use this exercise with brand-new groups, during one-shot guest appearances, or on any other occasion when some foundation of appreciation for students hasn't been established beforehand. We always guard against letting this session become an "Ain't They Awful" gripefest.

Yet despite our hesitation, we still do use the exercise. One reason we accept the risk is because this workshop so handily surfaces the subject of the "Literacy Crisis," which is supposed to be rampant in the schools of our land. Over the past decade or so, the American popular press has tirelessly proclaimed and bemoaned the supposed decline in student facility with language, hammering away at the literacy issue to the extent that practically everyone now blithely accepts the nostrum that "Johnny Can't Write." This, needless to say, is a concept which writing teachers ought to examine and understand.

The press certainly does have some evidence to work with, and it has not been difficult for critics to multiply the evidence of bad writing loose in the land: fuzzy business memos, governmental doublespeak, bureaucratic jargon, pulpy fiction, and error-ridden student essays abound. There can be no argument that the writing of most American children (and adults) needs improvement, and that if all of us did eventually come to write more fluently and effectively, the quality of our lives would be significantly improved.

But agreeing that the present level of writing needs improvement does not require us to accept the broadest accusations and most doomful predictions of the popular press and its "literacy crisis." The generalities—often the exaggerations—of outside commentators can be of little help to teachers, whose job is to discover the specific nature of their students' writing problems, and to devise teaching strategies which will both draw upon strengths and overcome weaknesses. Indeed, for teachers to operate from the perspective of the gloomy critic would have them so disregard and discourage their students' efforts, that the whole "crisis" prophecy would be brought much closer to fulfillment.

It is important, therefore, that teachers begin to draw a distinction between popular worries about "illiteracy," and the complex cluster of behaviors, attitudes, and cultural patterns which seems to make writing a problem for so many people. The main value of this more concrete, constructive approach, of course, lies in its potential usefulness for teachers who need to work with and understand real students. But there is another reason for teachers to detach themselves from the current sense of panic over the inadequacies of student writing. Despite the certainty with which the literacy crisis has been announced as a new and ominous development, there is considerable evidence that worry about writing is an old, continuing problem. We can get some perspective on the antiquity of these concerns by looking briefly at some past language and literacy crises.

If we go back to the invention of writing itself, about forty-five hundred years ago in ancient Sumeria, we find clay tablets recording the anguished reports of writing instructors about the sudden drop-off in their students' writing abilities. Teachers and writers in subsequent millenia have filled the pages of educational history with similar complaints about the deterioration of language in general, and writing in particular. William Caxton, who set up England's first printing press in 1474, argues that the language of authors had deteriorated and fragmented badly since he was a boy, and bemoaned the difficulty of printing works which represented such a divergent and decaying tongue. Jonathan Swift (and a whole line of others who followed him) lobbied vigorously for the establishment of an English Academy which would perfect the language, fix its rules, and oversee the production of writers who threatened to confound its purity.

In America, we have experienced forerunners of our current crisis which have a strikingly familiar sound. During the 1870s, there was a widespread and worrisome "writing crisis," with the president of Harvard complaining about the tedious and mechanically flawed writing of incoming freshmen. Several Ivy League professors recounted in the popular press their depressing experiences in reading the shamefully illiterate essays of "the picked youth of the country." After World War I, there was another, even larger language crisis which led to the establishment of a number of remedial programs, ranging from "Better Speech Week" in the public schools to the opening of a writing clinic for "undergraduate illiterates" at Princeton University. And even as recently as the late 1950s, American educators announced a crisis in literacy and, as a part of the post-Sputnik retrenchment, large infusions of federal funds were allocated to improve instruction in language, and particularly in composition.

In spite of this ample foreshadowing, the present "Literacy Crisis" is typically treated as a uniquely modern and utterly novel problem. Anyone who questions the smugly doomful commentaries of the literacy "experts" is greeted with the same blend of curiosity and contempt reserved for proponents of the Flat Earth theory: how can anyone argue with a reality which is so obvious, so fully proven? In an apparent attempt to close off any last gasps of debate, the *New York Times* recently editorialized that "The Decline in Literacy is No Illusion," and went on to counsel: "Rather than belittling the information, it would be wiser to absorb it, and to inquire pointedly why it is happening and how to reverse the trend."

History suggests that the contemporary literacy crisis may neither be so obvious nor so fully proven as the *Times*'s editorialists would have us believe. But whether or not the current panic about writing stems from a rational assessment of real behavior informed by an accurate historical perspective is largely beside the point. We believe we have a crisis, and so we are stuck with it. Obviously, the main goal for schools and teachers under these circumstances is to take full advantage of the opportunity to expand and improve their students' performance in this valuable skill.

But for teachers, the horrified reports of a crisis in student writing present a special problem. Not only are teachers as susceptible as the rest of the public to the general run of oversimplification and guesswork in the popular press, but in this particular case, they are usually identified as the villains of the piece. The American media generally blame illiteracy on bad schooling and bad teachers. And while most teachers are understandably quick (and usually right) to relocate some of that blame, they are also quite ready to nod in sad agreement with much of the commentary about their students' inadequacies.

Under the pressures of negative publicity and limited time, teachers are being tempted to overlook some important things they know about learning:

that blaming and complaining do not usually solve problems; that the skills of students need to be carefully and individually assessed; and that problems in writing (or in any other subject) are rooted not just in the students and schools, but also in a social context which may or may not support the achievement of particular educational goals. In the present period of hand-wringing about literacy, then, it is vital for teachers to move beyond the downbeat generalities of the popular media and try to determine just what their students' problems with writing really are.

More than we need simply to correct and complain, we need to study students' writing at close range; to attend to details; to search for patterns of skill and sets of difficulties; to ask questions and listen to the answers; to see students' writing problems from the inside and experience them with empathy as well as professional concern.

Developmental Issues

Researchers have not yet identified the stages in the development of writing ability, and probably never will, given the immense complexity and variability of this remarkable human activity. In many ways this lack of an official developmental schedule is a blessing; just think of all the taxonomic innovations we won't have to study, adopt, try out, and find wanting. On the other hand, teachers are invariably discouraged when they hear how little is known about the processes and milestones in writing development. One good way to cure this frustration—and, not incidentally, the best possible way to study the development of writing ability—is to have the workshop participants immerse themselves in a large number of age-graded natural writing samples, and to devise, so far as they are able, their own informal schedule of development.

The Appendix (pp. 219–235) is a collection of samples we have used for this workshop. It includes "compositions" from the oral fantasy narratives told by preschoolers in a Yale University research study (samples 1–10) on through to high school writings. The samples come from various places and times; some were spontaneous and others were done as school assignments. The whole group tends *slightly* toward the better-skilled students at any given age. Your best move as a workshop leader, though, is to slough off any quibbles about the representativeness of the sample. If people insist, "These kids are so much better than *my* nine-year-olds," just ask them to momentarily assume that what's in the packet *is* normal, rather than debate the matter.

1 Distribute the packet of samples. Talk people through the contents, pointing out that the first ten compositions are oral ones, that there are usually four to six samples at each age level, that all have been typed verbatim from the originals. Explain that the eventual goal of the workshop will be to identify threads, lines, directions, or milestones of development in writing—based on these samples as well as on what the teachers know from their own students. Explain that after a while they will be asked to study the packet with specific criteria in mind, but that for now, they are free to familiarize themselves with the samples—to read, browse, and talk among themselves informally about what they're reading for about thirty minutes. An excellent way to heighten the appreciation of these materials is to have volunteers read the first ten entries aloud.

2 After they've reviewed the materials, divide participants into four groups. Each group will be asked to look for growth in a particular dimension, though everyone is encouraged to note any ideas, trends, or milestones they discover outside their own assignment. The four tasks and some elements of each are:

- *Content* (subject matter, location/setting, characters, events, problems addressed, themes, feelings, implicit vs. explicit material)
- *Organization* (structure, order, logic, arrangement; evidence of planning; sense of audience and purpose; use of story conventions)
- *Spelling, Vocabulary, and Usage* (invented vs. conventional spellings, consistency, relation to oral vocabulary; word choices; metaphors)
- *Grammar and Mechanics* (punctuation; sentence length and complexity; grammar/copyediting issues)

This assignment always results in some uncertainty, and so it is good to restate the central tasks: one is to search for milestones or lines of development in the area assigned to your group (e.g., content). Another is to be open to discovering and discussing other patterns of development from age to age which happen not to fall into the group's assigned territory. Each group will want to elect a reporter, and the amount of time available for the job should be made clear (about forty minutes).

3 When groups have completed their discussion and notetaking, reassemble to share reports. Map on the board the main points of each report, making connections to previously suggested items as you go. By the end of the reporting period, you will have a ragged but serviceable outline of the development of writing. Though it will not yield clearcut, definable stages, it will indicate a number of subskills in which development occurs, and will suggest in what direction development goes.

If you wish, you can shift at this stage to the handout called "Constellation of a Writer's Concerns," which is simply another way of representing all the demands a writer must juggle in any writing act, and also suggesting how these abilities develop. The center of the model refers to "Executive Function"; this merely means that there has to be some mental agency which allows a writer to shift his conscious attention from one aspect of composing to another—clearly, no one is able to devote explicit efforts to all these concerns at once. The "Genre Schemes" near the center represent the sets of conventions which writers gradually learn; patterns of structure, tone, word choice, level of formality and so forth for certain kinds of writing—recommendation letters, poetry, grocery lists, newspaper articles, etc. (For terminology, see Carl Bereiter, "Development in Writing," in L. W. Gregg and E. R. Steinberg, eds., *Cognitive Processes in Writing*.) Mature writers have mastered the patterns of a number of genres largely unconsciously, much as they have mastered the lower-order skills like handwriting and punctuation. What the chart means to suggest, above all, is the enormous complexity of writing as a cognitive act, and this, in a roundabout fashion, also helps explain why we do not yet have a dependable schedule of how it develops.

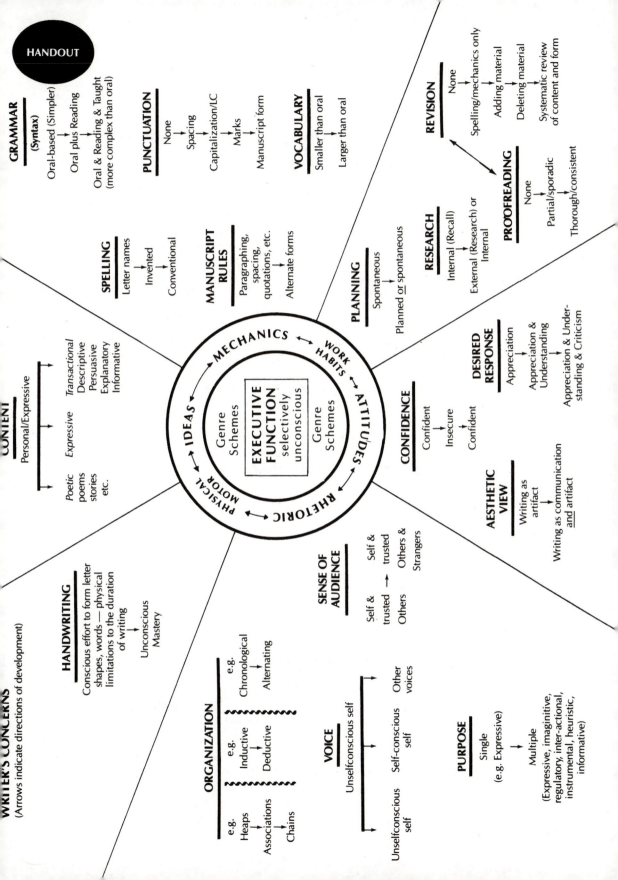

HANDOUT

WRITER'S CONCERNS
(Arrows indicate directions of development)

EXECUTIVE FUNCTION selectively unconscious

Genre Schemes — Genre Schemes

MECHANICS ↔ WORK HABITS ↔ ATTITUDES ↔ RHETORIC ↔ PHYSICAL MOTOR ↔ IDEAS

GRAMMAR (Syntax)
Oral-based (Simpler) → Oral plus Reading → Oral & Reading & Taught (more complex than oral)

PUNCTUATION
None → Spacing → Capitalization/LC → Marks → Manuscript form

VOCABULARY
Smaller than oral → Larger than oral

SPELLING
Letter names → Invented → Conventional

MANUSCRIPT RULES
Paragraphing, spacing, quotations, etc. → Alternate forms

REVISION
None → Spelling/mechanics only → Adding material → Deleting material → Systematic review of content and form

PROOFREADING
None → Partial/sporadic → Thorough/consistent

RESEARCH
Internal (Recall) → External (Research) or Internal

PLANNING
Spontaneous → Planned or spontaneous

DESIRED RESPONSE
Appreciation → Appreciation & Understanding → Appreciation & Understanding & Criticism

CONFIDENCE
Confident → Insecure → Confident

AESTHETIC VIEW
Writing as artifact → Writing as communication and artifact

CONTENT
Personal/Expressive
- Expressive
- Transactional: Descriptive, Persuasive, Explanatory, Informative
- Poetic: poems, stories, etc.

HANDWRITING
Conscious effort to form letter shapes, words — physical limitations to the duration of writing → Unconscious Mastery

ORGANIZATION
e.g. Heaps → Associations → Chains
e.g. Inductive → Deductive
e.g. Chronological → Alternating

VOICE
Unselfconscious self → Self-conscious self → Other voices
Unselfconscious self

SENSE OF AUDIENCE
Self & trusted Others → Self & trusted Others & Strangers

PURPOSE
Single (e.g. Expressive) → Multiple (Expressive, imaginitive, regulatory, inter-actional, instrumental, heuristic, informative)

VARIATION   Instead of dividing people into groups according to aspects of writing, you can divide by *grade levels*. In this case, the task for the groups is somewhat different. Ask each group to look over the writings for their own grade, for two years above it, and two below. They should then list *all* the developmental changes they perceive for children coming into and departing from their grade level. As with the first method of organizing the groups, there will be overlapping of results when the groups report. However, this approach seems especially helpful for elementary teachers, who need to think about the wide range of children's developmental levels in a given grade. (Our thanks to Cara Keller, of North Palos School District, for this variation.)

COMMENT   The young children's fantasy narratives are very special and often have quite an impact upon a group: as the leader or group members read a few of them aloud, the elementary teachers will chuckle knowingly and high school people will chuckle in wonderment. Anyone who happens to be skeptical of traditional Freudian psychology will have a tough time denying the underlying content of these charmingly primitive tales. If people show interest, we like to spend a little time discussing the content and structure of these stories, not only for whatever light they shed on the inner workings of children, but also for what they may imply about learning to write.

We've come to think that these oral fantasy narratives (which kids produce naturally, as well as in research studies, of course) are really their first composing experiences: when children of four or five search out an audience for a "story," (a parent, sibling, friend, or teacher) and then proceed to deliver a narrative monologue, they have performed a "composition" that is definably different from the conversational forms of language they have previously mastered. They have taken and held the floor, creating a complete, structured discourse without expectation of interruption or assistance from the audience. These are some of the critical elements of *written* communication as well; it seems to us no coincidence that youngsters who are good oral storytellers so often learn to write early and well.

Many effective elementary teachers recognize and exploit this bridge between speaking and writing. Knowing that kids have a natural foundation for writing in their vast experience of oral narratives, teachers encourage pupils to develop their writing in autobiographical and fanciful narrative forms. This offers an enticing and developmentally appropriate starting point for most children.

Ironically, after a few years of schooling, this strategy for getting writing done starts to backfire. As kids are assigned more and different modes of discourse, they have less success and take less pleasure in the work. What goes wrong? A closer look at the nature of the fantasy stories offers one possible explanation for this phenomenon. The oral narratives in the sample packet, as well as the early stories and autobiographies that primary school children write, have several underlying characteristics. They are *spontaneous*—they are

EXAMPLE *Report of the Content Study Group*

age	content	purpose
Preschool, Kindergarten 2–5 years	Family: Mom, Dad, baby Animals Bad behavior and punish- ment "Immanent justice"	To describe To work through feelings: loss, hurt, anger, fear, jealousy
Primary 6–9 years	True stories Growing awareness of self & world Forming clubs and joining groups Children's literature Awareness of future	To give information To clarify To express feeling of confi- dence in self as active participant To imitate literary forms
Intermediate 10–12 years	Concept of past/future, dis- tant time Expanded universe Creatures treated as charac- ters Scientific knowledge Jokes, riddles Assumption of authority roles Knowledge of societal prob- lems (drugs, violence, etc.) Sports Abstract concepts Friends	To affirm importance of friends To defy authority To struggle with morality and personal values
Teenage 14–16 years	Description of "hateful and cruel" action Awareness of fate Personal territory (i.e., bed- room, importance of pri- vacy) Self-degradation Controversial issues (i.e., val- ues, summer school, bus- ing) Love letter to teacher Literature analysis	To recall To engage in introspection (to examine motivation, guilt) To evaluate self-worth To examine and evaluate choices To express confidence in opinions and desires To influence others To communicate feelings (i.e., sex, love, loneli- ness) To clarify the meaning of a story

95

Report of the Organization Group

age

2–8	Story told with beginning, middle, and end, and with conventional story sequencing (#1–#13)
2–9	Contrast noted in #6 (babies)
6	Two ideas dealt with separately in #14
6	Simple topic sentence, comparison, and explanation in #15
6	Words written on each side of drawing that helps child organize thoughts in #13
6	Inconsistent use of margin (some indenting used) similar to that of a poem in #17
7	Evidence of preplanning directed to a specific audience (Mom) in #19
7	Conscious statement of "the end" in #20
7	Title and signature in #21
9	List in #26
11	Two distinct paragraphs; use of comparison and concluding sentences in #33
12	Assumption of the role of an inanimate object in #37
12	Use of ellipses (. . .) and capitals for emphasis in #38
12	Three separate paragraphs in #39
15	Cause and effect development, topic sentence, and conclusion in #48
17	Conventional letter organization (introduction of position, body, conclusion tying it together) in #54

Report of the Grammar and Mechanics Group

age

2–5	Cannot be judged because the sentences dictated; standard dialect
6–7	Short, simple sentences; use of periods, but no commas
8–9	Run-ons (more detail given); many *ands;* titles often appear; questions asked but no question marks used; complex sentences, but no commas
10	Capitals and commas still a problem; run-ons still evident; compound and complex sentences used (without commas); unnecessary verb tense shifts; titles always used
11	Dialogue attempted (poorly punctuated); many compound sentences; vague referents for pronouns
12	Capitals still a problem; little use of exclamation marks
14	Consistent verb tenses (appropriately changed); semicolons and hyphens used; some run-ons still evident; commas missing in compound and complex sentences

15   Commas still bothersome!
16   Conventional letter form; use of infinitives; parenthetical phrases and apposi-
     tives used with appropriate commas
17   Colons, semicolons, interjections, and commas are all used correctly; also
     parenthetical expressions used correctly with appropriate punctuation; *who*
     and *whom* used correctly

Report of the Spelling and Vocabulary Group

age

2–5   Vocabulary limited to experience; very literal; little description
5–6   Vocabulary even more limited as a result of the challenge of spelling the
       words; spelling inhibits flow of ideas; invented spellings; attempt at logic
       (*cuz* in #17)
6–7   Vocabulary still egocentric and literal; some use of imagery and transitions;
       use of some adjectives; invented spelling is phonetic; but more adventurous
       with spelling (#20, 21)
8–9   Vocabulary broader but not more sophisticated; improved spelling; use of
       more transitions, even more description (#25)
10   More sophisticated verbs, use of adjectives and technical terms such as
       "eclipse"—which they *can* spell; fewer spelling errors; errors not always
       consistent (#31)
11   Realistic but expressive vocabulary; developing command of language; very
       specific use of simile and metaphor; variety of imagery
12   Very reasonable; assimilation of adult language; values and judgment emerg-
       ing; spelling errors careless, not the result of ignorance
14–15 Sophisticated verbs (i.e., "distinguishes" rather than "is different from";
       "peer" rather than "look"; obvious differences based on socioeconomic
       background (#45 vs. #46); however, still capable of describing complex sit-
       uations; awareness of feelings of others, awareness of society and opinions,
       awareness of class distinctions; maturation of vocabulary to match matura-
       tion of self
16–17 Attempts at eloquence and precision; sometimes attempts successful (#51);
       support of opinions by argumentation involving sophisticated vocabulary
       (#53); explicit use of vocabulary to express feelings (#53); spelling seems to
       be sacrificed for the use of splendid, mature vocabulary to convey an opin-
       ion (#54)

created on the spot, and often the teller/author doesn't even know the ending when she begins. They are *personal;* whatever guises the protagonists may wear, it is always evident that the subject matter of these narratives is "me, my experience, my feelings." These stories are always strongly *reflexive,* meaning that they are told as much for the teller as for the audience; the purpose, in other words, is not so much communication as exploration. They are *symbolic,* often in a rather private way; we can't be exactly sure what the teddy bear and the milk mean to Keith M., but they are clearly personal symbols of some power. These stories are also *ritualistic* or, in a sense, unoriginal; once you become familiar with the work produced by primary-age children, you quickly recognize that they employ a limited number of underlying story structures— structures that are closely related to the content issues they wish to address. And, finally, the oral and written narratives are usually *unedited;* children are much more likely to compose another one before they'll go back and revise a story they've just finished.

Notice that each of these characteristics is the opposite of the elements called for in later school writing. When students arrive in junior high and high school, we want and expect them to do writing that is planned, not spontaneous; that is not about themselves but about material in the real world; that is truly informative to a reader, and not primarily for the amusement of the author; that is not laden with personal symbolism, but explicit and accessible to the "general" reader; that is not a ritualistic rehearsal of an archetypal theme, but something unique and "original"; and, at the very least, that is closely edited.

What does this imply for teaching? It certainly doesn't mean that starting out with stories is wrong. Teachers must begin where kids are, and tap into the motivation and energy that kids do have. What these contrasts suggest to us is that schools fail to help kids construct the bridge they need a few years later in school, when new kinds of writing begin to be assigned, modes for which students may lack an effective model of how to proceed with the work. We need to show kids, for example, how to gather information from outside as well as from inside their own heads. We have to show them ways of planning a piece of writing, preparing for each step of the work. We have to help them imagine the needs of an outside, sometimes unknown audience. We have to teach them to see their work as tentative, malleable, rearrangeable, and to practice revision. In sum, we need to provide kids with a rich and continuous experience in the full range of expository modes of writing—along with the guidance and intervention they need in order to build the bridge from expressive to expository forms.

13

Leader Presentation —Development

The line between the previous discussion and the start of this session might be quite hazy. In fact, this segment may well begin with the leader's commentary on the "Constellation" chart. In any case, the opportunity here is for the leader to present twenty minutes or so of material about recent research on the development of children's writing. While there are a number of alternative sources to choose from, we have found that an article by Julia Falk called "Language Acquisition in the Teaching and Learning of Writing" (*College English,* December 1979), effectively raises the central developmental issues for the participants. Many teachers are put off by the academicky tone of the article, and we don't necessarily recommend assigning it (though a disclaimer about the jargon in advance will be helpful if you do assign it). You as leader should be prepared to present its major ideas in outline form, whether your group has read the piece or not.

The basic premise of Falk's article is that learning to write is an act of language acquisition much like the native oral language-learning which all children do, and therefore we can discover much about how people learn to write by looking at how they learned to speak. She raises eleven major assumptions of child language researchers and then goes on to extend each of these principles, speculatively, to writing acquisition. In most cases, Falk's ideas are rich and insightful; on a couple of issues, she's since been contradicted by other people researching children's writing development. We include both her hits and misses on the following handout, which gives an annotated summary of the article's main points.

If you work your way through this list of ideas, it almost always generates a lively discussion. One of the nice things about the article is that it is speculative itself, and invites its readers to speculate as well—it is not a piece of research that says, "Here's how it is, buddy, take it or leave it."

VARIATION One good way to think about the sometimes unexpected connections between oral and written language development is to look at the writings of very young children—five- and six-year-olds—kids who are not yet officially able to read, but who sometimes create startlingly complex written texts with invented spellings. Glenda Bissex has written a lovely book about this subject called *Gnys at Wrk: A Child Learns to Write and Read.* It is not by mistake that Bissex puts writing before reading in her title, since her study shows that children's experiments with writing often go far beyond their "reading comprehension"—and that writing, for many kids, is the driving force in their acquisition of literacy.

The literature on children's early development in written language is burgeoning, and a number of works are filled with fascinating, concrete data—

Lucy Calkins's *Lessons from a Child,* Denny Taylor's *Family Literacy,* Robert Gundlach's forthcoming *How Children Learn to Write,* and, of course, Donald Graves's *Writing: Teachers and Children at Work.* While Graves focuses on practical methods (especially built around conferences) for encouraging elementary children's writing, he uses numerous examples of children's work, frustrations, and progress to illustrate his suggestions.

These books are full of wonderful samples of children's writing, and you might like to compile some of them for the workshop group. Or you could hand out copies of the following story, written by a five-year-old kindergartner who is the daughter of one of our students:

oNce thr
wos A Boy
Namd MichEaL
hiy haD a
GoD FiSh
AND a BRD
AND hiy WET
to hES MOM'S'
WOK hiy Kam
BaC AND the
goD Fish AND the
BRD WOR JOPiN OP AND
the BRT WOS
To the goD
Fish is out
uv the BOL
AND the Cat
is Com in
SoD th hos
wot wol the Fish
Do the cat
pot the Fish in
the BoL.

—*Annie Higgins*

Participants might want to consider some of these questions: How can a child who "cannot read" write such a story? (Of course, Annie recognizes many individual words in her environment and has been read to a good deal, though she hasn't yet studied reading in school.) What strategies does she use to generate spellings? What is signaled by the shifts between upper- and lowercase letters? How well-formed is this story as a narrative? What kinds of experience and knowledge underlie the construction of this story? What would be a helpful response for a parent or other adult to offer to Annie?

HANDOUT

What we know about the acquisition of *Oral Language*	What this might mean about the acquisition of *Writing*
1 Children have much exposure to language before they speak; they hear many samples, gather much raw material.	1 In order to become writers, kids need wide experience with written language; they need to be fairly accomplished readers. [Falk's emphasis was too narrow here: we now recognize the significance of children's exposure to written language in the first few years of life, before they formally learn to read. Kids who know their letter names and can translate/comprehend single words appearing in their environment know a lot about writing *and* reading.]
2 Children learn the dialects, styles, registers which they hear used around them.	2 Children will only be able to write in styles or dialects that they have often heard or read.
3 Comprehension precedes production; at any given age, kids will understand more than they can say.	3 Children will be able to read more complex texts than they can write. [Research by Bissex, Chomsky, and others shows that Falk overstated the case here. Children can and do write texts that are far more complicated than anything they could decipher in a book. For many kids, experiments with "production" (writing) *do* precede "comprehension" (reading) and are, in fact, the leading activity in the process of becoming literate. The degree to which Falk is wrong on this point depends on the degree to which one equates reading with comprehension.]
4 Learning is holistic; kids don't first learn sounds, then words, then syntax, but all at once: milk!	4 Children probably learn to write holistically, too; will perform quite differently on exercises than on real writing.

5   Acquisition largely unconscious and untaught; learn mostly without direct instruction; the unconscious internalization of rules and patterns of language.

5   Writing also probably learned by the unconscious internalization of rules and patterns. Argues for reading and practice, not drills and exercises.

6   Learn mostly in real attempts to communicate something (except crib monologues).

6   Instruction should offer real chances to communicate; not just to generate verbiage.

7   Main strategy is hypothesis-testing, not imitation; *goed, taked,* other overgeneralizations exemplify this.

7   Must write to test hypotheses; effect on audience, achievement of purpose, etc.

8   Must practice a great deal; make many, many mistakes.

8   (Same)

9   Parents normally respond to the truth of their childrens' utterances, not the form.

9   Teachers should respond to content of writing, not just form.

10   Sociolinguistic rules (politeness, dirty words, etc.) are learned relatively late; kids can express more than they know when to express at any given childhood age.

10   Usage rules may be learned late, by reading, practice, instruction.

11   Different children learn their language at different rates, and employ different approaches to the task.

11   (Same)

14
Key Concepts
Agenda

At this point in the program—especially if there has been a time lapse between the Developmental Issues workshops and this session—it is useful to review the major concepts which have emerged to date. Every group will show some differences in their interests, but some of the likeliest topics are given below. As you review and discuss these issues, it is not necessary to close the door on their implications; these ideas are still under investigation.

Fluency	Revising	Vulnerability
Practice	Audience	Idiosyncrasies of writers
Writing as a process	Purpose	Demands of different modes
Prewriting	Correctness	New views of students

As you will have said earlier, and will probably want to say again here, the remainder of the workshop series is generally patterned after the steps in the writing process model which the group itself devised. Accordingly, the next few sessions will deal with matters of prewriting and assignment-making. And those usually burning issues which lie further beyond—like grammar and grading—will indeed be addressed when their turn comes up.

VARIATION Use a "short write" to focus discussion at the start of this session. "The two most important (or surprising, or confusing) ideas we've dealt with so far in this workshop are. . . ."

VARIATION A somewhat more dramatic way of reviewing key concepts—and flushing out beliefs—is to write a "manifesto." Ask each participant to make a list of five things he or she believes about writing or the teaching of writing. Encourage blunt honesty, idiosyncrasy, and even personal prejudices—this is a major opportunity to surface disagreements. Go around the circle, asking each person to read one belief. Write the belief (or its abbreviated essence) along with the name of its contributor, on the board, but do not encourage discussion. This is a kind of sequenced brainstorm in which commenting on the others' ideas is forbidden. People may pass if they wish. You can either terminate this exercise arbitrarily after a certain number of circuits or you may continue until all beliefs have been expressed. The list can then be reviewed, conflicts noted, and overlaps pointed out—intersecting, more or less, with the final phases of the tamer discussion session outlined above.

EXAMPLE   What we believe about WRITING:

1   Writing is communication, not just drills.
2   Writing grows out of, and is intimately related to, thinking, talking, and reading.
3   Writing is a planned, conscious activity.
4   Writing does not always follow the writer's plan.
5   Writing is a process.
6   Different writers and tasks require different processes.
7   Writing is a solitary social activity.
8   Writing is risk-taking.
9   Writing satisfies the need to create.
10 Writing is a tool for learning.
11 Writing is hard work, and therefore is often fun.
12 Writing is important.

What we believe about TEACHING WRITING:

1   Writing can be taught.
2   Teaching writing involves risk for teachers and students.
3   Writing grows in a climate of genuineness, encouragement, empathy, and trust.
4   Students need to learn that prewriting and revising are natural and essential parts of the writing process.
5   Expressive writing is the base from which transactional and poetic forms develop.
6   Students should have many opportunities to write.
7   Teachers should take every opportunity to write.
8   Students should write for real purposes and audiences, and in a variety of modes.
9   Productive writing tasks reflect the teacher's awareness of the writing process, and identify the writer, reader, audience, and purpose.
10 Most writing requires some kind of response; not all writing needs to be corrected.
11 Evaluation is a necessary activity, and is useful when it responds to content as well as form.
12 The mechanics and conventions of writing are important, and should be taught in the context of real writing, in logical sets or patterns, and at developmentally appropriate times.
13 The writing teacher should be a student of language, and particularly of the nature of oral language acquisition.
14 Teachers should involve parents and administrators in their writing programs.
15 As with all other forms of advice, each teacher must sift these ideas into his or her own classroom reality and needs.

—IWP Summer Institute, 1980

Assignment-Making

15

In chapter 3, we defended our practice of using writing assignments in teacher workshops while simultaneously acknowledging the truth of Donald Graves's view that kids will never develop their own voices unless they're free to select their own subjects. It seems to us that there is a legitimate middle ground on this issue: it is fine for teachers to do some assigning and guiding as long as they are aware of students' fundamental need to own their work. Teachers who always dictate their students' writing topics *are* performing an act of theft—but teachers who sometimes ask students to address a particular topic (for a report, a test, for a class creation) aren't necessarily criminals. They may even help some kids to build confidence, break through stuck-points, or discover new forms. And, to be ruthlessly realistic for a moment, most teachers *do* give writing assignments and will not have this habit entirely broken by their participation in some writing project. So, let's at least try to do it well.

This workshop has three sections: the *Village Voice*, Cereal Box, and Re-making. All are linked together for a cumulative effect—the sequence demonstrates that there should never be a shortage of writing topics in school, and that no teacher needs a pile of commercial "story starters" to help her students find subjects.

Part I

There are writing topics around us everywhere, quietly waiting to be noticed. One way of confirming this richness is to take some artifact out of the real world and consider it as a stimulus for writing. A group can experience much success—and much ribaldry—by using a photocopied page from the *Village Voice* classified personal advertisements to make this point. The personal ads from any major newspaper, though usually less steamy, can serve the same purpose for those who do not have access to, or a taste for, the *Voice's* poly-sexual marketplace. The essential goal here is for participants to study the document at hand and try to develop out of it as many worthwhile writing assignments as they can imagine. Once this imagining starts, there is usually no clear-cut end.

Procedure: Give the teachers ten minutes or so to peruse and gossip about the want ads (if you don't permit this much time, they will take it anyway). As they read, you can offer to translate the various abbreviations. Then ask them to think up and write down five writing assignments which are based on the *Voice* ads—rush them; tell them how easy this should be; say they have two

HANDOUT

PERSONALS • 258

DWM, very attractive, 41, 5-9,slim, jogger, professional, warm, considerate, easy to be with, flexible, MS degree, from L.A., now working and living in Spain, seeking pretty, slim, nice female, wanting a positive change, to share life in beautiful Spain with transportation provided, address only, photo

Earthy attractive blonde SWF, 32, professional interested in the arts would like to meet sincere man with sense of humor.

ENTERTAINMENT EXEC
Aesthetic, attractive, droll SWM 33, 5'9, trim, with no time for illusion or play outside of business, seeks scrumptious simpatico woman 20-35, of artistic career & temperament, for special arrangement. Be slim, sharp, articulate, funny, affectionate, tactile, hungry for Chinese or Italian food & available upon request. I offer great dinners, interesting people, spiritual & contactual support, friendship, Moofkie Poofkie & more. Please be free of any commitments, except to yourself & me. Reply with phone & photo.

"ESPIONAGE AGENT"
Seeking romantic female undercover accomplice. I am 32, WM, 5'10', well-carved, 155lbs, wavy hair, piercing brown eyes. Rugged looks, writer/film maker with brilliant potential. If you're kind, very attractive and highly sensuous, maybe we can form a spy ring. Age no barrier. Enclose photograph and confidential data.

Exotic looking, down to earth SWF, 26, 6'2, smoker, seeks a politically aware open minded WM, thin, into music, longish hair, serious but fun. Photo

Financially secure, WM, 40s compassionate & communicative looking for a woman who is tall & athletically inclined to share in playing sports, dining, movies, good conversation and travel. Your race is unimportant.

FUNNY ROMANTIC
Tall, handsome, professional SJM 29 who is kind & considerate wishes to meet a bright SJF 20-37 for a mutually caring relationship. Let me put a rainbow in your life.

GBF, 33, honest, active, college grad likes outdoors, dinner dates, theater, shows, disco and traveling. Seeks same.

GBM 21 5'6' 135 Brooklynite with cute yet Grace Jones type appearance seeks creative friendly and sincerely masculine counterpart. Must be willing to look beyond that game of one nighters and fast time. For a change at a sincere relationship. Partial to Latin sunny smiles and nice physique. Photo or phone a must. Sincerity given and prosperity assured.

GM, appealing, trim, 42, well educated successful businessman looking for slim, quick witted, sensitive and physically attractive M companion. Phone requested.

GOOD CATCH
Handsome successful businessman, East side Manhattan, SWM, 41, 5'7, 140 lbs, enjoys sports, travel, theater, dining

PERSONALS • 258

GWM late 40s goodlooking 5'11' 175 lbs, extremely successful & super intelligent, searching for stylish bright counterpart. Preferably in 30s. Monogamous only & in perfect health. I have a fabulous lifestyle I would like to share. Please write & if possible, photo. Sincere replies only.

GWM, late 40s, trim, attractive, bright, friendly seeks G or BIWM, 30's to 50's, slim, educated, sincere for friendship, caring, sharing pleasures.

GWM making list of New Year's resolutions. Number one: change single status! What better time for romance than the Christmas Season. If your wild oats are sewn, your wondering eyes focused, and you know the difference between a fling and a relationship, then haul out the stationery! I'm 33, 6', 165, brown hair, blue eyes, handsome, into the arts, but not arty, adventurous romantic evenings for two and travel. Would like to meet a guy with individuality who knows how to share and prefers Fifth Avenue to Christopher Street. Please include phone and photo, if available, with your work of non-fiction to

GWM 22 Italian, straight acting & living, looking for same for friendship or more. Photo/phone to

GWM 22, 5'11', 165, brown/blue, healthy, inexperienced but not inept, college grad, straight acting & appearing non-smoker, goodlooking seeks same for one to one relationship. Pref Manhattan.

GWM 24, straight appearance, discrete. Tall, well built, enjoy travel, music, sports. Honest, sincere, good sense of humor. Seeks guy 18-25 Photo/tel#. No fats or fems.

GWM 25, 6'3, 195lb. Very attractive, cute face, good body, intelligent, fun-loving, professional in Huntington Village L.I. Looking to meet a goodlooking straight acting guy with interest in Art, theatre, movies, keeping fit & laughing with a friend. I look forward to receiving your letter & photo.

GWM, 26, HANDSOME, IVY LEAGUE educated professional, 5'10', 160lbs, into physical fitness, straight acting seeks similar background, handsome, straight-appearing, M, 20's. Please be sincere-I am. Send phone #, photo if available.

GWM, 26, 5'5", 130, goodlooking, friendly, sincere, humorous, healthy, straight acting/appearing seeks similar 20-30 for good times & possible relationship. If you are in control of life & know how to enjoy it, write to me. Photo/phone if possible.

GWM, 31, writer, broad-shouldered, sensitive, healthy, fit, seeks GWM, 25, actor/painter with spiritual openess, athletic build, and straight manners. Object: relaxed sharing. Phone, photo

GWM, 33, 5'8, 133, hazel, brown, moustache, professional, seeks GWM 28-38 to share interests, enjoy times, possible relationship. Write about yourself. Photo/phone

GWM 43, 6', 210lb. Brn hair/eyes/mustache, football player build. Sensitive,

PERSONALS • 258

Just ended with someone because she put business before me. NY Tech WM is looking for right F for good times.

Just turned 30 SWJF, pretty, physically active, 5'4, with master's degree in international affairs, a dry wit & gentle soul. I seek a SWJM 26-35 who is ambitious but not lost in the upward climb; confident but not arrogant. He has both feet firmly on the ground but is a dreamer, never the less; with a kind heart & ability to laugh at himself & life's absurdities.

LAIDBACK
Manhattanite, SJM, non-religious, 30, 5'6", who enjoys long walks, jazz, dancing, Yiddish, The Honeymooners, and just plain fooling around, seeks SJF with same or similiar interests.

LATE SHIFT
SWM 26 professional college educated seeks SWF 22-30 who works an 11-7 AM shift. I'm very good looking (really) diverse interests, great sense of humor. Our fun will begin, when everyone else is at the office. Photo please.

LET'S DANCE!
Your a caring, sincere, attractive F who smiles easily & enjoys pleasing her M. Not interested in your education, job or background. I'm an attractive DWM 6', 175lb, dark hair & mustache, looks 35 who enjoys Movies, walking in the city, drives in the country, Discos, good conversation, quiet eves at home & more. If you'd like to dance thru life together, holding hands & sharing hugs please write. NY or NJ OK.

Long Island BIWM, 35, very attractive, clean, discreet, seeks BIM, BIF or couple with similar qualities for friendship and sensual encounters.

LOVE TRIANGLE
A good-looking, very well-built WM 26 seeks an attractive couple for an eve of relaxed sensual pleasure.

MALE, single 50s, successful professional seeks intelligent, robust female who enjoys concerts. Write

MANHATTAN PALADIN
Very attractive M (John Denver resembles me) straight, 5'9, 36, slim, nicely muscled, tight bod, gainfully employed, sharp clear intellect, tempered with good humor and honest, joyous passion. Seeks very attractive lady for mate. Photo exchange a must.

Married NYC entrepreneur, M, 30s, seeks married/divorce NYC woman, 35-50 for discreet daytime affair. Include phone number or no response.

MWF, Blonde, blue eyed, 35, 5'6, 130lbs, desires a married White or Black Man, 30-35. For discreet, Lively love affair. Am seeking a playful passionate Man. Photo and Phone a must. Clean, no drugs, diseases or crazies. Write to

MWM Good looking, age 44, tall, slim, blond, athletic. Seeks discreet affair with lady in north Jersey area for occasional intimate afternoons

minutes to do the job (allow three or four). Next, talk around the room collecting examples—there should be a wide range of topics; your job here is to
point out and praise the breadth. Topics you are likely to discover (or can add
yourself) include:

1 Write the dialogue of a telephone conversation between two of the advertisers
   on this page. Write the letters these two people might exchange if they
   couldn't meet.

2 Describe what happens when a dozen of these people meet for a drink at Joe's
   Tap. At the New York Athletic Club. In the lounge on a 747. On a blanket in
   the park.

3 Write a profile of the typical *Voice* advertiser. What seem to be the most common, shared qualities? What do these advertisers appear to value in other people?

4 What do these ads say about the problem of loneliness in our society?

5 Try to find a page of personal advertisements from fifty to a hundred years ago,
   perhaps in a big city newspaper. In what way do the older ads reflect their
   times, and what, if anything, do they have in common with the modern *Voice*
   ads?

6 To what extent do you think these people's descriptions of themselves are true?
   If they tend to lie, what sort of lies do you think they are telling?

7 What relation can you see between these advertisements for individual people
   and the more familiar kinds of advertisements for commercial products and services?

8 Write an editorial for the *New York Times* in which you attack these ads and
   call for their being banned. Write an editorial for the *Voice* responding to the
   Times.

9 Select any one person who has placed an ad here and write a brief account of
   his or her childhood. Or write about this person's job and relations with his or
   her coworkers. Or write a detailed description of his or her apartment. Or tell
   what happened to him or her on the day before the ad was placed.

10 If one of these ads was really made up as a joke by a group of college students, which one would you think it was—and why?

11 Assume the voice of one of these advertisers and explain to a sympathetic
   friend exactly how you decided to place your ad.

12 Write an ad for yourself. For someone you would like to meet. For your
   teacher. For the president of the United States.

13 Write an account of what would happen if someone tried to place one of these
   ads in a small-town newspaper.

14 You are the *Village Voice* staff member in charge of personal ads. Tell about
   your job and how you feel about it.

15 If the *Wall Street Journal* carried such personal ads, what would they sound
   like? What about the *Christian Science Monitor*? *Field and Stream*?

16 If someone (or something) from Mars landed here and had to learn about the

human race's idea of *love* only on the basis of these ads, what might he, she, or it say?

17   Which person on this page would you be most interested in getting to know, and why? Which would you most like to avoid, and why?

Obviously, the value of this exercise lies in the process of the brainstorming and not in promoting the use of this sexual billboard in the schools. But, in a way, the fact that most teachers would not choose to use this particular artifact as a source of writing ideas is a kind of advantage: it emphasizes the need to find your own treasure troves, your own special sources of material and ideas which suit yourself, the students, and the school.

Often, talk about the *Village Voice* can lead to a discussion of small-town newspapers as a source of writing topics. We've talked about the curious way in which a stranger can learn a great deal about a community just by reading a single issue from cover to cover. The weekly paper, like the *Village Voice* personal ads, and like scores of other stimuli lying around loose, is a rich, almost endless source of ideas for writing. But what is even more important than sensing the richness of the *Galena Gazette* is developing the openness which helps us to see reasons to write everywhere, every day.

Part II

During the *Voice* exercises, you've undoubtedly had to apologize for the fact that most teachers could not use these want ads in their classrooms because of their salacious content. "Here," you can now announce as you plunk a box of sugary kiddie breakfast cereal on the desk, "is an artifact from the culture which students *can* write about in your classroom." Walk around the room slowly, holding the box up for people to see, and reading aloud from some of the panels as you go around (be sure to read ingredients, contest rules, nutrition information, etc.). Offer people a sample taste. Spend a good five minutes showing the box and reading from it. Then ask the people to jot down five writing assignments, using this cereal box as a source or starting point. Allow three to four minutes for the writing, and then collect examples, just as with the *Voice* assignments. Some potential topics using Cookie Crisp cereal:

1   Invent your own brand of cereal. What would you call it? What would it taste like? What color and shape would it be? What ingredients would it feature? What would the box look like? What mascot would you use? What would you give away free?
—Draw and letter a box for your cereal (all sides).
—Write a TV ad for your cereal.
—Write a story about a kid (your Mom, a dog, a Martian, etc.) tasting your cereal for the first time.

2   Does your Mom let you eat cereal like this? For lunch? When you're sick? What does she say about this stuff? How do you respond? Write a dialogue in which you try to convince your Mom to let you buy this cereal.

3   Make a list of things that would be fun to find in a box of cereal as premiums . . . *not* fun, etc.

4   Make up a recipe for something else, using Cookie Crisps as one ingredient.

5   Write a story about the "Cookie Wizard" and/or some other cereal-box characters.

6   Read the ingredients. Which one surprises you? Why do you think it's there? What's the main ingredient? What do you think of some of the chemical-sounding names?

7   Make up your own quiz and illustrate it. Why do you think the quiz is on the box at all?

8   Think of some questions you'd like to ask the makers of Cookie Crisp. Write a letter to the president of the company voicing your opinions, asking your questions.

Part III

Here's a bit of showmanship that should establish once and for all the infinity of writing assignments out there for the plucking. Distribute the handout "Remaking Assignments," and briefly discuss what it shows. Then have participants select any one writing assignment someone suggested during the Cereal Box brainstorming (or else you can daringly ask anyone to suggest *any* writing assignment, right now, right on the spot). *You* then take the suggested assignment through the chart, showing how it can be recast according to most of (sometimes all of) the different entries on the handout. Encourage the members of the group to help you out, to toss in their own suggestions as you work through the list. Alternatively, ask the group to brainstorm a few dozen kinds of assignments, using the chart.

VARIATION   This workshop session encourages an across-the-curriculum approach in elementary and secondary language arts. If you have a group that includes secondary teachers of other subjects or a workshop that is focused especially on using writing in other subjects, you may wish to redirect Part III of this session. Teachers interested in particular subjects can meet in small groups to brainstorm lists of writing activities relevant to their own goals. Or they can be given the list of ideas below and asked to choose one in their field that appeals, in order to flesh out details for designing a full assignment, providing prewriting activities, audiences, revising guidelines, and so forth.

   The concept of writing for learning in all subjects will probably need more explicit attention than it has received thus far, though its implications will no

HANDOUT   REMAKING ASSIGNMENTS

Change the Audience:

Parents, classmates, visitors to the class, the principal, children in other classes or other schools, children of other ages, politicians, businesses, readers of newspapers and magazines, etc.

The range is from close and trusted, to people with whom we must be careful, to distant and unknown audiences.

Change the Purpose:

Expressive—language close to the self; desire to share feelings, ideas.

Poetic—language itself an object of beauty, contemplation; poems, drama, etc.

Transactional—language for getting things done in the world:

—explanatory   —descriptive
—persuasive   —regulatory
—scientific   —evaluative

Change the Medium:

News article	Song
Story	Proverb
Script for TV, radio, slide show	Fable, myth
Editorial	Traditional fairy tale
Letter to the editor	Diary
Cartoon strip	Letter
Transcript of hearing, event	Advertisement
Interview	Lab report
Poem	

Change the Point of View:

Another character or participant in the same scene/event

A chance observer of the scene

A character remembering this later in life

An archaeologist digging up relics of this event

Looked at from across the street; the other side of the tracks, etc.

An object in the setting ("if walls had ears")

What the president, priest, lawyer, milkman might say about this doubt have come up in previous discussion. Teachers in other subject areas often need help distinguishing between the use of writing to clarify ideas (writing which may often be disorganized and more intelligible to the writer than to any reader) and writing to present ideas to others (which usually needs to be more focused on a reader's needs, more organized and polished). This distinction is made best and most clearly by James Britton in *Language and Learning,* and *The Development of Writing Abilities, 11–18.* Groups can explore this distinction explicitly by evolving writing assignment variations first for writing-to-learn goals, and then for more external goals. They may also need to review the writing process they experienced in earlier sessions to realize that they too may feel this distinction.

You can find specific ideas for various subject areas, including detailed lesson outlines, relevant prewriting activities, and critiquing guides in the three-volume set, *Teaching Writing in the Content Areas* (Elementary volume by Stephen Tchudi and Susan Tchudi, Middle School/Junior High by Stephen Tchudi and Margie Huerta, Senior High by Stephen Tchudi and Joanne Yates; NEA, 1983). Model units in the Elementary volume, for example, are on "Families," "The Foods We Eat," "Our Town," "The Sea," and "North American Indians."

Following is a list of topics that several groups of teachers have brainstormed. However, the leader may decide that it is most meaningful to have teachers create their own lists rather than studying this one.

HANDOUT

SAMPLE TOPICS FOR WRITING ACROSS THE CURRICULUM

(Note: These are only *topics*. Each would need explaining, discussion, creatio of context and audience, prewriting, etc., to be come an *assignment*.)

Art

reports on past or present artists
response/critique on a single work of art
explanation of a work of art by its maker (the student)
comparisons of various techniques: oil vs. acrylic, etc.
extended journal assignment: "What is art?" Students keep a record of obser-
    vations, emotional and esthetic reactions to various "art" pieces, all leading
    to student developing her own definition of *art*.
can graffiti be art?
can art be graffiti?
report of a gallery visit
how-to paper, telling how to work in an unusual medium
letters to artists

Business/Consumer Education

resumés, letters of application
starting a small business—is there hope? how? where? why?
computers in business
computer literacy in the future—who needs it?
responding to newspaper want ads
writing newspaper want ads
feature stories about people and their jobs
job descriptions, real or ideal
script of a job interview, real or ideal
investigative report: how local businesses are faring in the present economic
    climate
profile of a new (old, odd) business in the community
advertising gimmicks, tricks, lies exposed
product safety reports
editorial on planned obsolescence, reliability, workmanship
street-corner market research
interview of a local entrepreneur: a success story

Foreign Language

portraits of historical figures or events
report on religions of the country

visit and interview the local consul
correspond with a foreign pen-pal, business, relative
"survival guide" for traveling, living in the country
plan a dream trip to the country (3 days, 1 week, 1 month) and give detailed
   daily itinerary with reasons for choices
review of a foreign film
report on a magazine from the target country
one of the most interesting cultural differences between the U.S. and . . .
reports on a region or city
find evidence of patriotism, nationalism in foreign publications—compare to
   U.S. examples
review foreign-language soap opera on cable TV

Health

stress and cancer; is there a connection?
para-medicine; how much can nondoctors do?
health careers—what are the prospects (interviews, research)
editorial on euthanasia, artificial organs, abortion
story or play depicting a health issue
the most important health issue to teenagers is . . .
article on the #1 cause of teen death (accidents)
news article on a health discovery, issue
monitoring one's own health—in a log
the story of my diet (exercise program, aerobics class, etc.) and observation of
   its effect on my health
narrative of a time when first aid was crucial—or a failure
comparisons of five health clubs
research on health effects of food additives, pollution, radiation, etc.

History/Social Studies

interview with a historical figure (answers based on researched plausibility)
diary of historical figure—or fictional amalgam person from a particular era
"review" of a form of government; strengths, weaknesses
predicting the future, based on the past; schools in 2085
artifacts: studying objects from the past
dialogue of famous events
man-in-the-street interview regarding historical event
the biggest myths, lies, in history
editorial on social changes in progress: divorce, feminism
the most important social change now in progress is . . .
report of historical event written as contemporary newspaper article

Home Economics

running the home as a small business
satire on the homemaker's day
diary of a frontier homemaker; homemaker of the future
recipes
spouse roles; task-swapping, problems
issues in child care; should mothers work full-time?
reviewing new products for the home
Foxfire-type how-to articles on unusual crafts, cooking done by local people
essay on fashion trends
report on the economics of designer vs. bargain apparel
advantages of different fabrics (compare and contrast)
interview with cooks on their life and work
report based on visit to small food or catering business

Shop (Wood, Machine, Auto)

advertisement or pamphlet on importance of safety in the shop
video spot about what happens when safety rules not followed
instructions: how to use a particular machine effectively—read and then im-
    prove on manufacturer's instruction manual
how-to: step-by-step directions for making a particular object or performing a
    particular operation
history of the hammer (drill, awl, other tools)
different styles of joining (or sealing, or other process) around the world
profiles of shop-related jobs; interviews with workers in each specialty
editorial: how much should the average person know about making and repair
    ing things?
fraud and deception in the auto repair business; how much? why?
cartoon dos and don'ts (shop rules)

Math

story problems, especially ones which illustrate some actual human problem
calculators and mathematical literacy: a contradiction in terms?
should the U.S. adopt the metric system? Will it ever do so, no matter what it
    says it plans to do?
written descriptions of the relationships between concepts—in formal reports o
    in a learning log
geometry: find real-life illustrations of theorems; ways in which the principle
    may be practically applied
how to lie with statistics; use examples from real advertisements, make up you
    own

profiles of famous mathematicians, computer folk
write the same BASIC program in two or three different styles, and compare
  these with literary styles
write an explanation for newer students comparing closed with bail-out loops
write an improved version of the last textbook chapter covered

Music

reports on great composers of the past or present
why I like Van Halen even though my parents hate them
why I like the Chicago Symphony even though my friends say I'm a wimp
folk song lyrics, for new or traditional melodies
expressive writings stimulated by various musical passages
essay on the different approaches to teaching music to young children (Orf, Su-
  zuki, etc.)
my favorite instrument
the role of music in my life
comparisons of different musical genres
national anthems; history of ours; write a new one for your town
musical learning/practice log

Physical Education

portraits of sports stars, present or past
pros and cons on the social significance of sport
comparisons of the ethos of different sports: golf vs. football
script for a fictional TV sportscast
interview with a player, official, coach
review a professional game or contest—or study an amateur version
parody of game rules
make up a new sport
how to avoid sports injuries
write entries for a sports dictionary
why_____should be the next admission to the Hall of Fame
exploitation of college athletes—investigate, research
pressures on child athletes; Little League, pro or con?
obligations of sports stars as public figures
describe precompetition stream-of-consciousness; feelings of winners, losers

Science

letters to famous inventors
portraits of great scientists
autobiography of a failed scientist (pick your own era and specialty)

editorial on a problem caused by technology; nuclear waste disposal
step-by-step description of a lab experiment
evolution vs. creationism; my side of the story
mystery stories in which the solution depends upon a scientific test, principle,
   or understanding
laboratory tips, instructions, for future students
product comparisons; testing the Ph of shampoos
the most important scientific advances in the next decade will be (should be)
   in the field of_____because . . .
the worst scientific discovery of all time was . . .
interview a scientist

General

the use of a journal or learning log is appropriate in every class
setting the agenda for the day in class; three things I'd like to find out today
summing up work: the main thing I learned today was . . .
listing questions, problems
stopping and reflecting; interrupting discussion to jot notes
communication between teachers and students: I appreciated your comments;
   thanks for the extra frog to dissect

Compiled by Sherrill Crivellone and
the faculty of Blackhawk Junior High School

Purpose

16

This session is meant to remind participants of the many kinds of writing used in the real world, and also to show how few varieties are permitted or taught in schools.

1 Have participants take out a piece of paper. Ask them to try to list all of the different purposes they have ever used writing for, all of the kinds of things they can remember using writing to accomplish. Tell them that the goal is to have a long list; they shouldn't discriminate or edit, just include everything which comes to mind. If they get stuck (but only if they're really stumped), you can lob in a few suggestions: recommendation letters, mash notes, grocery lists, etc.

2 Once they've got their list assembled, ask them to circle or star the three entries which were the most personally significant uses of writing for them. After a pause for the circling, ask them to mark next (with a check, perhaps) the three least important uses of writing. Go around the group, having volunteers share pairs—a valued and an unvalued use of writing from their own lives. With a little luck, you'll get to hear about some love letters, proposals, and condolences in the valued category, with some school assignments falling into the insignificant category.

3 Now have them make another list, this one including all the kinds of writing which kids are asked to do in school. (Do not include illicit uses like note-passing). This list will presumably be much shorter than the previous one. The questions to discuss, then, are these:

- Why is the school list shorter?
- What additional kinds of writing should be added to school curricula; which should remain outside of it?
- How can we teach a greater variety of modes and styles of writing in schools?

COMMENT Those familiar with the work of James Britton will recognize that this activity brings up many issues he has researched and written about. Britton has proposed categories for writing that are more clearly differentiated and more descriptive than the traditional rhetorical terminology ("narrative," "descriptive," "persuasive"). He divides writing by *purposes*—"expressive," "transactional," and "poetic"—and argues that all these are language uses important to human beings, and especially to growing, learning children. "Expressive" writing is not just private psychologizing, but is the language in which ideas often first develop. It is also the language we use for exploring values and for altering our world picture—i.e., for real learning. "Poetic" language includes all language

117

used with a focus on the words themselves. "Transactional" is language used to get things done in the world.

When he turns to pedagogy, Britton stresses the importance not just of variety of purposes, but of writing for real communication. In this regard, it is all too easy for teachers to create "pseudo" categories for writing assignments—"expressive" or "poetic" writing that is only meant to earn a grade. Such writing actually falls into one narrow branch of *transactional* language. Britton's research has shown that the range of assigned purposes and audiences for school writing narrows steadily as students get older. Increasingly, the classroom seems cut off from the outside world, both in the purposes and the audiences to which writing can be directed.

There are, of course, internal purposes and audiences—the students' own learning of new subject material, writing for oneself, writing to be shared with classmates and with the teacher. While these are central and powerful kinds of writing, most of us also want our students to relate to a larger community. However, in their attempt to help students connect with this larger community, many teachers stress only expository writing. Britton argues that this does not help students learn to write, to understand the needs of various audiences, *or* to use writing for their own learning. He suggests that a balance of assignments for many purposes would be wise.

While it may seem that the activities in this workshop series have primarily stressed expressive writing, they also bring up the importance of real audiences and real purposes in a multitude of ways, and participants will have been thinking about them whether or not they've read or heard of Britton. However, the exercise on purposes can open up a whole set of issues that may not have been explicit before. Most of them don't have cut-and-dried answers, but will be worth hashing out in the group. They include the following:

- To what extent does a teacher wish to encourage writing for learning (which may be messy, confusing, and incomplete) vs. learning to write?
- To what extent can teachers use writing to test students' knowledge and still be able to encourage writing for other, more communicative purposes?
- To what extent can teachers grade writing and still be able to serve as a meaningful audience for other writing purposes students may have?
- How important is writing across the curriculum? In what ways can teachers of other subjects use writing for helping students learn their subject matter? In what ways can these teachers encourage or discourage students' writing?

Many of these issues will be elaborated in the sessions just ahead.

Audience Shift

17

This is the first of three short sessions on the role of audience in writing. The purpose of this initial experience is to dramatize the adjustments writers make, often unconsciously, to accommodate differing audiences.

1 Ask participants to think of the student who has caused them the most anguish in their teaching careers. You may wish to use some version of the guided imagery prewrite from the Memoir session here. Help them to visualize this student and recapture a few details about how the child made their life difficult, upset them, caused them grief, or challenged their desire to be good teachers. After a couple of minutes of this preparation, ask them to write a note to their best friend about the problems they have had with this child. You will have to help clarify what "best friend" means. You want them to address their note to the person to whom they feel closest, who is most sympathetic, most likely to understand their feelings in this matter. This might be a spouse, a fellow teacher, an out-of-town friend. Whoever they'd feel most comfortable writing to about this problem is the right audience. The assignment is: *Tell this person about the problems you've had with the student you've chosen.*

2 After allowing about eight to ten minutes for the writing, tell the group to stop and prepare to start another page. Now the assignment will be: *Write a note to the student's parents, telling about the problems you're having with their child.* After the groans have died down, allow about ten minutes for the writing.

3 Have examples of pairs read aloud. List elements of the writing that change to accommodate the changes in the audience. Usually, people will be quite impressed to see that almost everything changes, at least in some way, in response to the shift in audience. This is another nice demonstration of how direct instruction can never be the key to learning how to write. How could any teacher, no matter how skilled, ever detail the enormous number of adjustments that get made from one piece of writing to the next? Instead, it seems clear that the key to learning how to make these subtle, deeply embedded shifts is by practicing many different kinds of writing on many different kinds of audiences. Some changes typically noted:

Grammar	Sentence structure	Use of 1st person	Jargon
Vocabulary	Level of formality	Slang	Qualification
Neatness	Tone	Content/facts	

COMMENT If you have actually been following the sequence of the plan, this will be the first time in several sessions that you have asked the participants to do some

119

writing in class. One lovely complication may develop at this point: the participants may not be able to do the writing assignment without your taking them through an extended formal prewriting exercise of the type you used in the Accident and Memoir sessions. Of course, you should slow down in such a case, drawing out the prewriting to whatever degree the group requires. Later, though, don't neglect to use this as a focus of discussion—point out to the group their own desire for explicit prewriting activities.

VARIATION Here is another, quite different way of raising fundamental issues about audience, and how the writer's ability to anticipate readers' needs is a crucial writing skill. This session could replace workshop 17—or could be used in any combination with sessions 17, 18, or 19.

The exercise is often called "one-way-two-way communication" (J. William Pfeiffer and John E. Jones, *A Handbook of Structured Experiences for Human Relations Training*). A volunteer is given a diagram to look at but not to show the group. Instruct the volunteer to describe the diagram in such a way that the rest of the group can reproduce it on paper as accurately as possible. Here is a drawing that presents interesting problems for describers:

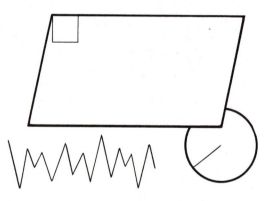

The volunteer can use any words he or she wishes—no tricky restrictions are involved with the language itself. However, to eliminate the role of the listener's response in revising communication, the volunteer is asked to stand with his or her back to the group and to answer no questions from the listeners. The listeners are instructed to follow the speaker's instructions as best they can but to communicate in *no* way with him—no questions, no groans, no chuckles, no requests to wait or continue.

Typically, the frustration of both volunteer and group mounts as he attempts to describe an image without either gestures or the input of responses from those receiving the directions. The situation for the volunteer is similar to that of a writer who sits alone at his desk trying to guess whether a reader will be able to visualize what he is explaining.

After the drawing is over and diagrams are compared, to the amusement of the participants, a fruitful discussion can ensue on the problems the exercise poses. Ask the describer what difficulties she encountered as she carried out the task. How did the describer feel while doing it? What problems did the listeners experience and how did they feel? When groups consider these questions, they usually raise some of the following points:

- Describer wasn't sure what geometrical terms listeners knew—or perhaps didn't know the terms herself. For some figures, simple terms don't exist and the describer may resort to metaphor.
- Describer couldn't judge the pace—when were the listeners finished drawing and ready to digest more information?
- Describer failed to consider a general question or problem, such as overall size or angular orientation, and simply went on without discussing it.
- Describer felt lack of confidence because geometry wasn't a subject he was prepared to talk about. The situation thus becomes one of exposing the speaker's ignorance, instead of communicating about the diagram.
- Describer felt cut off from listeners and thus cut off from the task itself.
- Listeners often get just one chance to catch vital specifications.
- Noise or low voice may blot out part of what the speaker says.
- The listener is faced with a problem of interpretive process: should she follow the directions step by step or listen to the whole account completely before writing, in order to get a larger picture? (The describer may also wonder about this issue of providing context vs. providing details.)

A workshop group discussing those difficulties will soon notice that these are all problems of writing in an explanatory or descriptive mode. Issues of how much detail, how to establish an image in its context, how to help a reader perceive information without misinterpreting clues, how to be aware of all the possible ways words might be interpreted—all these are embedded in this task.

The volunteer who describes the diagram is dramatically confronted with his egocentricity. When he looks at the drawing and begins to talk to a wall instead of another person, he realizes that egocentricity is a problem in *all* writing and not just that done by young children. When one can't check on the reception of information as one proceeds, one can only guess at the reader's thoughts. One can *try* to imagine a reader and this is what writers continually do; but the fact remains that in most writing tasks, the writer is alone.

As discussion proceeds, the leader can point out that the activity shows why writing is different from speaking, and why it causes anxiety for most people, even good, experienced writers. We realize how much we depend on an audience for adjusting and perfecting communication. We can begin to perceive the particular resistances students feel toward writing, and how a supportive audience and contact with many audiences, rather than just with a teacher, can be important in learning to write.

18

*Revising a
Child's Story*

This session turns to look at the role of audience in childrens' writing, raising issues of egocentricity and the child's developing ability to anticipate the needs of readers. We have most often used this tale by seven-and-a-half-year-old Mark, which is entry #21 in the sample packet:

Wons thar was a sell. He was cappshrd.
But he could swim. So he puld and puld.
And he got louse. And a sharck came along.
But he was smart. So he dru a pictur
another syle. Then the sharck ayt the Rokc.

1 Divide the people into groups of three or four and have them work together to produce a revised version of Mark's story which "anybody could fully understand." Allow about ten minutes for the work.

2 Regather to share samples of the revisions, and to begin discussing the process. We usually ask the group to consider what questions their revised versions answered that were not explained in Mark's original story. We tend to come up with a list like this one:

What is the story about? (title)
What is the name of the protagonist?
What did the characters look like?
What were the characters thinking?
How did the characters feel?
How was the seal captured?
How did he escape?
When did the events happen?
What was the setting?
What was the weather like?
What happened before the problem developed?
Who drew the picture?
How did the seal draw the picture on the rock?
Why is it important that the seal could swim?
Who was smart?
Why did the shark eat the rock?
How did the story end?

Answers to questions like these provide details of setting, character development, agent of the action, cause and effect connections—the list goes on and on. What the adults soon realize is that they are able to improve on Mark's story because they are more aware of a reader's needs. If you ask teachers to categorize the problems Mark has, they usually focus on the fact that he did not provide enough information and what he did provide was not adequately connected. Both of these problems stem from his egocentricity. Mark does not yet have the maturity to role-play the reader and imagine his needs.

Yet these problems of Mark's are essentially developmental. Elementary teachers immediately recognize the cleverness of the plot and the fact that the story has a beginning, middle, and end. All agree that if you were to talk to Mark, you would probably not find *him* confused about what happened or how it happened. The images of the story are clear in his mind; he just hasn't yet learned how to translate these into words. Teachers often suggest that each of his sentences could be a caption for one in a series of pictures he has drawn—in reality or in his imagination. The skillful teacher could even ask Mark to illustrate his story, and then make further suggestions to him about the writing based upon details which appear in the pictures.

Whatever direction the ensuing discussion takes, there is one vital realization which participants should share: that the ability to imagine, consider, and accommodate the needs of one's readers is one of the most sophisticated and demanding of the writer's tasks—and that our expectations of students in this area need to be reasonable and well-informed.

EXAMPLES   THE SMART SEAL

Once upon a time there was a seal. He was captured by a fisherman's net. But he could still swim. He pulled and pulled and got loose. Then a shark came along and wanted to eat him. But the seal was smart. He drew a picture of another seal on a rock. This fooled the shark, and the shark ate the rock. The smart seal got away.

The End

VERY LIKE A THURBER SEAL

Once upon a time there was a seal with a lot of pull. He got along swimmingly. By and by there came a loan shark who wanted the seal of approval for his inflationary appetite. But the seal was smart. He tricked the shark. Instead of the seal of approval, the shark got a piece of the rock.

19

By now, the participants have seen that learning how to address different audiences is one of the central tasks of writing development. It is just as important for a teacher to be able to suggest various audiences for kids to address as it is for the teacher to dream up different subjects for their writing. In keeping with these ideas, you can now offer the "Forty Audiences for Student Writing" handout, which gives some specific suggestions.

For this short session, two main activities are usually helpful. First, simply go through the list focusing on and giving personal examples of audiences you have used successfully in your own teaching. After this has been completed, you should ask people to think for a few moments and jot down three more audiences which might be added to the list of forty. Then go around the group, listening to new audiences, and adding them (mentally or actually) to the "master list."

HANDOUT

FORTY AUDIENCES FOR STUDENTS' WRITING

1   Each other (narratives, autobiographies, instructions, reflections, inquiries).
2   Students in other classrooms.
3   Students/classes in other local schools.
4   Students/classes in other states (your fine friend who teaches in Oregon—set up an exchange).
5   Write stories for students in lower grades: twelfth graders write stories for eighth graders; sixth graders write tales for third graders; third graders write to-first graders. Visit and read aloud. Get feedback and write new stories.
6   For the principal/administrator(s): set up a mailbox—encourage administrator to respond to students' writing. Selected exchanges can also be posted.
7   For the cooks, custodians, crossing guards, secretaries, coaches, and other school staff.
8   For other subjects: write math limericks; physics poems, etc. Have these teachers judge students' writing.
9   For the School Board/Parent Committee—report from Room 222. Here's what we're doing. What are *you* doing?
10 For hall displays: interests, holidays, wanted posters.
11 For the classroom bulletin board: each student can be responsible for a week, filling the board with his/her own autobiography, grade-school writings, family history, neighborhood news.
12 Write home: to parents, brothers, sisters.
13 Establish correspondence with a distant relative, friend.
14 Find out about a shirt-tail relative you've never met; write and introduce yourself and your branch of the family.
15 Write for the community newspaper: prepare news releases about school activities; propose a literary supplement; write letters to the editor.
16 To workers in the community (may be parents of class members): "What's it like to be a firefighter (plumber, accountant, pharmacist)? What do you enjoy most about your job? How did you learn about your work?"
17 Write to city officials on issues affecting students—getting a pedestrian crossing light installed.
18 Write to state/federal representatives and senators—state views, ask questions, request information—they will answer, especially to students.
19 To local TV/radio stations, personalities. "How do you decide which news is most important?" "Why don't you show more episodes of Sesame Street?" etc.
20 Government officials—every classroom in America should have posted on the wall a letter from the president, vice-president, chief justice, attorney general, etc. They will answer (eventually) and autopen a signature.
21 Corporations—especially public relations offices. You can get answers to questions as well as free samples of all sorts.

22   Civic, fraternal, social service, and other organizations—most are public relations conscious and scrupulously respond to student writers.
23   Travel bureaus/tourist bureaus: free samples, posters.
24   Chambers of commerce: they will send you reams of folders, flyers, and freebies. Try resort towns like Aspen, Ft. Lauderdale, Bar Harbor.
25   Local historical societies—Reading *Huckleberry Finn?* Write to the historical society in each town that figures in the book. Some wonderful local historian will answer.
26   Foreign embassies (also consulates) for information about other countries: it is their job to inform Americans about their countries.
27   Publish student writing in books—bind, cover, place in the library with card in catalogue, etc. Other students can check out.
28   Start a literary journal (comic, historical) and distribute around school (all you need is a ditto machine to do this).
29   Put copies of your student magazine in doctors'/dentists' waiting rooms around town. Also, the bus station, motel lobby.
30   Put up a display of students' writing in a store in town, the public library, etc.
31   Submit entries to student writing contests (ACUTE, *Scholastic Magazine*, NOTE).
32   Start your own contest. Get a local business to put up $25.00 or $50.00 prize money. Have many categories, many honorable mentions. Have an awards ceremony. Invite the local press. Display winners at City Hall or district office.
33   Write skits and plays for production in your own classroom, or for videotaping; do a radio play to broadcast on the school/local station. For cable TV?
34   Write to the authors of the books students are reading—both text and literature. (Charles Dickens may not answer—others may.)
35   Pen pals (an old, good idea).
36   Fan mail.
37   For a time capsule.
38   For martians, other planetary folks.
39   For historical figures: "Dear Abe, I just wanted to ask you about why you really decided to grow that beard. . . ."
40   One of the most appreciative audiences of all—have students write for themselves: private diaries, journals, notes, poems.

—Compiled by Rachel Faries and the IWP Summer Institute of 1981.

20

Leader Presentation— Prewriting Activities

This is the facilitator's chance to give a minilecture on prewriting activities that have worked for her—or activities which other sources have suggested. Often at this stage of a workshop, teachers agree that, yes, prewriting is a valuable and important thing to do, but they freeze up and feel uncreative when asked to devise prewriting activities for different sorts of writing tasks in their own classrooms. If your group has these feelings, it is often empowering simply to remind them how many classroom activities and structures can be used as prewriting. Each of the following activities can be arranged to prepare students for writing, to structure opportunities for them to gather and organize information prior to writing.

1   *Talking*—with another person, with a group, with people who know something about your topic. You can talk about the subject or you can talk about your goals, needs, worries, as an author.
2   *Interviewing*—one of the best ways to gather information, ideas, opinions; surveys are a subtype. Also a writer could discover what she has to say about a subject by having someone else interview *her*.
3   *Brainstorming*—following the formal rules of brainstorming (no criticizing, quantity over quality, etc.).
4   *Drama*—role-playing, creative dramatics, oral reading.
5   *Mental Exercises*—internal research, visualization, meditation, self-hypnosis (as in the Accident assignment).
6   *Experimenting*—manipulate objects, people, situations; study the changes.
7   *Experiencing*—putting yourself into the activity you wish to write about (e.g., riding a bike, running for office, lying in wet grass).
8   *Reading*—either to gather information about the topic *or* reading other pieces in the same mode, genre, or style, as models.
9   *Free Writing*—continuous stream-of-consciousness writing as a way of searching for ideas (see Peter Elbow, *Writing Without Teachers*).
10   *Focused Free Writing*—continuous, nonstop writing on your intended subject, as a way to crystallize your ideas and feelings. (Also see Elbow.)
11   *Writing Leads*—creating three or five or ten different opening sentences as a way of feeling for the shape and scope and limits of the topic.
12   *Doodling*—drawing models, flow charts, cartoons, or other graphic representations of the subject or of the writer's plans.
13   *Outlining*—there are many ways of laying out raw material in a helpful display. Formal academic outlining with Roman numerals, charts for data, clustering techniques.
14   *Listing*—natural and effective; a list of all the things you want to get in.

In addition to describing these activities in a lecture, the leader will want to remind people that they've already experienced activities 1, 2, 5, 7, 8, 12, and 14 (and probably a few others) in the workshop itself. Members of the group may wish to add other entries to this list, which would be helpful.

As a second step in this session, the leader can demonstrate one prewriting technique that's applicable to a wide variety of writing courses, topics, and students. Here's an example. Credit for the following activity goes to Donald Murray.

Ask participants to tear an 8½ × 11 sheet of paper into four small rectangles—or if you are *very* well organized, provide each person with three or four note cards, preferably 4 × 6 inch size. Then give the following instructions:

Think of a place that has been important to you, a place you recall vividly. It may be a place you remember with pleasure or one with negative associations. (Pause a few moments to make sure everyone has chosen their place.) *Now on the first card make notes—just words or phrases, no sentences—about your place.* (Ask slowly:) *What do you remember about how it looks? . . . What events occurred there? . . . Who was with you? . . . What do you see close by? . . . In the distance? . . . If you fill the front, feel free to use the back of the card, too.* Participants will, of course, recognize the prompts, but there's more to come.

Give the group a few minutes of silence to complete the task, and begin on it yourself. When many have put down their pens, apologize to those who are still writing and suggest that even if they aren't finished it's best to go on to the next step. Instructions for the next step: *Now look over your card and choose one thing you'd like to talk more about. You can select on any basis you wish—you don't need to stick with your original descriptive aim. Circle the word or phrase you have chosen and write about it on the second card, now using full sentences. Again use the back if you find you've filled the front and want to continue.*

Allow five to ten minutes for writing, and do the task yourself. Then as people finish—or if you have a limited time, as the limit is reached—give instructions for a final step. *You have a few choices for the last step. You can circle a word or phrase on your second card and write about that on the third card. Or go back to the first card to find something new to write about. Or if you were really going strong on the second card and want to continue, you can do so on the third card.* Then allow another five to ten minutes to write. Pushing on the time doesn't hurt, for this particular exercise.

Obviously, this process could continue *ad infinitum*, but three cards are enough to make the point. Reading aloud will then show everyone the results of the work. Readers have the choice of sharing one, two, or all of their cards. Then come the questions:

- What was your experience in doing this task?
- What in the method helped you (or hindered you)?
- How widely did each writer's three cards vary in their focus?

Most groups will remark how the small cards help avoid the "blank page syndrome" and how the successive steps permit brainstorming without worry about a focus, while focusing becomes easier once some words are down. People may speculate about the multiple branching of choices in the writing process and notice the mental relief that results from giving each of several choices a brief run on a separate card to see its possibilities. They'll realize the opportunity for helping writers who have trouble elaborating topics. A further turn might be to ask the group how they can adapt this procedure to more expository writing tasks.

One implication of this exercise is that students can discover they don't need to *wait* for inspiration when they write. Being a good writer does not necessarily mean being blessed by some mysterious muse. There are actions one can take to jog and direct one's thoughts, and writing involves learning how to structure mental activity effectively. Students who have difficulty with a task often feel helpless, or blame themselves or their intelligence, whereas methods like this one show them that the blank page syndrome is simply one more problem they can learn how to solve.

Drafting: "How I Write"

21

This session is closely related to session 9, Modeling the Process, and on some occasions we've used it as an introduction to session 9. However, as you work through the writing process, it makes sense (if you've got enough time) to progress from the prewriting of the previous session to the actual process of drafting, which this session examines. The primary difference between this session and Modeling the Process is that this one invites a full awareness of the *idiosyncrasies* of writers, whereas Modeling presses the group toward a single pattern meant to represent "writing" in general. If you have a talkative, take-charge group, you may never find time for this session. This is not a problem, because the writing activities and model-making do introduce the same issues, and many other crucial ones lie just ahead. But some groups really enjoy the self-observation this activity calls for, and some may need to make earlier experiences of their writing process more explicit.

It is appropriate to point out to your group what a relatively small amount of attention the workshop series itself gives to actual drafting. What this implies, clearly, is that much of the real work of writing does indeed go on during prewriting and revision. Yet there is another factor as well: writing research tells us relatively little about how teachers can successfully intervene and help during the writing itself.

The main work of this session is to have teachers compose a short piece on the subject, "How I Write," and go on to make connections with the needs of their student writers.

1 *Think about yourself as a writer. I want you to focus on your own needs, on all the things you have to have, all the conditions that have to be right, in order for you to write comfortably. Feel free to make some notes as I talk. Where do you like to be when you write? Any special kind of place, or perhaps one specific place? What do you work with—pencil, pen, typewriter, word processor? What time of day do you work best? What conditions do you need—quiet, music, the pitter-patter of little footsteps? What kind of lighting? Do you need any food or drink or other things to ingest? How do you get yourself started? How do you motivate yourself? What happens when you get stuck? How often do you take breaks? What do you do during your breaks? How long can you work at a stretch? How do you usually feel when you're writing? What is special about the way you go about writing?* (Allow about fifteen minutes for writing.)

2 Share a few examples, read aloud by volunteers. People are usually very interested to hear about each other's idiosyncrasies. Then work your way a bit more methodically through the list of questions you asked in the assignment.

Take note of the many differences between people's needs (e.g., some require quiet, while others play the Rolling Stones, etc.). The aim of this discussion is twofold: first, to demonstrate the range of conditions which different writers need while drafting; and second, to assert that these needs are legitimate—that writing *is* hard work which requires appropriate conditions.

3 The last step in this session is to focus on school as a place for writing, a topic which may be raised in a couple of ways. Have the people make a list of all the drawbacks of school classrooms as a place to write, and then share their lists with each other. Or, simply let the discussion from section two carry you right on into this set of implications. What you will find, naturally, is that school is not always the best setting for writers at work—and this leads into a discussion of ways to accommodate the needs of different students and different stages of the writing process.

EXAMPLE   HOW I WRITE

I look at the ceiling a lot. That is, a large part of the time that I'm supposedly writing is spent staring out above the desk, above almost everything. I don't register what I'm looking at. Whether I'm communicating with my muse or simply daydreaming, a large part of my composing seems to find its source in the upper regions of the room I'm sitting in.

If the writing is of a more interesting kind—"creative," perhaps, or at least not impersonal busy-ness—I'll "set up" for it. There'll be two or three wooden pencils (I insist on writing in #2 yellow pencils), paper, a hard chair, sometimes music (recorded) and sometimes a glass of Scotch. The pipe burns continually.

At a certain point in the first few lines I'm either "hooked" or I'm not. If "hooked" I could write for hours—at least I feel that way; I've never tested it. If "hooked" I don't tire. Actually, my energy increases, this despite the innate laziness that has guided and protected me all these years. Yes. Despite a firm belief in procrastination, a veritable faith in snow days and canceled classes, I'm able to write with alertness and purpose.

I prefer the flow of a whole sentence, longish and peppered with commas. There's a certain pleasure, I guess, in the sound of the pauses. I've noticed that a string of short sentences can provide a similar, but not identical rhythm. This seems to indicate an oral base to the writing I do. As I scan the upper walls and the ceiling, I hear whole sentences (or at least the parts before the first comma). It's difficult for me to revise whole sentences. Revision seems to be of words and phrases. However, the eraser part of my cherished yellow pencil is quite active as the sentence moves across the page.

My limited quantity of writing indicates a preference for descriptive composing, although I can move through a lively bit of argumentation. (The latter kind of writing becomes caustic and sarcastic very easily.) Description, especially more personalized describing, frees me from the desire to win a point. It allows me to feel more creative and, at times, good-humored.

I wish I could feel more responsibility and discipline myself to write at length. Almost all the writing I've done has left me with an abrupt feeling. I cannot take the time to develop the writing to a completed stage. Despite the rambling sentences, the pieces of writing have an abbreviated, if not incomplete, aspect to them. Interestingly, my letter-writing and my conversation have this same effect on me.

I've always been comfortable in the mechanical aspects of writing—grammatical structures, spelling, punctuation. I admit that I have ignored every lesson on topic sentences I've had since elementary school. Paragraphing has always been intuitive for me. I guess I noticed it in my early reading and it seemed a most reasonable thing to do. But I have consistently refused to "develop" a paragraph in any other way than simply indenting whenever I felt it was time to do so.

People have never complained about my writing, either in its lack of clarity or its lack of interest. I suppose that has freed me from worrying about how I write.

James M. Wicklund

DIGRESSION A couple of years ago, it occurred to our friend Bob Gundlach to poll *students* about their writing process and attitudes, so he devised a simple three-item, open-ended questionnaire and distributed it through teachers in six Chicago-area high schools. Two hundred and seventeen students responded. The following tables show the distribution of the kids' responses to three questions:

What makes you want to write?
Where do you like to be when you write?
Who would you choose to read your writing?

As a workshop leader, there are several things you might do with this data. You can simply study the tables yourself for what they reveal about teenagers' writing attitudes (they do believe in the personal usefulness of writing, they are very sensitive to the conditions they work in, they are pretty shrewd about picking their audiences, etc.). You could briefly present these results to your group, contrasting and comparing them with the teachers' writing attitudes. You might even encourage your participants to replicate the study among their own students—or better, devise a new one which gets at more detailed information.

Table 1
What Makes
You Want to
Write?

answer	#	rank	% of students
Express feelings	89	1	41
School assignments	59	2	27
Correspondence, notes	50	3	23
Get ideas down, understand things	30	4	14
Don't like to write	26	5	12
To remember	16	6	7
Boredom	14	7	6
To share ideas	7	8	3
Don't know or no answer	3	9	1
TOTAL	294	(multiple responses)	134

Table 2
Where Do You
Like to Be When
You Write?

answer	#	rank	% of students
Alone, solitude	104	1	48
Quiet place	48	2	22
Outside	30	3	14
With music or noise	28	4	13
Home	21	5	10
Anywhere	18	6	8
At a desk	14	7	6
At school	13	8	6
In bed	9	9	4
Someplace comfortable	9	9	4
Nowhere	4	10	2
TOTAL	298	(multiple responses)	137

Table 3
Who Would You
Choose to Read
Your Writing?

answer	#	rank	% of students
Friends	74	1	34
Teacher	34	2	16
Restricted by contents	33	3	15
Family members	30	4	14
No one	21	5	10
Anyone	20	6	9
Someone understanding	20	6	9
Corrector	13	7	6
Addressee of writing	9	8	4
Don't know or no answer	6	9	3
TOTAL	260	(multiple responses)	120

Content vs. Correctness

22 There are a number of very important and pressing questions that teachers in this writing workshop have more or less held off asking for the past sixteen hours. These questions have become even more urgent as teachers have encountered new ideas about the process of writing and re-experienced it for themselves. Now they want to know:

What is good writing, anyway?
How are you supposed to grade students' writing?
How does grammar fit in?
How can I reorganize my classroom to make writing happen?
Do kids really have as much to say as we adults?
Are autobiography and storytelling legitimate writing activities for my class?
What's the connection between storytelling and formal writing?
Is writing a skill or an art or a craft?
Are we supposed to believe that any kid can write?
What are my responsibilities as a teacher, and as an audience?
What's the relative importance of form and content? In real writing? In school?
What's the best way to help writers grow and improve their skills?
Am I always supposed to support and praise my students (as we've done in this workshop) and never criticize them?

Rather than addressing these questions one at a time, we've found it helpful to let them all come out at once at this moment in the course. Focusing on the special problems of a poor, nonstandard-dialect-speaking inner-city kid seems to open up the pent-up concerns about these issues in a dramatic way. It doesn't matter whether inner-city teachers are represented in the workshop group or not; the materials in the next three workshops invariably serve as a strong catalyst for honest discussion about what *any* writing teacher ought to do for *any* kid.

This session is designed to raise questions about the relative importance of correctness versus content. The workshop also helps introduce nonstandard dialects and related teaching problems. Jan's story (see p. 231; number 45 in the Appendix) which is the centerpiece here, works best when the leader uses it open-endedly; the group can take discussion of the sample in many different directions, all of them worthwhile. We almost always find that time is much too short to deal with all matters raised in this session.

1 Hand out a copy of "The Five Dollars" to each participant or have them use the one in their packets. Tell them to imagine that they are this student's

HANDOUT

The Five Dollars

Once when I was 7, I saw my mother bag on the drawer. So I went to the drawer and look in the bag and seen a roll of money. I got five dollar out and told my boy and sister that I had got it. So we went to the store and bought lot's and lots of candy. We eat most of the candy. Went we got home my mother was sitting on a chair she told us that she want to speak to us. We went over were she was and she ask use did we take five dollar out of her bag we said we didn't so she said OK. It was lunch time when this happen. So we went back to school and went we got home she ask us again we said no we didn't see the five dollar. Then she said that when she went to the store she asked Mrs Heard did we bring five dollar and she said yes we did. She told use to go up stairs. We went up stair and she beat use. While she was beating use my sister and brother was said they didn't take the money but she said you two went with him to spent the money. After she beat use I told her that I was going to run away. So I went out side and walked around the block and went back to the house. When I got in my mother was up stair in bed and my brother told me that my mother said I would come back home. So I did, So I did.

English teacher. It is ninth grade, and this is the first writing assignment of the year. *The assignment you have given is "Write a story about the last time you cried." This is Jan's (he's a boy) submission, and now you are supposed to do whatever you think it is your job to do with this paper.* (This direction is *supposed* to be opaque—don't answer any questions about it.)

2 After participants have finished working (no more than ten minutes), tell them to assign a letter grade to the student paper, regardless of whether they would actually do so in their own classrooms. Note: You may very well find that ten minutes is not enough time because people are trying to mark and correct every single error on the page. If this is holding people up, after about seven or eight minutes you should say: *If you have started to correct all the mechanical errors, then you have established that this is one of the things which you would do. In the interests of time, however, I'd suggest that you move on now to add any note or comment you might wish to put on the paper.*

3 The first step in the discussion is simply for the leader to take a poll on the letter grades assigned by the participants, recording the number of As, Bs, Cs, Ds, and Fs. Usually, the results of this tabulation tend to obliterate any notion of teacher objectivity. The next step is for the leader to ask: "What did you think of the paper?" and then to stand back. Generally the discussion will lead itself into issues of form versus content, standard versus nonstandard language, and the like. Teaching issues also arise: What's the right thing to do to motivate a kid on the first assignment of the year? Should you ever red-pencil personal writing? How important is it to literally fulfill the terms of an assignment? It has always been our experience that the issues spin themselves out with little prodding by the leader.

On the other hand, there is one kind of question which seems extremely helpful in this session: "What is it in the paper that makes you say that?" In other words, as people use "The Five Dollars" as a basis for generalizations about student writing (which is certainly fine), it usually serves them well if you as the leader constantly call them back to the level of the concrete, the particular, the specific. If people say, for example, that kids today don't know their grammar, then ask them to come up with several specific examples of grammar points that Jan doesn't know. The idea is not to one-up the participants, but to get them to look closely at what Jan does and doesn't know. The distinctions are not always obvious. As the discussion continues, most groups find more and more to like about Jan's story. Their objections tend to moderate or evaporate as they come to understand his frame of reference and to understand what he has accomplished.

Over the seven-year life of the Illinois Writing Project—and for five years before that—we have been using "The Five Dollars" in various teacher-training workshops. By now, more than 2,500 teachers from all levels and all types of schools and colleges have rated Jan's paper. The single most striking thing we have learned from spending all this time with one essay is how much can be learned from a single piece of student work. This story rewards almost limitless study; each new group of teachers immediately recognizes the many crucial issues it raises, and each new group also manages to discover one or two new points which previous teachers have somehow overlooked.

Jan's story introduces a couple of issues that the leader needs to be prepared for, and perhaps to stress if the group tries to skirt or deny them. "The Five Dollars" is a competent piece of work for a 14-year-old inner-city boy writing impromptu, in class, in one draft, on the topic "The last time I cried." The plot is clear, the details are ample, the writer's engagement with the topic is palpable, and the theme or message of the tale is conclusively illustrated. The fact that these qualities will be obscured, for teachers, by the many surface errors in the text, is a response that requires serious investigation. Why is it, in other words, that so many of us—teachers, parents, taxpayers, citizens—automatically equate "good writing" with correctness, and that we just as instinctively assume that anything written in a dialect other than Standard English is probably not valuable or important?

Jan's mechanical errors fall into three main categories. The first type are those mistakes produced by mismatches between Jan's natural oral dialect and the Standard English dialect favored by most teachers. Sometimes this is a simple and obvious problem; Jan uses a few idiomatic Black English forms, omitting, for example, the possessive marker in *my mother bag* and the plural marker on *five dollar* (which in Jan's speech community is dropped only with two nouns: *dollar* and *cent*). At other times, phonetic differences between Jan's dialect and standard English cause the problem: this explains most of the incorrect verb tense markers (*look* for *looked, spent* for *spend, ask* for *asked, happen* for *happened*), as well as the confusion between Jan's homonyms *when* and *went.* The second group of errors includes troubles common to all beginning writers: run-on sentences, punctuation problems, confusing the spelling of similar words, even hedging one's bets by rendering a dubious item once each way (*lot's* and *lots*) to ensure that the author will be at least 50 percent correct. The final set of problems—a smaller group than the other two—contains those errors which cannot be ascribed either to Black English or to universal writers' pitfalls (*boy* for *brother, was said* for *said*). These are mistakes which a teacher will only be able to understand by understanding Jan as a writer.

Looking at the patterns of Jan's errors provides other useful insights. With almost all errors that repeat (*dollar* for *dollars, went* for *when, use* for *us*), Jan gets it right the first time and deteriorates later—either losing confidence in his initial instinct or not bothering to check one incidence of the word against another. There is some support for the latter theory in Jan's handling of the title. Here is the only time in five opportunities when *dollar* earns an *-s,* and it seems significant that this would happen at the one point when any author takes extra care with both the form and content of a single phrase: making a title. The run-on sentences are also fascinating, revealing not just a failure to insert punctuation marks, but a kind of breathless, headlong enthusiasm—the sound of a person spilling out his story as fast as the words come to him. Indeed, the teacher-corrector who tries to remediate the run-ons by simply inserting quotation marks around the dialogue is in for a big surprise: those quotations are deeply embedded oral-narrative constructions which will not yield to a few punctuation marks.

This commentary on Jan's problems could go on for pages—and in a workshop discussion, teachers may similarly persevere—or perseverate. To some extent, such exhaustive study is valuable; it reminds us, quite dramatically, of how much we can learn by scrutinizing a single piece of student work. It also dramatizes the fact that, in order to respond helpfully to any student's written work, teachers need to understand their students' background, culture, dialect, experience, values, and personalities—as well as the usual assortment of academic criteria. Such understanding directly informs teaching behavior, and this is why it is so important. For example, a teacher reading "The Five Dollars" might casually assume that Jan didn't understand the meaning or formation of past tenses, and might begin *teaching* him about these things. But a close study of the story (noting the correct handling of irregular forms like *got, told,* etc.) combined with some sense of the rules of Black English, helps the teacher to see that Jan does understand the concept of past tense, uses it correctly most of the time, and needs to be coached to use *-ed* markers in phonetic environments in which he'd drop them in speech. Similar lessons can be derived from studying nearly all of the patterns of error which Jan displays. He is a student who has a considerable, though inconstant, command of many Standard English forms—and who needs to be helped to edit without having his promising authorial talent and drive squelched.

4 For groups that, as a result of this session, request specific help on how to teach grammar more constructively, you can find excellent suggestions at the elementary level in Hennings and Grant, *Written Expression in the Language Arts.* The chapters on grammar and technical skills in their book focus especially on oral methods of building sentence awareness and exploring sentence patterns, transformations, expansions, and condensations. They suggest work that achieves pattern and repetition through word-play and poetry, rather than in dull drills. More advanced work moves to sentence combining. Extensive, interesting materials for sentence combining at the secondary level can also be found in William Strong's *Sentence Combining* and Daiker and Morenberg's *The Writer's Options.*

Marty Gliserman's "An Act of Theft: Teaching Grammar" (*College English,* March, 1978), outlines a constructive approach for older students. The "theft" occurs when teachers mark all grammatical errors themselves, thereby "stealing" the students' responsibility and opportunity to make their own improvements. Gliserman's strategy is based on teaching only to each student's actual grammatical weaknesses, as indicated by his or her inability to pick up certain kinds of errors in the proofreading stage of composing.

Sometimes workshop groups—especially those with a high proportion of secondary English teachers—will want to talk extensively about the teaching of grammatical terminology and sentence diagramming. This particular kind of instruction presents high school teachers with a profound ambiguity: most of them are aware of the vast body of experimental research showing that such exercises do not improve student writing, but at the same time they often feel that teaching about the structure of language is one of their most sacred duties. Those who fall into the latter camp will find a spirited ally in Frederica Davis' "In Defense of Grammar" (*English Education,* October 1984), including an interesting letter to the author from Noam Chomsky. A good counterpoint is Elizabeth Haynes' review of the unpromising research results from grammar-centered classrooms ("Using Research in Preparing to Teach Writing," *English Journal,* January 1978). We've often distributed both of these articles to teacher groups and let the fur fly. The key outcome for teachers in a writing project is *not* a rejection of language study as a humanistic discipline, but an awareness that the transfer to writing ability is unproven in spite of centuries of dogma, tradition, and "common sense."

Guk-Bo

23
Here is one of our liveliest sessions—and one which you should vastly enjoy leading. There are two tricks to getting the most out of Guk-Bo: introducing it at the right moment and hyperdramatizing the presentation.

You are looking for the moment when the discussion of Jan begins to go flat, to lose energy—or (rarely) to get sufficiently antagonistic that a change of pace is called for. When you sense the Jan discussion deteriorating in one of these ways, stop it: "Obviously, on a subject like this we could go on forever—and probably never find answers that would satisfy everyone." Next you can call for a coffee break if the schedule is right—it is a good moment to pause. (If not, plunge ahead; no problem.)

The key to starting Guk-Bo itself is to sound abrupt and authoritarian and to confuse people. Whether coming back from a break or not, adopt an increasingly autocratic tone as you move the group into "the next activity." Camp it up, ham it up—act the role of an overbearing, sing-songy, condescending, fuddy-duddy, grammar-obsessed teacher. Your act should be well over-done—so it's clear to everyone about four or six or eight sentences along that this is a joke, and that they're all playing along:

Now, class, we're going to do another short writing assignment today, but before we do, I must point out that on the last paragraphs your grammar was just atrocious. Frankly, I was shocked that after all the time we've spent reviewing these rules in class so many of you would forget the most basic forms of standard English. Two problems were especially prevalent. Many of you used the substandard dialect -s to mark plurals. Now, I understand that all of you come from culturally deprived backgrounds and that this may be the way you talk at home or on the street. But here in school, as all of you should know by now (acidly), *we mark our plurals with the correct, standard suffix . . . which is what, Bob* (Sue, etc.)??? (They won't know. Ask others. Even get angry.) *GUK! You see, you don't even remember, after all our work. The Standard English plural marker is Guk!* (Go through this list, calling for them to supply correct forms.)

1 boy,	2?	(boyguk)
1 cat,	2?	(catguk)
1 ball,	2?	(ballguk)
1 dog,	2?	(dogguk)—(note the double g)
1 man,	2?	(manguk)
1 duck,	2?	(duckguk)
1 mukluk,	2?	(muklukguk)
1 mother,	2?	(motherguk)—(watch your enunciation!)

The other problem which was just as common in your last set of very poor essays was the use of another substandard street form, marking past tense verbs with an -ed. Now class, you should all know at your age that we form past tense verbs with . . . what? (Repeat, with threats and abuse.) BO! -bo is correct!

Today I walk.	Yesterday I ____?	(walkbo)
" eat.	" ____?	(eatbo)
" jump.	" ____?	(jumpbo)
" steal.	" ____?	(stealbo)
" hoe.	" ____?	(hoebo)
" sew.	" ____?	(sewbo)
" know.	" ____?	(knowbo)
" am.	" ____?	(ambo)

When people try to supply the last answer, shout: *"There are no irregulars!"* Act heartbroken. Review the past conjugation of *to be:*

I ambo.	We arebo.
You arebo.	You arebo.
He/She/It isbo.	They arebo.

Ask impatiently if they have finally got the rules straight. Then assign a paragraph on something that requires past tense (e.g., "What I did up to now today," "What my last birthday was like," something related to previous workshop sessions). Warn them not to avoid the target constructions or they will be punished for *that,* too. Allow ten minutes for writing.

Now it is time to drop your Fidditch role. Ask several people to read their paragraphs aloud. Next, initiate a discussion about (1) how they felt being abused about their dialect, even though it was clearly a put-on, and (2) how the unfamiliar grammatical forms intruded upon their attempts to write sensible prose. Some may argue that this experience doesn't perfectly match that of minority students in schools (which it certainly doesn't)—and it is worth reviewing what is and isn't parallel. In the end, this exercise should establish some degree of increased sympathy for—or at least understanding of—the static some students get from their teachers.

EXAMPLE   Last Fall, I gobo hunting with my friendguk Chuck and Doug. Two hourguk before dawn on a cold, crisp October morning, we assemblebo all of our gunguk, tentguk, backpackguk, and other materialguk on Chuck's porch. Chuck's dogguk arebo straining at their leashguk, eager to chase duckguk through the woodguk of Wisconsin.

Chuck's wife yellbo, "Good luck, you guyguk!" as we drivebo out of the driveway in Chuck's truck. We drivebo for five hourguk, until finally we getbo to some promising fieldguk and marshguk where we thinkbo duckguk might be hidebo. We pilebo out of the truck, turnbo loose the dogguk, and marchbo off into the fieldguk. The hunt bebo on!

Just five minuteguk later, we hearbo two shotguk. Unfortunately, none of us-guk havebo shootbo any duckguk; Chuck shootbo himself in the toeguk with his double-barrelbo shotgun. We havebo to take him to the nearest emergency room to get fixbo up. He isbon't hurtbo too badly; mostly his pride bebo woundbo. And also he havebo to pay 235 dollarguk for all the testguk and treatmentguk they putbo him through. So, just seven hourguk after our wonderful hunting weekend beginbo, we arebo heading home again, depressbo and disappointbo, without any duckguk to our nameguk. If only we havebo knowbo!

COMMENT You have obviously noticed by now that this group of activities centered on grammar and dialect, questions the teacherly tradition of red-penciling grammatical and mechanical errors, but doesn't require you as leader to denigrate Standard English grammar. Perhaps due to the reputation of writing projects, or perhaps because they are projecting their own secret doubts about it, your participants may be expecting you to oppose grammar instruction. However, it is especially important that teachers reach their own decisions to change in this area, since grammar is such a sensitive matter and is so deeply rooted in professional traditions. Most English teachers were, themselves, good and dutiful students who learned their grammar well, and who now enjoy teaching it.

In any case, we have never been against the learning or improving of students' grammar, and you may not wish to be either. We have, however, questioned the *transfer* of grammar drills to actual writing practice, and we've questioned whether teachers' *editing* of students' grammar is any more effective for inducing real improvement. From teachers' own complaints, it appears not to be. We have observed in our teaching that students' grammar improves as they become seriously engaged with writing. And we've discovered that all too many teachers believe students must study grammar *before* they write—which not only denies them the motivation for learning grammar, but results in their having far too little writing practice.

Grammar is important in its place—which is at the proofreading stage of writing. We want teachers to discover this, rather than have it told to them. The workshop activities provide more inductive experiences to allow this discovery.

24

Leader Presentation— Grammar/Dialects

This session may never identifiably occur. In the first place, it is possible—perhaps even preferable—that you will have found ways to embed your own material on this subject into the Jan discussion. Or, it may be that some of the partisans in a vigorous and informed Jan debate will raise research issues for you. Or you may simply have to sacrifice this short presentation in the interests of time, given the fact that once teachers start talking about dialects and standards, it's hard to stop them.

Let's assume that it is both feasible and appropriate for you to use the planned twenty-minute session here. What will you present? Obviously, if you have personal, academic, or teaching experience in this area (teaching inner-city kids, being bilingual yourself, having studied sociolinguistics in grad school, etc.), this material will probably offer you the strongest base. If you wish some preparatory reading to flesh out your own knowledge, here are a couple of suggestions. On the matter of Black English, you could consult *English in Black and White* by Robbins Burling or read William Labov's much-reprinted essay, "The Logic of Nonstandard English." Both of these sources date from the early 1970s when serious linguistic study of lower-class dialects was initiated, and both are still fresh and powerful.

Another useful way of looking at this session is as a mini-lesson in linguistics (well, sociolinguistics, anyway). Most of your teacher-students, whether they're English teachers or not, probably will have never had a college-level introduction (forget other coursework) in linguistics. Obviously you can't do the whole job here—but below is a string of basic linguistic principles which ultimately do relate to writing and to dialects. The list is adapted from Daniels's book *Famous Last Words: The American Language Crisis Reconsidered* (Southern Illinois University Press, 1983), and he's included inspirational quotes (other people's, mostly) where appropriate.

1   Children learn their native language swiftly, efficiently, and largely without direct instruction before they ever come near a school. Children learn the language(s) or dialect(s) they hear around them, and there are no exceptions to this: French children do not acquire Eskimo unless they are consistently immersed in it.
2   Learning one's native language means learning a vast, interrelated, largely subconscious system of rules for combining sounds, words, and strings of words. The rules are arbitrary and differ from language to language—but all languages and dialects are "logical" and rule-governed.
3   Everyone speaks a dialect: south side of Chicago, Scarsdale, Boothbay Harbor, Miami, etc.

144

4 All human speakers employ a range of speech styles and various jargons related to occupation, age, interests, community, and so forth.

5 Language differences between groups of people are initiated and maintained by degrees of separation and isolation between them. Total separation (geographical, social, political, economic) leads to linguistic bifurcation; partial separation maintains dialectical variation; free interaction breaks down differences.

6 All languages are intimately related to the societies and individuals who use them.

7 Value judgments about different languages or dialects are matters of taste.

To quote Daniels more directly, here are a few key paragraphs from his book.

. . . it is sometimes objected: "Well, you could never discuss Kierkegaard's philosophy in Eskimo or Black English, and so these languages are not equal after all." The implication here, of course, is that the discussion of Kierkegaard's philosophy, or any number of other complex intellectual topics, simply cannot be accomplished by people whose language is "too primitive" to handle them. The error in such thinking is to equate what is typically talked about in a given language with what *could* be talked about. Certainly few Eskimos, and probably few Black English speakers (or white ones, for that matter), typically discuss Kierkegaard's philosophy. And if they wished to do so, each group of speakers would have to add some new vocabulary and some new concepts to their language, which would take time, study, and adjustment. But no topic, in other words, is inherently beyond the reach of any particular human language. . . .

It is also important to realize that a language is not just an asset of a culture or group, but of individual human beings. Our native language is the speech of our parents, siblings, friends, and community. It is the code we use to communicate in the most powerful and intimate experiences of our lives. It is a central part of our personality, an expression and a mirror of what we are and wish to be. Our language is as personal and as integral to each of us as our bodies and our brains, and in our own unique ways, we all treasure it. And all of us, when we are honest, have to admit that criticism of the way we talk is hard not to take personally. This reaction is nothing to be ashamed of: it is simply a reflection of the natural and profound importance of language to every individual human being.

To summarize: all human languages and the concept systems which they embody are efficient in their native speech communities. The languages of the world also vary in some important ways, so that people sometimes falsely assume that certain tongues are inherently superior to others. Yet it is marvelous that these differences exist. It is good that the Eskimo language facilitates talk about snow, that the Hopi language supports that culture's view

of time, and, I suppose, that Chicago speech has ample resources for discussing drizzle, wind, and inept athletic teams.

It is easy enough to assert that all languages are equal and efficient in
their own sphere of use. But most of us do not really believe in this idea,
and certainly do not act as if we did. We constantly make judgments about
other people and other nations on the basis of the language they use. Of
course, some of these judgments have a basis in reality. If an American employer declines to hire a monolingual Japanese speaker to answer his telephone, he may be making a sound business decision since callers would be
unable to communicate with this person. But if the same employer declines
to hire an Alabama native because southern speech doesn't project the
"classy" image he wants, then he is using language in a somewhat different
way. The employer is saying to himself: "My customers (like me) have negative attitudes toward southern speech. I do not want to take the chance of
putting them off, even in the slightest, by having this Alabaman represent
the company." In each case the job applicants' natural, native, and "perfect" languages have been found inadequate. But they have been judged
outside the native context, and the employer's decision not to hire either
speaker proves nothing about the inherent worth of Japanese or southern
American speech.

Especially when we consider the question of mutually intelligible American dialects, we are able to see that most ideas about language differences
are purely matters of taste. It isn't that we cannot understand each other—
Southerners, Northerners, Californians, New Yorkers, blacks, whites, Appala-
chian folk—with only the slightest effort we can communicate just fine. But
because of our history of experiences with each other, or perhaps just out of
perversity, we have developed prejudices toward other people's language
which sometimes affect our behavior. Such prejudices, however irrational,
generate much pressure for speakers of disfavored dialects to abandon their
native speech for some more approved pattern. But as linguist Einar Haugen
has warned:

"And yet, who are we to call for linguistic genocide in the name of effi-
ciency? Let us recall that although a language is a tool and an instrument of
communication, that is not all it is. A language is also a part of one's personality, a form of behavior that has its roots in our earliest experience.
Whether it is a so-called rural or ghetto dialect, or a peasant language, or a
'primitive' idiom, it fulfills exactly the same needs and performs the same
services in the daily lives of its speakers as does the most advanced language of culture. Every language, dialect, patois, or lingo is a structurally
complete framework into which can be poured any subtlety of emotion or
thought that its users are capable of experiencing. Whatever it lacks at any
given time or place in the way of vocabulary and syntax can be supplied in
very short order by borrowing and imitation from other languages. Any

scorn for the language of others is scorn for those who use it, and as such is a form of social discrimination.''

It is not Haugen's purpose—nor is it mine—to deny that social acceptability and economic success in America may be linked in certain ways to the mastery of approved patterns of speech. Yet all of us must realize that the need for such mastery arises *only* out of the prejudices of the dominant speech community and not from any intrinsic shortcomings of nonstandard American dialects. (pp. 77–83)

25

This is a vital workshop which models the importance of revision, allows the participants to extend the pleasure of discovering their own writing process, and leaves considerable flexibility for the leader. It prepares participants for the discussions on evaluation that are just ahead—since evaluation, if it is to improve a student's writing rather than just label it, must fit into the process by which writers identify and carry out improvements they want to make.

In fact, some of the formal workshops and discussions about teacher response, conferencing, peer editing, and grading pressures which lie further along in the plan can appropriately be brought forward and embedded in the revising activities described here. At this stage of the workshop, time often seems to be running out; topics of interest are quickly proliferating within the group, and the enthusiasm for analysis can slow down the march through the agenda. For the sake of clarity, we'll keep sessions 25–31 separate here, but we'll also tell you that in real life they tend to overlap.

All through the workshop, participants have been reminded of this formal opportunity to revise a piece of their writing. Back at the end of session 10, the leader encouraged participants to consider whether they had a personal piece of writing that needed doing, and suggested that those with an urge to write such pieces get a draft started in time for this workshop. Other participants will have at least four rough drafts (a poem, an accident, a memoir, and a school review) from which to choose.

1 Have participants select the piece of writing which they'd like to revise—to expand, rewrite, polish, trim, in some way make more effective. At the beginning of this session ask each person to jot down a few notes in answer to these questions:

- What kind of revising does this piece of writing seem to need?
- What reactions did this piece of writing get when (and if) you shared it with others as a rough draft?
- How do you feel about the connections—or lack of them—between your answers to the two questions above?

2 Next, ask everyone to pair up with someone who hasn't been a significant individual audience for them thus far in the workshop—a fresh eye and ear, to whatever degree possible. Each person is to tell the other, as specifically as possible, what kind of feedback he wants from a critical reading. This may mean that the author will reveal some alleged flaws before the reader ever encounters them, or he may keep mum and request a more general response. (One lesson here is that student writers can be taught to *ask* for the kind of criticism they want—so that teachers or peer readers can go hard or easy depending on what students feel ready for.) The two people exchange papers, read, and take turns offering and discussing the asked-for feedback.

3 The leader now makes a few remarks before everyone goes off to the next stage of work: *For this exercise, I'm going to ask that you now try to implement one or more of your reader's suggestions—to make the kinds of changes he said (or implied) were necessary. In other words, even if you're skeptical about the value of the feedback you've just gotten, or if there's something else you'd rather work on first, for now, be guided by your reader's response. Try to make some useful revisions grow out of his feedback. You'll have thirty minutes to make a start on this. Very likely it won't be possible to do everything during this session, but by the end of our time, you should have some idea of where your revision is headed—and whether it is going to work.*

4 After a half hour, give the writers this instruction: *Now, I'd like for you to get back together with your critic-collaborator and talk about how the revision is going. You can spend about ten minutes each talking about what happened as you tried to implement each other's suggestions. Try to touch on attitude and morale issues, as well as technical and procedural matters.*

5 After the above twenty minutes, recall the group to the whole for some discussion. How did it feel to be reviewed? Were you comfortable asking for specific kinds of feedback? How did you react to the feedback when you got it? Was the feedback helpful? (Try to establish what types were generally most useful, if possible.) What problems did you encounter in trying to incorporate what seemed to be good ideas? Did your piece improve as a result of this revision? Did anyone have their work take off in an unexpected direction? As you worked on your revision, how was your morale and energy? Where would you like to go next with this piece? Then there are questions for the responders to consider: How did it feel to give a response? Did you feel constrained by the author's request? Did you want to raise other issues? Do you sense that there are any general principles or approaches that are helpful in giving feedback to other writers? Did you discover any ideas or procedures which seemed to connect immediately with the needs of your own students?

6 One of the most important tasks at this stage of the workshop is to be sure that a complex and deepening definition of *revision* has been established among the group. This usually occurs experientially, from the cumulative effect of all the writing and discussing that's gone on, culminated by this immediate experience of reworking a piece of one's own writing. If you want to make the defining more explicit, ask everyone to briefly jot down and then share two lists: (a) the kinds of changes they found themselves making, and (b) the steps they took to make these changes. Listing these on the board or flip-chart can create an important addition to the writing process model developed earlier.

Participants normally will offer enthusiastic testimony about their discovery that real revising is reseeing, revisioning, rethinking—all of which implies working with meaning, and not only with form. The group can make distinctions between the following levels of change:

- Reconsidering the whole topic.
- Changing one's mind about the meaning, the outcome, or the "side" one is on, for the whole piece.
- Adding, subtracting, changing, or improving specific arguments or chunks of information.
- Changing the organization of the piece.
- Changing the style or improving the clarity of a smaller part.
- Editing for style.
- Editing for grammar and mechanics.

These distinctions obviously have some significant classroom applications and call traditional grading practices deeply into question. While it certainly isn't necessary to comb through all these implications now (there are a half-dozen sessions on evaluation coming up), it is vital that the importance and complexity of revision are acknowledged here.

To add to your own insights on the revision process, you can find excellent discussions in Donald Graves's *Writing: Teachers and Children at Work* (especially chapters 13, 15, and 16), in Hennings and Grant, *Written Expression in the Language Arts* (chapter 8), and Peter Elbow, *Writing With Power* (chapters 12 through 16). Graves observes the complex paths by which children discover that it is possible to change what they have already done, and shows how conferences allow teachers to sensitively encourage children to reconsider what they have written. Graves says that elementary school children are willing to revise their writing in the following order:

1 Spelling
2 Motor-esthetic issues
3 Conventions (punctuation, capitalization)
4 Topic and information
5 Major revisions: addition of information, exclusion of information and reorganization.

In other words, young children are quick to adjust a spelling, but most unlikely to completely restructure a piece of writing. Graves asserts that kids are able to make changes in all five categories right from the earliest school year, but that this scale shows the most frequent categories of revision.

Anyone who has watched primary school children writing will recognize the truth of Graves's schedule. Many young writers labor tirelessly over individual spellings, wearing eraser holes in their papers in search of the right collection of letters. Similarly, children's painstaking attention to an illustration or to the look of their own name reveals considerable esthetic concern. Yet, in the early years at least, the basic piece of writing that a kid sets down isn't very negotiable. Children can sometimes be brought to *add* a missing bit of information or two, but there is a sense that an act of writing is like any other work of art: once it's done, it's done—and let's get on to the next one. This sense of inviolability is something that gradually breaks down over the years as kids come to see their writing (as so many other things in their world) as plastic, malleable, adjustable, and open to revision. In other words, young kids' resistance to comprehensive revision is natural and predictable.

At the same time, none of this is grounds for nonfeasance on the teacher's part. If working on microlevel spelling corrections and artistic adjustments are of natural interest to children, then teachers can certainly support such work; if children are developmentally more able to add elements to their writing than to cut things out, teachers can be guided by this fact as well. Hennings and Grant outline a variety of teaching strategies including group revision, oral rereading of written work, comparing alternative sentences, and using folders to collect and review students' work.

Teachers of older students may also learn from Graves's chart. In what ways, if any, are the revising preferences of adolescents different from the list Graves offers? How can we move high school kids up through some sensible sequence of revising skills—perhaps a sequence that recapitulates the natural order discovered among younger kids? Some of this can be illuminated by reviewing Peter Elbow's exploration of the psychology of revising, the difficulty of giving up words one has struggled over, and the threat of chaos involved in admitting that one has really changed one's mind about an idea.

26

Evaluation Expectations

Many people have an interest in the way teachers evaluate student writing—the students themselves, parents, department chairs, school administrators, board members, assorted taxpayers, and others. Practically every adult in America believes that he knows exactly how student writing should be evaluated, in spite of the fact that nearly every American adult feels inadequate about his own writing, avoids it where possible, and usually does write less well than he might. Teachers may not only share in these generally held attitudes about writing, but they have also inherited a professional tradition full of ideas about writing instruction, perhaps the most powerful of which is: ALL STUDENT WRITING MUST BE GRADED.

This is the first of six workshops about the various ways in which students' writing may be evaluated. In this session, teachers are offered a chance to detach and rationally examine the crossfire of advice amidst which they are expected to evaluate their students' written work.

1 The leader asks the group to brainstorm a list of every person who directly or indirectly has an influence (or would like to have an influence) on the way teachers grade student work. Some of these characters will be obvious; others will take more thought. Sometimes we as teachers imagine what some group or individual would think if they did visit or hear about our classroom—so, in anticipation (or fear) of this potential response, we adjust our teaching behavior accordingly. In other words, the list should include both immediate supervisors and more distant, shadowy influences.

2 Now the leader picks out four entries from the list (probably "parents," "students," "myself," and "my immediate supervisor"—perhaps the principal for elementary people and the department chair for high school teachers). Next, she asks each person to write an answer to each of these questions, impersonating each of the four people in turn:

- As a parent of a student in Ms. _____'s class, I expect her evaluation of my child's writing to be . . .
- As _____'s Chair (or Principal), I expect her evaluation of students' writing to be . . .
- When I hand in my writing to Ms. _____ , I want her to . . .
- When I evaluate students' writing, I owe them . . .

Allow just two to three minutes for jotting each answer. Encourage participants to write as the person in question—to earnestly try to impersonate not only the sentiments, but also the voice of each person.

3 Now, people should break into groups of four or five, first to share and then to discuss their notes and the attitudes they reflect. The groups should be asked to prepare answers to some of these questions: What are the typical attitudes toward evaluation among each of these four people? Did you have any trouble agreeing upon what each constituency typically expects? Which attitudes were hardest to define? What are the commonest worries related to evaluation among yourselves? What are the most anxiety-provoking pressures, procedures, or personalities? How do you cope with all of these sometimes contradictory expectations?

4 In large group reports, the leader can simply moderate the sharing, and perhaps the listing, of common concerns. Very likely, someone will report that they are forced to act contrary to their beliefs (e.g., put letter grades on personal autobiographical writing) because of community or administrative pressures. Someone will probably raise the point that: "We certainly haven't graded or evaluated each other's writing here in this workshop, yet we've gotten lots of powerful, useful feedback, and been helped to revise our work effectively." It is a positive development if all this testimony leads to a deeper and more explicit discussion of teachers' occupational obligations and the limits of their professional autonomy. The discussion should shift toward the positive as it winds down, focusing on the constructive things teachers are able to accomplish in spite of pressures, and on the ways some teachers have invented to sidestep unwholesome influences.

5 To crystallize the meaning of this exercise, and to summarize the points which people have probably made, the leader can give a short lecture here, reviewing the contrasts outlined below:

- **Grading** is the most common, but least often necessary or helpful kind of feedback teachers can give students. Putting a grade on a piece of writing finalizes it, puts it to rest, closes off discussion. No matter how we may try to qualify or buffer this message, the fact remains that affixing an official grade on a piece of writing usually ends its life as a growing thing. Grades, generally, are inimical to revision.

- **Evaluation** is often useful, and does not necessarily require a grade. "I don't understand your ending" is an evaluation; peers' reactions can be evaluative; transactional writing which fails to achieve its intended transaction has been evaluated, etc.

- **Response** is reading, listening, offering a reaction as some sort of audience. Almost all writing deserves a response. Nonjudgmental, content-centered response ("This made me sad," "Then what happened?" "What did she look like?") is especially valuable. Not only does this demonstrate the teacher's interest in what the student has to say, but it shows the student the effects her writing has had on a reader. In many cases this is far more useful than a grade or an evaluation, because it tells the student *what* was communicated. The student herself can then decide whether the writing was successful, achieved her aims, or not.

One key point emerges from these three definitions, as well as from previous activities in the workshop: teacher response must motivate students to revise. This is one of the toughest challenges teachers face, partly because students expect to be judged, measured, and assessed rather than encouraged to continue working. But constructive feedback for developing writers must be formative (as we say in the trade) as well as summative. Each student writer needs responses that help her see the work freshly and clearly; that help her refine her subject, purpose, audience; that help her decide whether the piece deserves further effort; that give her energy and strategies for pressing on with revision. Any teacher responses that obstruct these goals (like premature or relentless grade-giving) may work against the long-range development of student writers.

There is a related and perhaps less positive way of looking at teacher response to kids' writing. If a teacher believes—as many do—that it is her professional duty to mark every error on every paper every kid ever writes, she becomes, among other things, a bottleneck in the process. The amount of writing practice that students get is governed by the amount of time and energy the teacher has available for this kind of omnivorous evaluation. Usually, students of such a teacher will not write enough to get sufficient practice to really improve; ironically, this highly dedicated, serious, hard-working teacher may be blocking, rather than facilitating, the growth in literacy she is aiming for. As some of the upcoming sessions will dramatize, effective writing teachers must find ways of renouncing the bottleneck role; they must create classroom patterns, structures, and activities that provide students with lots of writing practice *and* plenty of response, feedback, evaluation, and even some grading.

27

*Response
Roles*

When responding to student writing, many teachers feel trapped by the notion that there is only one "right" way to read and comment. As the previous workshop acknowledged, many teachers feel that this one "right way" carries a very heavy emphasis on form and grammar, is quite authoritarian and critical, and requires a letter grade. Though teachers are not always comfortable in this taskmaster role, they often feel a nearly sacred duty to act it out anyway—so that "bad writing habits" don't get a chance to "take root." What this traditional kind of teacher response does, of course, is to silence and discourage many students without protecting anyone against error-production. Teachers need to reassure themselves that (1) there are many other ways to respond to kids' writing; and that (2) it is *right* (correct, sensible, appropriate, helpful, wise, rational) to have a repertoire of responses which can be selectively applied to different sorts of student writing. This workshop aims to build that much-needed sense of choice.

1 Ask the whole group to work together to brainstorm "all" of the possible roles which an instructor can play in responding to students' writing. List them on the board as they are offered, and ask each volunteer to briefly explain the role he's suggesting as you write it. You'll probably have to suggest an example or two to get the group started and to make clear what sort of roles you're talking about. (Some of the usual ones: Literary Critic, Reformer of Youth, Grammarian, Editor, Parent, Trusted Adult, Psychologist, Expert Reader, Collaborator, Friend.) Encourage funny, rare, or off-the-wall roles—a long list is highly desirable—and try to maintain syntactic/semantic parallels (we want *roles* here, not adjectives).

2 Next, distribute a copy of a sample student paper. We've often used piece #39 from the student writing samples in the appendix: "About one year ago I had a friend. . . ." Instruct the participants that they are to choose one of the roles listed on the board and respond to the paper in that role by writing comments directly on the paper, just as a teacher in that role would. Allow five to seven minutes' work time, then circulate another copy of the same paper and tell them to pick a different role and respond to the paper in *that* role. Allow five more minutes and then send around a third copy to repeat the process one last time. After about twenty minutes, everyone will have evaluated the same paper three ways, from three different perspectives, giving feedback of three different kinds.

155

EXAMPLE   ROLES TEACHERS PLAY AS THEY RESPOND TO STUDENTS

1	Savior	20	Avenging Angel
2	Order Keeper	21	Mediator
3	Genius	22	Task Master
4	Dictionary	23	Coauthor
5	Literary Critic	24	Encourager
6	Psychologist	25	Instructor
7	Parent	26	Student (a fellow learner)
8	Editor	27	Librarian
9	Corrector/Grammarian	28	Writer
10	Missionary	29	Orator
11	Stationer	30	Partisan
12	Social Worker	31	Cheerleader (for students)
13	Computer	32	Expert
14	Model	33	Priest (transmitter of community values and myths)
15	Trusted Adult	34	Teacher as a Person
16	Philosopher	35	Acculturator
17	Disciplinarian	36	Reader
18	Friend	37	Motivator
19	Audience	38	Censor

—Compiled by the IWP 1981 Summer Institute

HANDOUT

About one year ago I had a friend named David Bates, We were pretty good friends and we all ways went fishing to gather, and most off all we would go skiing, When

I could not ski he fought me, So ~~Now~~ I can ski very well. we allso would always take a ride to Mc Donolds oh are bikes, I also rember him for being very Reasonable He just wasent The kind of kid That did what he wanted to do

I remember one time when I was in a fight with two kid he came and heiped me a lot. Thare was even a time when he saved Another Kids life when he was caught under a boat

3 Ask volunteers to read all three versions of their comments, telling, of course, what roles they were trying out. Initiate some discussion about which sorts of response were more appropriate and helpful than others. Usually, you will find that there will be three or four kinds of responses that were genuinely appropriate to the paper at hand, and some others that would be patently useless or harmful to the student author. This reinforces the idea that there *are* legitimate alternatives in responding to writing, and yet that the response has to be tailored to the student, the subject, the teacher, and the moment. Discussion can proceed to take up the methodological issues: What changes do we most want to encourage in students' writing, and which types of response seem likely to elicit these changes, as well as allow students to continue making them independently in the future? What problems arise when you respond in different ways at different times to the same kid—or differently to various writers on the same assignment? How does a teacher balance her desire to respond in a way that's appropriate to the material without neglecting issues of form?

4 This session can end with a brief lecture drawing on some of the following material.

Several authors have written excellent analyses and suggestions for giving feedback to students. Peter Elbow, in portions of *Writing Without Teachers* (especially pages 117—121) and *Writing With Power* (pages 216—226) provides the base for this by looking closely at what a teacher actually experiences when she reads papers—the complex way in which impressions form, often separate from the technical error (or achievement) she may focus on. Elbow describes the difficulties inherent in the student-teacher relationship, directing his comments to student writers:

> You don't write to teachers, you write for them. You can feel the difference vividly if you write a regular essay assigned by your teacher and then go on to write something directly *to* him: write him a letter asking him to change your grade or to contribute money to your political campaign. You will find these writing tasks refreshing and satisfying compared to regular assignments—even if harder. It's a relief to put words down on paper for the sake of *results*—not just for the sake of getting a *judgment*. "Getting an A is results," you may say, but see how you feel if you write your teacher for a contribution and get an "A" instead of a check.

> —Peter Elbow, *Writing With Power*, p. 220

As a help in undoing this unreal relationship, Elbow's suggestions for responding to writing, in *Writing Without Teachers,* focus on the basic task of simply showing the writer what effect his words had on one particular reader: you. This is not judgmental but factual: "Here is what I heard and what your words made me think about." Both reader and writer learn to realize that no one sees all that is in the words, nor sees them totally "objectively." "You are always right and always wrong," he tells the reader of other people's writing.

Writing With Power offers two lists of questions for giving response to writing—"criterion-based" questions and "reader-based" questions. "Criterion-based" questions identify particular qualities many people consider important to writing—for example, "Are the parts arranged in a coherent or logical sequence?" "Reader-based" questions focus on the effect the writing has on a particular reader—for example, "Tell which words or phrases struck you most or stuck out or had resonance."

Dennis Searle and David Dillon, in "Responding to Writing: What Is Said or How It Is Said" (*Language Arts,* October, 1980), extend the range of response types and provide alternatives to the usual teacher-as-editor marking of errors on papers. Teachers can ask questions, can provide encouragement or instruction, can respond to the information as interested readers, can add their own thoughts on the subject. The range is most easily seen in their chart of types and examples, reproduced here.

HANDOUT   CLASSIFYING TEACHER RESPONSES TO PUPILS' WRITTEN WORK

type of teacher response	focus of teacher response	
	content	form
Evaluation	Good Story! Excellent! Poor ideas! Your best work!	Well-written! Good word choice. Poor sentence structure.
Assessment	I see that you know the subject.	You are beginning to use paragraphs.
Instructional		
a) didactic/correction	The way people treated the boy is an example of prejudice.	You have several spelling mistakes. Use indentations to signal this new idea.
b) encouragement	This was very exciting. You should write more.	You used a good variety of sentences. Keep up the good work!
	You haven't researched this very well—try harder.	Don't be so careless with your spelling and handwriting.
Audience		
a) clarification	I don't understand what happened here. Can you explain? What would this feel like?	Misplaced modifier. Where is your topic sentence? Use more descriptive vocabulary.
b) reaction	I enjoyed that. I felt what you would feel if that happened. I think that should be in the class paper.	You have beautiful handwriting. I'm impressed by your vocabulary.
c) taking action	Change a classroom procedure in response to a written request.	Have a lesson on quotation marks after seeing that most students in class could not use this in their stories.
Moving outside the writing		
a) extension	Tell me more! Have you considered what Bill says?	This anecdote would make a good starting point for a play.
b) addition	Let me tell you what happened to me. I disagree with what you say.	Your work reminds me of the poetry of e. e. cummings.

Dennis Searle and David Dillon, in Language Arts, *October, 1980.*

Conferences

28

This session and the following one ("Peer Editing") outline two of the most helpful classroom structures for providing students with immediate, meaningful responses to their writing. Both techniques are useful and adaptable for students of all ages. However, in the real world, peer editing is more commonly used by secondary-level teachers, while conferencing is more often seen in elementary writing classes. Without necessarily endorsing this stratification, we have followed this pattern in our own presentation. This workshop on conferencing is skewed toward the elementary level; the following session on peer editing has a more secondary flavor. You should help your workshop participants to make the connections, comparisons, and translations to their own level when the activities here do not exactly fit the age-level characteristics of their own students.

Both workshops also follow a similar, if somewhat unexciting format: the leader presents an example of how some teachers have implemented a promising classroom practice, and then leads an open discussion on the merits and potential problems of that practice. In spite of their uninspiring design, these sessions are usually pretty lively because some teachers in any group will have tried (and perhaps feel that they failed at) both techniques. And, of course, some version of each of these techniques has already been used during the workshop itself, providing participants with fresh, personal experience to draw from.

Donald Graves has collected many disciples with his detailed, sensitive, and lively program for teaching writing to elementary school children, outlined in *Writing: Teachers and Children at Work.* One key element of Graves's approach is the individual conference—between teacher and student or between students. Since teachers at all levels complain about the lack of time for individual conferences with students, Graves's solution to the problem is worth outlining for the group.

The initial assumption of Graves's approach (which sometimes comes as a shock to secondary teachers) is that individual conferences are a perfectly appropriate expenditure of class time, and that a one-on-one conference can accomplish a great deal in just two or three minutes. Given this starting point, it is a matter of setting up classroom structures and routines that permit the teacher to spend time with individual students while the others are engaged in productive work. Graves likes to divide a class period roughly into thirds, first seeing children who need immediate help with a piece of writing, then meeting with several regularly scheduled students, and finally seeking out four or five children who are at important stages in their work or who may be brought together with a few others for a short lesson on a common problem. What goes

161

on while the teacher circulates from kid to kid conducting these various kinds of quick conferences? The other students write, as they have become accustomed to doing. The teacher has established this class time as a serious writing workshop, and pupils draft, revise, think, or review their cumulative writing folders while the teacher meets with other students.

What gets talked about in these individual conferences? Graves stresses that the teacher, rather than reading the writing while the student sits by, feeling vulnerable, must allow the student to express her own view of the writing and the problems she faces. Three general and open-ended questions can help the teacher structure a conference: What's the writing about? Where are you in the work? What kind of help might you need now? When the teacher meets with the student in a scheduled conference, as opposed to a spontaneous one, she should have previously checked through the student's cumulative folder and have a good sense of what the child is working on. Graves insists that each child should be seen in conference once every week—or two weeks at the most—and that the teacher should keep records of the progress of the conferences.

The hardest thing for teachers to learn about conducting conferences, Graves says, is to listen. Teachers must give up their near-instinctive urge to teach, lead, instruct, remake, and purify the kids, and let themselves be instructed. Graves lists the behaviors he dreads in himself when he inadvertently starts dominating a student conference:

- I talk more than the writer.
- I try to redirect the writer to a subject that is more interesting to me.
- I try to redirect the writer to a more morally uplifting subject.
- I ignore where the writer is in the draft.
- I ignore the writer's original reason for writing the piece.
- I teach skills too early in the conference.
- I supply words, catchy phrases, and examples for the writer to use (I'm delighted if the writer uses *my* language).
- I ask questions I know the writer can't answer.

—*Graves, p. 128*

As tempting as these teacherly moves are, Graves insists that in effective conferences, they must be shunned. Instead, the goal for the teacher is to be a listener:

> The marvelous part about waiting for children, and helping them to teach us is what we learn ourselves. Seven year-olds will teach us about space, cats, dogs, prehistoric animals, their ills, and fantasies about wild creatures from outer space. They send us scurrying for reference books when they reverse roles and ask *us* questions. The top teachers, I've found, whether in

the center of the city, or in a rural school, have an insatiable appetite for learning. When teachers learn, the children learn.

—Graves, p. 128

Given this short description of Donald Graves's approach to conferencing, there are plenty of questions that teachers may want to discuss.

- How could this plan be adapted to work in your classroom, with your students? Could this structure work with students of any age, including high school and college? What institutional or attitudinal barriers might have to be dealt with at various levels?
- Are there certain kinds of students who would be more likely than others to benefit from this sort of instruction?
- Do you agree that individual conferences are a key element in learning how to write? Do you think that a couple of minutes' work can be powerful?
- How could you blend this conferencing/workshop model of writing instruction with a strongly skills-oriented curriculum?
- Can you think about how you'd add conferencing to a particular writing course or project that's already part of your regular teaching?
- What classroom management problems would you foresee if you were going to move your own students into a regular pattern of conferencing? How could you overcome those problems?

VARIATION Probably the best way to treat the issues involved with conferencing is to conduct individual editorial conferences with the teacher-authors, in the workshop. In fact, it is only because of time constraints that *doing* such conferences isn't a standard part of the master plan. If you decide to take this route, you will probably want to work with each participant's chosen personal piece of writing (see session 25) and you'll need to spend five to seven minutes per person to do a reasonably substantive, unrushed job. Even so, you may not have time to read each piece of writing, and rather will want to use Graves' three questions (see above) to structure the exchange. Meanwhile, you'll also need to consider the activities and expectations of the other members of the group while you're meeting with individuals—and you'll need to rearrange and prune several of the sessions between 25 and 31 to allow for this two to three hour departure from the schedule. This, by the way, is a variation that we tend to use often when we teach the program ourselves. Despite the abundant complications, the one-to-one exchange is as valuable 'with adult learners as it is with kids.

Peer Editing

29

Peer editing, because it has been extensively modeled during the workshops, can now benefit from a straightforward presentation and discussion, rather than our usual experiential approach. What we say draws on ideas from Daniel Fader's *The New Hooked on Books,* and from the rich experience of three teachers, Sherrill Crivellone, Bob Runtz, and Marilyn Wiencek, who have worked with and thought about the method.

For a discussion of peer editing, the following topics need to be covered:

1 What does "peer editing" mean?
2 What preparation do students need in order to do it successfully?
3 How large should groups be? How should their membership be determined?
4 When, where, how often should groups meet, and what procedures should they follow?
5 What should be the focus of peer editing groups (content, form, lists, what proportions)?
6 What sort of rating forms, comment sheets, or other written response should be used?
7 What role (if any) should peer editing groups have in evaluation?

We'll cover each of these topics briefly here, and the reader can consult other sources listed in the bibliography for more in-depth discussion of the alternatives.

1. What it means. Peer editing does *not* mean just correcting spelling, grammar, and technical errors. Students should respond to the *content* of one another's writing as well as the form. And it does not mean just *judging* that content. Each student critic needs to make clear to the writer what the writing tells her, what it makes her think about, so that the writer can discover how he has communicated.

Beyond the improvement of compositions, peer editing also increases students' sense of responsibility, rather than leaving evaluation and change wholly for the teacher to orchestrate. It provides a real audience of other students who need not just listen passively to the performance. Rather, critiquing groups can make writing part of a genuine dialogue among students about their topics. It can include prewriting before compositions are finished, as well as response afterwords. It allows for the *conversation* among students which Kenneth Bruffee argues is the key to developing and deepening students' thought processes (see "Collaborative Learning and the 'Conversation of Mankind,' " *College English,* November 1984).

164

2. **What preparation is needed.** Teachers experienced with the method stress the need for trust between students, so that students will be willing to put honest thoughts into writing, and so that comments are given and received constructively. This issue has, of course, been covered earlier in the workshop series. However, you can stress that one way to achieve trust is to encourage students to discuss their interests and values, tell about themselves, and listen to one another. Some teacher talk can be directed to matters of listening, mutual respect, and constructive vs. desctructive criticism. A good critic must learn to consider what the *writer* wants to say, and not just substitute how she, the critic, would approach the topic. Still, a teacher's lecture cannot take the place of students' actual experience of these processes. To model methods of giving response, a teacher can introduce a few sample essays for his class to comment on, while he gives guidance.

3. **How groups should be structured.** Methods vary from free choice by students to highly structured systems. Free choice can present problems if friends stick together or loners are left hanging. Fader suggests the following method. Collect writing samples early in the semester and *tentatively* rank students from (1) most well prepared—not necessarily most *intelligent*—to (30, or whatever is your total in class) least prepared. Arrange students' names in three columns, in number order, as follows:

1	11	21
2	12	22
3	13	23
4	14	24
5	15	25
6	16	26
7	17	27
8	18	28
9	19	29
10	20	30

Form groups of three by choosing laterally—one from each column, making sure each group has at least one representative of each sex. Some teachers keep the same groups together all semester, while others re-form them every month or so, to provide writers with fresh readers' perspectives.

4. **Frequency of, and procedures for, group meetings.** Crivellone uses the schedule given in the example on pp. 167–8 for incorporating peer critiquing into a typical week's work on writing. Two elements seem especially important in the procedure. First, reading aloud is valuable because both writer and listener get

to hear the character of the language. The human ear is usually far better attuned than the eye to the effect and clarity of syntactic structures. Having one of the *others* in the group read an essay back to its author is an alternative that adds still another level of consciousness to the review process. The second element: student signatures signal the responsibility that both the writer *and* her peers are taking for the words written down. If a writer has not done well, she can be reminded that her *group* should be more careful to give her helpful criticisms.

5. **Focus of groups' work.** As we've stressed, groups need to consider content as well as form. Crivellone and Runtz indicate three levels of group work. "First, they get together to discuss the assignment. Their second meeting is focused on editing each other's rough drafts. They also get together later, to proofread the 'final' drafts."

6. **Rating forms.** Much of the feedback given in editing groups is verbal, of course. But most teachers are also ready to create their own written guides for student critics, and students often benefit from support of this kind. In fact, most readers of writing, no matter what their age, find it difficult to give good, thorough responses covering all aspects of writing. Searching one's reactions and pinning them to specific spots in the text isn't easy, and is often rather speculative. *Why* does a particular sentence sound uncertain? What alternative would express the same idea better? Or is it the idea itself that bothers the reader? It isn't always easy to tell.

   A few guidelines for constructing peer response forms should be considered. (A) The form shouldn't be too long. A long list of criteria can be discouraging and can prevent the writer from focussing on any *pattern* to the problems in his writing. To cover more issues, new forms can be circulated later in the semester. (B) The guide should carefully balance concerns for ideas, manner of presentation (organization, elaboration, transition), and editing (grammar, mechanics, spelling). (C) Guides should include positive as well as negative items. Writing should not be made to appear like a trip through mined enemy territory. Two sample critiquing forms appear on pages 169–170.

7. **Role of groups in final evaluation.** Teachers differ on this matter. One way to make discussion of the issue interesting is to open it up to *other* evaluation options than just grading by teacher or by group. What about self-evaluation? Consider the use of writing *folders* containing all the work of the semester for each student, from which teacher and/or student and/or group selects some items, but not all, to be evaluated. The latter option not only saves time for teachers, but helps insure that each student's writing is viewed longitudinally, instead of piece-by-piece.

Finally, a note on trouble-shooting. Any sharp group of teachers will raise questions like, "What do you do if a student really brutalizes a peer with criticisms?" Or, "What if a group fails to operate because two members never do the assignment?" "What if the students are too easy on each other, or give very little or inaccurate criticism?" Or, "What if my department chairperson says I'm using too much time with these groups?" Numerous problems need to be solved to make this operation work, and teachers in the group who are experienced with peer critiquing—there are often one or two—should be consulted, along with plenty of general brainstorming.

EXAMPLE   WEEKLY SCHEDULE OF PEER EDITING GROUP ACTIVITIES

Mondays

1   Rough drafts are due for assignment given the previous Friday.

2   Groups meet immediately and begin work. Each paper is read aloud by its author. The other group members ask questions about the content of the paper, which the author records on his rough draft, without actually answering any of them at this time. Both positive comments and constructive suggestions are expected at this time. Students have the entire period for this purpose and are instructed to think over the questions that were asked and make any changes that seem appropriate before coming to class on Tuesday.

Tuesdays

1   "Final" drafts are due.

2   Ten-minute free writing.

3   Groups meet again, this time actually exchanging papers and looking over them silently. Their focus today is on content and grammar/mechanics. No marks are made on another person's paper; instead, group members are to point the problems out and allow the author to decide what he/she wants to do about them.

4   Papers are turned in, signed by the author and *cosigned* by the readers. Those who wish to do further rewriting simply sign a list on the teacher's desk and are automatically granted an extension.

Wednesdays

1   Ten-minute free writing.

2   People who have done further rewriting may have their group members go

over their new "final" drafts instead of doing the ten-minute free writing on this day.

3   Focus lesson on subject matter, writing process, or grammar item.

Thursdays

1   Ten-minute free writing.

2   Complete the focus lesson.

Fridays

1   Student-evaluation (alternating between self-evaluation and group evaluation).

2   Vocabulary due.

3   Students are allowed to work independently, reading their novels, working on the next paragraph, or revising papers. Individual conferences are held at this time.

This schedule developed and used by Sherrill Crivellone

HANDOUT

Cara Keller, who teaches fifth graders, uses peer critiquing sheets in the following way. She instructs her students first to read the story (poem, article, etc.) they are critiquing, and then to read it again, putting "faces" along the side margin:

—when something is well done

—when you don't understand something or have a question

—when something needs more work or should be taken out.

These faces are the only marks allowed on the author's work. The children then write out their comments on the following response sheet.

READ—READ AGAIN—PUT ON FACES—FILL IN BLANKS

_____

Author's Name _____

Project Title _____

Date _____

I like _____

_____

I need to know more about _____

_____

Do you really need the part about _____

_____

You might want to work on _____

_____

Other _____

_____

_____

Assistant's full name _____

HANDOUT   SAMPLE PEER CRITIQUING SHEET

Writer _____

Reader _____

Assignment _____

1 One thing you said that really interested me was:
   What you say makes me think about:

2 Questions I have about what you've said:

3 The main idea of your essay seems to be (quote it, if the writer has said it. Put it together if he or she hasn't said it):

4 The organization of your paper

   _____ is fine as it is.

   _____ could benefit from the following changes in order:

5 Paragraph breaks are

   _____ in sensible places.

   _____ would make more sense in places marked ''P'' on your paper.

6 Your sentences

   _____ are all complete.

   _____ include _____ (#) that are incomplete.

Proofreading

As the age of students and the formality of writing tasks increases, it becomes legitimate to attend more carefully to mechanics, to help writers find ways of eliminating errors from the surface of their work. Such a focus on proofreading can only be positive and helpful, of course, when writing has been looked at *first* for its meaning, its message, its content. Nor do we think that mechanics can be learned very well from drills, exercises, workbooks, dittos, or other materials which force students to fiddle with someone else's errors. The primary text for the study of copyediting must be students' own writing.

The following workshop is based on an idea we've forthrightly stolen from John Von Kerens of Hinsdale South High School. When John responds to student writing, he always comments extensively on subject matter first. Next, he has a handy way of focusing on mechanics so that the student can take increasing responsibility for her own efforts. For each student, he prepares a chart which lists all the course's writing assignments along one axis and some common classes of mechanical errors along the other. When the semester's first paper comes in, John charts each student's single most prevalent mechanical problem by number of occurrences. Other mechanical errors, though they may be marked, are not charted at this time. The student's job on the next assignment is simply to reduce the frequency of this charted error—say, run-on sentences—not worrying too much about other mechanical matters. Normally, this focus on a single pattern of errors helps the student to concentrate and attend to the problem, and the occurrence of problem #1 declines in the second paper submitted. But now, perhaps, there may be four run-ons and seven comma splices; according to John's plan, the student now shifts to work on the comma splices in the next paper. As the year goes on, the student has been made aware of his own particular patterns of error, one error at a time, and has been helped to overcome each kind of mistake by concentrating on each in turn. Generally, students working on this plan will steadily reduce their overall count of errors, without having error-reduction become an obsession which devitalizes meaning.

Once you explain the chart, the actual task for the participants, working in grade-level groups, is one of revision. The error list provided is obviously not appropriate for all levels, and some people may feel that, no matter what the level, important items are missing, less important ones could be deleted, or labels changed.

Questions or comments are likely to center on:

- Is it enough to work on one error pattern at a time? Won't other bad habits take root while we're working on some other error?

EXAMPLE

Error Patterns	Writing Assignment	#1—Last Summer	#2—Beowolf	#3—I Love School	#4—Elmo Zumwalt	#5—Wm. Shakespeare	#6—The Cubs	#7—Letter to Editor
Spelling								
Run-Ons								
Comma Splice								
Sentence Variety								
Paragraphing								
Diction/Usage								
Awkwardness								
Tense Errors								
Agreement								
Modification								
Pronoun Ref.								
Parallelism								
Transitions								
Punctuation								
Neatness								
Others								

- Don't kids forget what they've learned about one kind of error as soon as they move along to work on another?
- Isn't it an English teacher's duty to mark all errors in all papers at all times? What might the parents say?
- Won't the mere existence of these charts and all the record-keeping work they require imply to students that the teacher really does care more about mechanics than about meaning?

VARIATION   In some school districts there are official lists of mandated writing "competencies," usually mechanical skills, that students are supposed to master by certain

#8—Mark Twain	#9—How to Get to Moon	#10—Dear Principal	#11—Herman Melville	#12—Ralph Nader	#13—Poem	#14—Movie Review	#15—Term Paper	Comments

grade levels. In other districts, subscores on standard achievement tests (like the Iowa tests) provide an implicit agenda for writing instruction. If teachers in your workshop group feel that they are forced to teach such an externally imposed menu of mechanics, you could substitute that list or test for the chart offered here. The session's activity could be brainstorming ways of embedding the necessary instruction in work with students' actual writing, rather than succumbing to drills.

Dealing with Grading Pressures

31

If this session seems redundant, that's because it is. We've found, over years of working in schools, that we get the most frequent "callbacks"—invitations to do a brushup workshop—on one topic: grading. Teachers often need to be reassured that it isn't necessary to put a grade on every piece of writing every kid ever does, or to mark every single mechanical error on every paper every time. They have returned to an environment in which the pressures to behave in these ways are so strong that their resolve to try alternatives wavers. This session recapitulates earlier ones in some ways—and may be slipped in just about anywhere between session 26 and session 30.

To reset the scene: The grading issue has already come out quite dramatically. Many, perhaps most, of the teachers come to the workshop with the belief that grading each piece of student writing and marking all mechanical errors are simple God-given baseline minimal competencies of being a writing teacher—and that they will be swiftly and stoutly punished if they fail to do these things. Yet, the teachers also probably see the wisdom of doing otherwise—of letting rough drafts alone mechanically, of not grading intimate personal reminiscence, of allowing kids a chance to polish only chosen pieces, and so forth. They now need ways of defending these new ideas in their old environments; they need logistical support, protection, plausible explanations, and camouflage.

Grading, however, is not the only issue involved here; it is merely the point at which teachers can be most vulnerable. If a parent sees her child's paper returned without every spelling and grammar problem duly marked in blood, she may conclude—since this is all the evidence she has, and the only method she knows—that the teacher is not doing his job. But many project-trained teachers have found that if they inform parents fully about the new program for teaching writing, the parents appreciate the effort, understand the marking policy, and cease to use it as the only measure of what is being done for their children. The Handouts on pages 175–178 show how this public relations effort can be carried out.

Hand out the NCTE pamphlet, "How to Help Your Child Become a Better Writer." Allow people about eight or ten minutes to skim its contents. It supports many of the concepts that have been discovered in this workshop, sounds pretty authoritative, and is fairly well (not perfectly) addressed to the average concerned parent. Discuss how this flyer could be used by a teacher planning to try new techniques of writing instruction, especially nontraditional approaches to evaluation. The second phase of the discussion can build from this point: talking about how teachers can devise their own version of the pamphlet and supplement it with a personal letter to parents. Let the group brainstorm

HOW TO HELP YOUR CHILD BECOME A BETTER WRITER

Things to Do at Home

1   Build a climate of words at home. Go places and see things with your child, then talk about what has been seen, heard, smelled, tasted, touched. The basis of good writing is good talk, and younger children especially grow into stronger control of language when loving adults—particularly parents—share experiences and rich talk about those experiences.

2   Let children see you write often. You're both a model and a teacher. If children never see adults write, they gain an impression that writing occurs only at school. What you *do* is as important as what you say. Have children see you writing notes to friends, letters to business firms, perhaps stories to share with the children. From time to time, read aloud what you have written and ask the children their opinion of what you've said. If it's not perfect, so much the better. Making changes in what you write confirms for the child that revision is a natural part of writing, which it is.

3   Be as helpful as you can in helping children write. Talk through their ideas with them; help them discover what they want to say. When they ask for help with spelling, punctuation, and usage, supply that help. Your most effective role is not as a critic but as a helper. Rejoice in effort, delight in ideas, and resist the temptation to be critical.

4   Provide a suitable place for children to write. A quiet corner is best, the child's own place, if possible. If not, any flat surface with elbow room, a comfortable chair, and a good light will do.

5   Give, and encourage others to give the child gifts associated with writing.
—pens of several kinds and pencils of appropriate size and hardness
—a desk lamp
—pads of paper, stationery and envelopes—even stamps
—a booklet for a diary or daily journal (Make sure that the booklet is the child's private property; when children want to share, they will.)
—a dictionary appropriate to the child's age and needs. Most dictionary use is for checking spelling, but a good dictionary contains fascinating information on word origins, synonyms, pronunciation, and so forth.
—a thesaurus for older children. This will help in the search for the "right" word
—a typewriter, even a battered portable will do, allowing for occasional public messages, like neighborhood newspapers, play scripts
—erasers or "white-out" liquid for correcting errors that the child wants to repair without rewriting.

6   Encourage (but do not demand) frequent writing. Be patient with reluctance to write. "I have nothing to say" is a perfect excuse. Recognize that the desire to write is a sometime thing. There will be times when a child "burns" to write,

others when the need is cool. But frequency of writing is important to develop the habit of writing.

7 Praise the child's efforts at writing. Forget what happened to you in school, and resist the tendency to focus on errors of spelling, punctuation, and other mechanical parts of writing. Emphasize the child's successes. For every error the child makes, there are dozens of things he or she has done well.

8 Share letters from friends and relatives. Treat such letters as special events. Urge relatives and friends to write notes and letters to the child, no matter how brief. Writing is especially rewarding when the child gets a response. When thank you notes are in order, after a holiday especially, sit with the child and write your own notes at the same time. Writing ten letters (for ten gifts) is a heavy burden for the child; space the work and be supportive.

9 Encourage the child to write away for information, free samples, travel brochures. For a great many suggestions about where to write and how to write, purchase a copy of the helpful U.S. Postal Service booklet, *All About Letters* (available from NCTE @ $1.50 per copy).

10 Be alert to occasions when the child can be involved in writing. For example, helping with grocery lists; adding notes at the end of parents' letters; sending holiday and birthday cards; taking down telephone messages; writing notes to friends; helping plan trips by writing for information; drafting notes to school for parental signature; writing notes to letter carriers and other service persons; preparing invitations to family get-togethers.

Writing for real purposes is rewarding, and the daily activities of families present many opportunities for purposeful writing. Involving your child may take some coaxing, but it will be worth your patient effort.

Things to Do for School Writing Programs

1 Ask to see the child's writing, either the writing brought home or the writing kept in folders at school. Encourage the use of writing folders, both at home and at school. Most writing should be kept, not thrown away. Folders are important means for helping both teachers and children see progress in writing skill.

2 Be affirmative about the child's efforts in school writing. Recognize that for every error a child makes, he or she will do many things right. Applaud the good things you see. The willingness to write is fragile. Your optimistic attitude toward the child's efforts is vital to strengthening the writing habit.

3 Be primarily interested in the content, not the mechanics of expression. It's easy for many adults to spot misspellings, faulty word usage, and shaky punctuation. Perfection in these escapes most adults, so don't demand it of children. Sometimes teachers—for these same reasons—will mark only a few mechanical

errors, leaving others for another time. What matters most in writing is words, sentences, and ideas. Perfection in mechanics develops slowly. Be patient.

4   Find out if children are given writing instruction and practice in writing on a regular basis. Daily writing is the ideal; once a week is not often enough. If classes are too large in your school, understand that it may not be possible for teachers to ask as much writing practice as they or you would like. Insist on smaller classes—no more than 25 in elementary schools and no more than four classes of 25 for secondary school English teachers.

5   Ask if *every* teacher is involved in helping youngsters write better. Worksheets, blank-filling exercises, multiple choice tests, and similar materials are sometimes used to *avoid* having children write. If children and youth are not being asked to write sentences and paragraphs about science, history, geography, and the other school subjects, they are not being helped to become better writers. *All* teachers have responsibility to help children improve their writing skills.

6   See if youngsters are being asked to write in a variety of forms (letters, essays, stories, etc.) for a variety of purposes (to inform, persuade, describe, etc.), and for a variety of audiences (other students, teachers, friends, strangers, relatives, business firms). Each form, purpose, and audience demands differences of style, tone, approach, and choice of words. A wide variety of writing experiences is critical to developing effective writing.

7   Check to see if there is continuing contact with the imaginative writing of skilled authors. While it's true we learn to write by writing, we also learn to write by reading. The works of talented authors should be studied not only for ideas but also for the writing skills involved. Good literature is an essential part of any effective writing program.

8   Watch out for "the grammar trap." Some people may try to persuade you that a full understanding of English grammar is needed before students can express themselves well. Some knowledge of grammar *is* useful, but too much time spent on study of grammar steals time from the study of writing. Time is much better spent in writing and conferring with the teacher or other students about each attempt to communicate in writing.

9   Encourage administrators to see that teachers of writing have plenty of supplies—writing paper, teaching materials, duplicating and copying machines, dictionaries, books about writing, and classroom libraries of good books.

10 Work through your PTA and your school board to make writing a high priority. Learn about writing and the ways youngsters learn to write. Encourage publication of good student writing in school newspapers, literary journals, local newspapers and magazines. See that the high school's best writers are entered into the NCTE Achievement Awards in Writing Program or the Scholastic Writing Awards or other writing contests. Let everyone know that writing matters.

By becoming an active participant in your child's education as a writer, you will serve not only your child but other children and youth as well. You have an important role to play, and we encourage your involvement.

National Council of Teachers of English

ways in which communication with parents can not only head off complaints and criticism, but actually get them involved in their kids' development as writers.

LETTER TO PARENTS

Dear Family,

I want to let you know at the outset of this school year some of what your student will be experiencing in Independent Junior English. This course will be primarily a writing course. In the face of mounting criticism that kids at worst can't write at all, and at best "aren't as good as they used to be," we want to address the problem. Suffice it to say, kids *can* write and, frankly, I don't find them significantly less talented than my students from past years.

What I do find is a growing feeling among kids themselves that they are failures as writers and therefore are fearful of the endeavor. My approach is a positive one in which kids are reminded that school is for success, and that they can experience success with their writing.

We will approach the craft of writing as a process, not as a series of individual exercises which may or may not help a student when real writing is called for. Real kids need real writing for real audiences. Since we view all writing as creative, we will be doing both expressive and expository pieces. The students and I will be working and writing together. They will learn to share and value not only their individual writing, but also the writing of their peers. I will write with the students to model the process; they will see me struggle too. Building this mutual trust and sense of community is central to feeling successful.

This approach to writing may be new to you, so I ask you to look through the outline for the course. You will see that the emphasis is not wholly on the product; your son or daughter will not be getting each paper back completely obliterated with red ink. Instead, we will work through one or two problems at a time with a more positive, teacher-response evaluation system. Student papers will be kept in a folder in the classroom; you are welcome to come at any prearranged time to review your student's progress. This approach, too, is quite different from what you and I experienced in our own high school years. However, you may wish to ask yourself how comfortable you feel when you must communicate in writing.

Please call, come in, or send a note if you have questions. I begin this year with great enthusiasm that I can spend an hour a day with your son or daughter. Would you please sign the "coupon" at the bottom of this letter to show your willingness to join our team and to extend positive support to your student?

Sincerely,
Marilyn Wiencek

Toward Expository Writing

32

This is the introductory experience for a three-session cluster on expository writing. Since schools stress transactional more than expressive writing—and since this emphasis increases with school grade levels—it is important to address the participants' need to instruct students in reporting, describing, persuading, explaining, and the other expository modes, as well as in storywriting and autobiography.

On the other hand, the dichotomy between creative and expository writing is vastly exaggerated by schools and teachers. Almost any piece of decent expository writing contains strong elements of personal expression and creativity; and almost all creative writing executes some transaction with its audience. So one main task of these next few workshops is to blur arbitrary distinctions between modes, and help teachers to see the many theoretical and practical bridges between expressive and expository writing.

This first session provides a whimsical—and perhaps familiar—demonstration of semi-expository writing in action.

1 Without any initial ado, the leader dumps a bag of potatoes on a table. She asks each person to come up, pick one, and take it back to his seat. Next, she says something like: *Your job now is to study your potato extremely closely; to get to know it intimately; to commune with your potato. In a few minutes you'll be asked to write a description of your potato that is sufficiently detailed and distinctive that anyone reading it could pick your potato out of a whole pile of other spuds. So you really need to study all the details of your potato—its shape, size, color, texture, smell, markings, and other features. You may want to study it scientifically or figuratively, cataloguing, or analogizing—whatever works best for you and your potato. Feel free to make notes as you study, and you can begin writing your description whenever you're ready. You'll have fifteen minutes to finish writing, and then we'll shuffle potatoes and descriptions and try to match up the right sets.*

2 After fifteen minutes, collect all the potatoes and dump them back in a pile. Then collect all the papers and give them out randomly. Allow everyone to read, get up, paw potatoes, mingle, ask "Who wrote this one?" argue with each other, and *ad hoc*ly figure out which spud is which. This procedure should take about fifteen minutes. Encourage those who find the correct potato to confirm it with the original author and then take the potato and get out of the way of the remaining seekers.

3 Discussion can center on some of these questions:

- How did you feel while doing this assignment?
- Do you see any immediate connections between this assignment and your own classroom or students?
- In what ways was this an *expository* assignment?
- In what ways was this a *creative* or *expressive* writing task?
- How common are such hybrid or in-between modes of writing?
- Why do we so steadfastly maintain the creative/expository dichotomy?
- Why is "creative writing" sometimes a dangerous term to use in certain company?

Also, this is a good opportunity to simply review whatever terminologies the group has chosen to use in talking about various modes of writing (e.g., creative, expressive, transactional, expository, personal, reflexive, extensive, descriptive, explanatory, persuasive, argumentative, scientific, reporting, etc.).

33

Want Ad for a Teacher

This is a second, somewhat more powerful example of a satisfyingly personal expository writing assignment—this time, in a persuasive mode.

1 Ask participants to imagine that they are going to write an advertisement about themselves to run in a newspaper that is religiously scrutinized by school personnel directors. Tell them this is a fantasy exercise in an idealized world—they needn't be obstructed by the way teaching jobs are actually sought and brokered, by the poor job market, by riffings, or whatever. Help them to imagine a situation in which they could advertise *themselves* to schools that were free to respond to the ads and hire them. Tell them that they have an absolute maximum of 150 words to make the most enticing, most distinctive picture of themselves and their qualifications. Once the assignment is clear, and you've built up some enthusiasm for it, set them to work for about fifteen minutes. People will probably pass each other's ads-in-progress around and giggle some. After this first phase, announce that they have to cut their ads down to 100 words ("because of a steep increase in the price of advertising space"). Allow another ten minutes or so to do this revision.

2 You can now have people share their want-ads aloud. An even better idea may be to tape them up around the walls and let people circulate and read—in this way, everyone's ad would be read by almost everyone else.

3 Discussion: This assignment reaches back to the personal writing done earlier in the workshop, and the first stage of discussion may relate to risk-taking, self-disclosure, being honest, and so forth. Or, the discussion may move toward hard times in the world of teaching; such a digression is relevant, of course, and deserves some time. But the leader should eventually aim toward issues of expository writing. Some of the same questions from the last phase of session 32 will be appropriate here. The intention is to further confound and break down the notion that creative and expository writing are highly distinct, and especially that expository writing is dry, impersonal, and generally a pain to work on.

4 Using the principle that all kinds of expository assignments can be full of vitality and allow for great personal creativity and individuality, you now want to help the group brainstorm some more ideas for teaching transactional writing. Ask each person to work individually for about five minutes, to come up with three expository assignments or activities which might work with their own students. Then allow some time for the sharing and discussion of these ideas.

34

Leader Presentation— Expository Writing

Here's your own chance to offer a few ideas on energizing writing tasks that fall into informative, descriptive, explanatory, persuasive, or scientific modes. Naturally, you'll want to concentrate on your own favorites. Just for your own thinking and planning, some of the kinds of expository writing which teachers find exciting to apply to their own classrooms include:

- Instructions and directions; telling how to get to some place either in the real world or on a map; writing directions for making a peanut butter and jelly sandwich or some other confection—directions which are then followed literally by the teacher or students, to see if they work.
- Process papers: explaining how something operates or occurs (e.g., how a four-cycle engine works; how to crochet, etc.), by drawing on students' own expertise.
- Product research paper; have kids investigate and conduct "scientific comparisons" between different brands of one product (yogurt, shampoo) and report the results in prose, tables, statistics. You can use a few articles from *Consumer Reports* as models.

Materials on writing-across-the-curriculum (discussed on pages 109–116) and from the *Teaching Writing in the Content Areas* texts are relevant here, if you haven't covered them earlier.

You can point out that one important way to bridge the gap between expressive writing (which most students find engaging) and informational writing (which can seem more distant and difficult) is to help students make the material, the "territory," their own (as Donald Graves puts it). This can be done either by choosing topics about which students are already experts (shell collections, car repairs, game rules, etc.), or setting up activities that help students *become* experts (as in the product research paper, above). The "Foxfire" projects that have taken place in so many schools reflect the same important principle. Students who interview someone about an interesting trade, hobby, or piece of local color become its emissaries, bearers of valuable knowledge about which they know more than do their classmates, readers, or teachers.

Perhaps as important as a good topic, however, is the context in which an expository task is developed. When students are involved in communication with each other and with outsiders about their topics, and when they are encouraged to choose their own purposes for communicating, they begin to discover a real need to explain what they know—as has been observed in the progression of students' writing by teachers such as Nancie Atwell of Boothbay Harbor, Maine (National Council of Teachers of English conference presentation, Detroit, 1984). Visits by live outside experts or trips to significant locations obviously help to break the isolation of the classroom, to make research vivid and "real" to students. Later, sharing final reports with other students and outside audiences turns "practice" at informational writing into true use of language to inform.

Even writing about literature can be transformed as much by altering the classroom context as by dreaming up a clever new assignment. For example (at the high school level), each individual (or small group) can be asked to analyze the role of a different character (or scene) and *report* to the whole class about how it affects our understanding of the work. The result is that students are helped to perceive more than they usually do in their individual reading, for they hear how perspectives are influenced by many parts of the work. Differing interpretations of a poem can be compared, not to decide who is "right," but to analyze how a given set of words can suggest a variety of meanings, and to see what elements in the writing or in the reader's background may inspire particular interpretations. When this is the goal, all students' writing contributes to the learning process of the class, and thus becomes truly "informative" rather than just a test of whether the student read the material or not.

35

Curriculum Fair— Participants' Sharing

This is a very important workshop. A large amount of time is set aside here for the participants to share their own successful teaching ideas, assignments, projects, procedures, or materials with each other. Obviously, a good deal of planned and spontaneous idea-sharing will have already occurred throughout the program, but it is also vital to schedule this special, explicit sharing session to build upon, expand, and confirm all of the previous exchanges. Though the focus obviously should be on writing, you will find that some teachers will want to present larger units, multi-disciplinary, multi-skill plans they've used with good results. This should all be encouraged, of course—with appropriate attention directed to the writing activities that are (or could be) embedded in such unit plans.

The leader may at first be disappointed to find participants sharing teaching ideas they'd used *before* the workshop series—implying, perhaps, that their teaching approaches haven't really changed or that no new ideas have been generated. Remember, though, that risk is involved here: teachers asked to share a favorite plan will want to offer something they can recommend with the confidence of their own repeated experience. Nevertheless, the lesson they choose to present, as well as the way they describe it, is likely to have been strongly influenced by the workshop curriculum.

How can this sharing be conducted? With a broadly mixed group (K–12 or across-the-curriculum-type gatherings), this seems a fitting moment to subdivide by interests—perhaps Primary, Intermediate, Junior High/Middle, High School English, and subject-area groups. Although teachers will enjoy the rare chance to meet with their own grade-level-mates, everyone should remember the moral of session 15 on remaking assignments: almost any good first-grade writing project can be reworked to offer worthwhile activities for high school students, and vice versa. So, after special-interest groups have had a chance to share ideas at their own level, they can reassemble, share examples with the large group, and brainstorm on re-leveling some of the more promising ideas.

However the "fair" is organized, the leaders should see that each person has a roughly equal opportunity to share her teaching idea, whatever the size of the group that is acting as an audience. You should offer a time-budgeting suggestion based on a little mathematics of your own (e.g., "You'll have time to spend eight to ten minutes on each person's ideas—so try to keep track of the time as best you can.") Also, it helps a great deal to have people bring enough copies of teaching ideas to distribute one to each participant. This way even if time is short, everyone's idea can get eventual scrutiny—not to mention the advantage of people being able to simply talk through the highlights of their plan without having to explain it step-by-step to note-taking peers. It's nice for participants to leave with a tall stack of new teaching ideas.

VARIATION With a group that is predominantly working at one age level, or a group that wants and needs to share everything together, the idea fair can be conducted in the whole group. Obviously, this will cut down on the time available to each presenter and will make copied versions of the plans a virtual necessity. It offers, on the other hand, all the usual advantages of a large-group approach: conviviality, support, the quick derivation of alternatives, laughter. Before asking each person to comment on his/her plan, you can lay out stacks of the plans buffet-style, to let everyone collect and read for ten to fifteen minutes, even to allow people to seek each other out to ask questions for a while. This can even end up being the largest part of the session; it isn't essential to emphasize the formal talk-through of each plan or idea.

36

Curriculum Fair— Leader's Ideas

Depending upon how you structured the participants' curriculum-sharing sessions, this may or may not be a separate, differentiated workshop. You may, in other words, have simply decided to mix your own ideas in along with everyone else's as groups met to exchange ideas. If you do want to conduct your own show, this is your chance—and, obviously, you'll have to figure out the contents of your own session. Generally, it is a good idea to emphasize teaching ideas which are different from ones the teachers themselves have already introduced, which means that you'll want to arm yourself with a wide variety of material.

Owning Activity

37

If you study the literature of group dynamics, you will find that attitude and behavior changes are facilitated by public declarations. In other words, when a person seriously wants to begin doing something differently, it can strengthen her resolve to say so clearly to at least one other person. So it is with teachers and teaching. Toward the end of the writing in-service program, participants may need an opportunity to "own" their new or revised views of composition and students and to state what they wish to do in responding to these ideas.

The leader must have a good sense of her own group in order to figure out just how direct and self-revelatory this activity can or should be. Your way of handling the activity will probably fall between the following two examples: the first is a mild nonthreatening approach for a generally coolish group; later comes the purer owning exercise for a more open or committed group.

Version 1 The leader makes some remarks about the workshop coming to a close, reviewing some of the main concepts and interests which have emerged during the sessions (five minutes or so). Then she asks the participants to jot down three new ideas or approaches discussed in the workshop which they are most eager to try with their own students and to list some ideas they are *not* going to try, no matter how strongly they were endorsed in previous workshop sessions. The sharing of these pro and con lists can be the basis of a useful discussion, utilizing whatever is the group's most comfortable format (small-group, whole-group, etc.).

Version 2 The leader makes some remarks about the workshop coming to a close, reviewing some of the main concepts and interests which have emerged during the sessions (five minutes or so). She is careful also to review the affective and interpersonal history of the group. Next she asks people to write a few notes on the topic, "One thing I'd like to change in my classroom next year (semester, etc.) is. . . ." (Notice that this invites a much broader range of responses than just "nifty teaching ideas I want to try.") The leader helps teachers to focus on the question: *It could be something about your unit plans, your textbooks, your decor, your attitude, your writing lessons, your grading system, etc. It should be something you really want to change and which seems possible, though it may be difficult.* Next, the leader asks each person to make a list of all the problems, hinderances, difficulties, oppositions, stumbling-blocks, or hostile people standing in the way of this change. After these lists have been made, the leader asks each participant to cross off, one by one, each item she can see herself overcoming. Finally, the leader says: *Considering the change you want to make and the obstacles before you, by what* specific date *do you*

187

think you will have accomplished this change—or made a personally satisfying start toward it? On a new sheet of paper, incorporate the date into a statement like this: 'By January 15, 1985, I will have stopped carping about my students' tastes in music, TV, and other popular entertainments.' Sign your name to the statement. Next, find one (or more) other person in the room to read and also sign your statement. This last requirement helps to formalize the development of a mutual support system among the participants as well as reinforcing the degree of commitment to the written statements.

38

Appreciation—Enjoyment

Near the end of the program it is nice to save some time for mutual appreciation which is still loosely related to writing. One useful technique is to go around the group giving everyone one minute to make one final statement, share one additional activity, or express something about an individual or the group. We call this session "Famous Last Words." You should announce it well enough in advance so that people will have time to really plan their last words well. This sounds simple, but it has often been a memorable, deeply meaningful session.

VARIATIONS **1** Have people write comedic or satiric pieces and share a few in this session (one good topic is: "The stupidest idea I've heard in this workshop"). The humorous pieces have to be written outside of class, obviously, since there is no extra time available. Given the large number of shared references which the class has by now developed, some quite funny in-group comedy is likely to result. Such humor usually seems to center on issues which have been of serious concern to the group—and the laughter often seems to summarize the group's struggles.

2 Another approach is to have a "Circle of Appreciation." Go around the circle one by one, giving each person a chance to thank one other person for something she has done or been or exemplified.

EXAMPLE   TUNNEL VISION

```
Those   junior  high   teachers  should   teach   sentences...
Those  elementary  teachers  should  teach   sentences..,
I've   been   in   this  building  for   eighteen  years.,
High   school   teachers  are  so  subject   oriented.
Those   parents  should  read  to  their   children.
Why   don't   you   English teachers  teach  spelling?
But   I've  got   to  get  through  long   division
This  is   fine,  but  how  does  it  apply to me?
But   I   don't   need   to   read   the  experts
But  when  we  go  back  to  our   schools
But  the  administration  would   never..
Those  theories  mean  nothing  to  me
But  that  means  more  work  for  me
You'll  never  get  the  parents to
English  teachers  act  superior
Not   that  inquiry  stuff   again
They've  tried  that   before
But   I  can't  help  it  if
But   I've  always  done  it
But   I'm  too  tired  to
It's   the  only  way
I  hear  you,  but
Warriner's  says...
Piaget  says....
Caldwell  said
Britton  says
Moffett says
KIDS TODAY
But   I
Can't
(See the forest for the trees)
```

Wendy McPherrin

39

Evaluation

It is important to save a substantial chunk of time toward the end of an Institute for participants to do some written (naturally) evaluation of the program itself—and, as a kind of natural by-product, some summarizing of their own experience in the program. In keeping with everything that has come before, it seems important for the teacher-evaluators to begin with an open-ended rather than a statistical multiple-choice or ranking question. We've often used "One thing I'd like to say about this program is. . . ." This prompt allows people to address their own most important, sometimes most personal, concerns at the outset. More focused and specific questions can appropriately follow. Here's an example of an evaluation form we've commonly used.

EVALUATION

_____
Name (optional)

IWP Writing Workshops

1 One thing I'd like to say about the workshop series is . . .

2 Value of the various activities to me (5 = highest, 1 = lowest).
Doing my own writing __
Sharing my writing with others __
Getting to know some of my colleagues better __
Instructor's presentations/remarks in small groups __
Large-group lectures/sessions __
Small-group discussions __
Readings __ (Please note special favorites or unfavorites)

_____

_____

Practical classroom teaching ideas and assignments _____

Other (please specify) _____

_____

3 Comments on my small-group leader:

4 Some drawbacks/disappointments during the workshops:

5 Here's what I'd like to see done as a follow-up to this experience:

Summary and Celebration

40

Unless you suffer from a rare psychological ailment called aneuphoria (inability to experience pleasure), you will undoubtedly be able to figure out some happy and appropriate way to conclude the work of your group. While the manifestations of these celebrations tend to vary, a few of the constants appear to be food, drink, and laughter. Many of us like to conclude with some sort of awards ceremony—often including bogus diplomas, ribbons, prizes, etc. Another popular party game (assuming you *do* have a party going) is the world-famous homemade Mad Lib. If you don't know how to make up your own Mad Libs (which make wonderful parts-of-speech lessons, by the way), pick up a few of the books published by Price, Sloan, Stern which are available at card shops, party stores, and other outlets of frivolity. A sample starter for this occasion:

Dear Dr. _____ (your Superintendent),

Well, when we started this _____ workshop, we never thought that a
       (Adjective—"a")

_____ like (Leader's name) could teach a course at all _____. But now,
(Noun—"b")   (Adverb—"c")

after _____ hours of _____ work, we . . . .
      (any number)   (Adjective—"d")

Chapter

The Summer
Institute

The Illinois Writing Project summer institutes are designed to prepare teachers to lead in service programs for colleagues back in their own and other districts. Unlike most other sites in the National Writing Project, we train our teacher-consultants to lead a whole 30-hour inservice course (alone or in teams), rather than to develop a single, specialized presentation that they can give as a part of a longer workshop program that features various presenters. Obviously, the leadership demands on our teacher-consultants are tremendous, and the summer institute must prepare them in depth and in detail for the complex work they will face.

At the core of the summer institute activities is the curriculum of the IWP's school-based 30-hour inservice program. It is vital that these prospective inservice facilitators fully experience the dynamics of the program they will later be called upon to lead. The institute runs for four weeks, four days a week, five hours a day—for a total of eighty hours. Here is a brief outline of elements that build upon the basic core.

First, the writing and sharing that occupy the initial nine hours of the thirty-hour plan take up the first two-and-a-half days—thirteen hours—of the institute. More time is available for writers to read their work in small and large groups, so that everyone experiences both the anxiety and the growing trust involved. Discussions about implications of the writing experiences are also fuller. Participants have the luxury of taking writing seriously, immersing in it fully for at least a few days.

On the afternoon of day three, participants in pairs discuss their own deepest feelings about teaching, using a structured set of questions. The last day of the first week, a professional writer visits to read his work and discuss his own writing process.

Week two includes a morning devoted to the Developmental Issues workshop (session 12 in this book), and a morning for the drafting and reading of compositions entirely of individuals' own choice, accompanied by conferences with the leaders. From here, the institute diverges further from the thirty-hour plan, with two mornings given over to discussion of readings.

We've used a variety of texts for readings over the years, and have found that Donald Murray's *A Writer Teaches Writing* still stirs the most discussion and bridges the gap between theory and practice most fully for high school teachers—even though we argue with its sometimes preachy tone. Other texts people have found especially useful: Donald Graves's *Writing: Teachers and Children at Work,* Charles Cooper and Lee Odell's *Evaluating Writing,* and Peter Elbow's *Writing With Power.* We've often included selections from James Britton, even though teachers find his British indirectness frustrating. We usually end up giving one or two brief lectures on essential theories about the writing process.

For most of the second and third weeks, afternoons are devoted to participants' own presentations. Some of these take the form of discussions on other relevant texts, some demonstrate methods and strategies participants have used successfully, and some are issue-oriented debates. Usually these sessions are *not* practice runs for presenting workshops back home, because everyone is too immersed in new ideas for that. Instead, the sessions allow participants to process their thoughts from the work of the institute, while the leaders observe how people are internalizing new understandings and/or clinging to old ones. The sessions are sometimes uneven in quality, reminding everyone that change comes slowly and that even when people do adopt new ideas, they don't immediately transfer all the implications to their teaching.

Mornings of week three cover most of the applied and practical issues presented in sessions 15 through 34 of the thirty-hour plan. Parts of one or more afternoons are also needed to complete this work. The "Curriculum Fair" (session 35) culminates the classroom application cycle of the institute, and we try to get to it by the last morning of week three. On the last afternoon of this week, or the first one in week four, several old-timers, seasoned workshop leaders, visit to discuss their experience as teachers and as in-service facilitators. This dispels a lot of anxiety about the business of running workshops for other teachers, a concern which looms large in participants' minds as the last week of the institute begins.

Week four is devoted to strategies for promoting writing in participants' districts, and methods for running the thirty-hour in-service program (though usually we are still trying to fit in a few practical issues we didn't get to in week three). We introduce the leadership issue through a "hidden agendas" role-play activity, a mock meeting of teachers, administrators, and school board members gathered to discuss a controversial proposal affecting teachers' work and salaries. Each participant is given a specific secret role to play, and the ensuing enactment always highlights the teachers' showmanship as well as the complexity of the system we are all working to change.

Participants spend time discussing *this* book, identifying sessions they feel confident to conduct, those they need help with, and those they'd like to change or improve. Interestingly, when people first read through the manual, they are often shocked by the extent to which their own institute experiences were anticipated. Even good teachers, professionals who know they must be well prepared in advance, want classes to be magic, to be "spontaneous" when *they* are the students. An important discussion often ensues here about the difference between "planning" and "manipulation." The fact that most groups of teacher-learners have many things in common and that a leader may repeat actions and words used before doesn't mean that the newest group isn't making "real" discoveries or that the leader doesn't "really" care about *this* particular group. In other words, recognizing certain uniformities of social dynamics does not deny the reality of human freedom, individuality, and uniqueness.

Much of this week is focused on alleviating prospective workshop leaders' worries about a hostile reception from their colleagues. A lively activity that demonstrates resistance to new ideas is one we call "freeze groups." In groups of five or six, participants plan out dramatic scenes in which a leader is faced with some form of resistance as he or she presents a workshop. These are then acted out for the whole institute. Anyone in the audience (or among the actors) can call out "freeze" at any time, stopping the action while we discuss alternate ways to deal with the problem dramatized.

Since summer institutes are usually populated by pairs, threes or fours from the same districts, participants need to meet in district groups to discuss strategies for their own communities. Loners from assorted districts can pair up and serve as sympathetic listeners for one another. The groups must consider several questions. Are enough of their teachers ready to commit the time for a thirty-hour workshop? Must groundwork be laid first, among friends, administrators, key people in other buildings? Since not every institute participant intends to give workshops afterward, an equally relevant topic is the building of support with colleagues, one's principal, parents and others, for one's own classroom efforts. The leaders get around to every district group to listen, learn how we can help, and give encouragement. At least two such sessions on separate days are needed for this.

The last day of the institute is usually crowded with final consultations, handing out and admiring the collection of teachers' writing (produced by a few gung-ho volunteer editors), activities for expressing appreciation to everyone, evaluations, and a celebration picnic (see sessions 37 through 40 in the handbook). We're always amazed, exhausted, and moved when it's over.

There are many reasons why we might present research to "prove" the effectiveness of an inservice program on teaching writing. These reasons differ considerably from one another, and call for quite different kinds of data to support them. One obvious purpose would be to convince readers of this book, particularly those new to its ideas, that the workshops we describe are effective—that they result in changed classroom methods and improved writing by students.

There are several ways to regard such an attempt to persuade. On the one hand, we have an obligation to provide proof, to be accountable. On the other, no amount of proof precludes further questions. A doubter could justifiably expect us to present our work in the best light, and could imagine that, over the seven years of our program, we had sifted out the most favorable data. Such research is obviously not "pure" scientific inquiry in which the observer has no preference about the outcome. Given that many educational improvement programs have "impressive data" to back them up, it is easy to be cynical about accountability research.

If the reader already has some faith in what we've described, perhaps the research is actually more helpful. It then serves as a confirmation, through one kind of observation, of patterns the reader has discovered in her own experience. This really makes more sense to us as a purpose for presenting research. Over decades, educational methods have been tested and proven again and again, while government agencies and new generations simply doubt and ask for proof once more. We will be more realistic, and perhaps more helpful, if we think of our research mainly as providing confirmation and confidence to those who agree that our methods are valuable.

Accountability remains important, however, and our research can provide a model for sensible data-gathering by school districts. We cannot escape the need to show other teachers, administrators, and the community some results. Even if "proof" can't convince everyone, it is wrong to insist that improvement in teaching and writing is mysterious and can't be studied at all.

A somewhat different purpose for research is more *descriptive*. Rather than ask a "yes-no" question like "Does it work or not?" we may want to consider more interesting matters: How do teachers and students change? What sorts of things are student writers in a school system doing well, and in what areas do they need more help? Answers to such diagnostic questions will be more complex, impossible to summarize with simple numerical averages. Such research is more expensive, involving collection and analysis of a large number of student writing samples.

Still another issue is long-range, schoolwide development. How widely does an effective new approach spread in a school system? After three or four years, has the program gained acceptance, faded away, or been left isolated in a few classrooms? We should be careful, however, when we define success in this area. Helping good teachers survive in unsupportive surroundings may be as important as having a broader influence.

Perhaps the best thing we can provide in this chapter, to respond to these various views of research, is a variety of sources and kinds of information. Our own evaluation effort includes a statistical analysis of pre- and post-test writing samples, something relatively few projects have attempted. Teacher testimony and a narrative of school-wide development offer a descriptive view of growth and change. Other writing projects around the country have achieved results similar to ours, and we'll review several of their key studies as well.

No matter how we present this material, however, it is likely to sound self-serving. We can only protest that:

1 Credit for results in schools goes almost entirely to the tenacious, thoughtful, caring teachers (and administrators) who have generated and adapted ideas for their own unique settings, and who have kept working to spread these ideas throughout school systems. In fact, much of our data is several levels removed from us, for it includes performance of students whose teachers were trained by teacher-trainers, while only the trainers themselves were in summer institutes.

2 What "works" in the workshops themselves is not some personal quality or wisdom we possess, even though personal involvement and judgment are needed from workshop leaders. Rather, the magic derives from a set of concepts and methods, patterns that reflect universalities about human learning (or at least learning within *our* culture). Writing projects have tapped into—often stumbled upon—structures that many good educators, writers, parents, psychologists, businesspeople, have known and used either consciously or subconsciously for years. Participants tend to project their feelings of success upon their leaders and overstress the leaders' role in making workshops successful, but we are convinced there is more to the workshops than strong personalities. One piece of evidence of this: comments about workshops are remarkably alike, no matter who conducts the sessions or where they take place. Personalities of leaders differ; workshop plans differ; but serious writing and sharing that writing with peers results in the same kinds of discovery and renewal again and again.

Illinois Writing Project Study of Student Writing Samples

During its experimental phase (1979–81), the Illinois Writing Project (originally called the Chicago Area Writing Project) trained teachers in grades 2 through 12 in six target school districts. These districts represented a broad socioeconomic mix, from poor, inner-city minority populations to affluent exurban

areas. We conducted a summer institute for thirty-one teachers and then offered thirty-hour in-service programs for additional teachers in the same districts, run by those trained in the summer. We then matched the teachers and
their students to a control group and collected writing samples from both
groups with a pre-test each fall and post-test each spring. We employed a writing stimulus and primary trait scoring guide used by the National Assessment
of Educational Progress and compared groups statistically.

The outcome was that, on average, students whose teachers were trained in
the summer institute made over twice as much improvement from pre- to post-
testing as did control group students with essentially equivalent pre-test scores.
Students of second-level workshop teachers (teachers in workshops led by
those trained in the summer institute) made similar gains. During both academic years involved, significance for the summer institute group's students
was at the .012 level or better. Significance for the second-level group was below the .001 level. This study was validated by an out-of-state review panel for
the Illinois State Board of Education in 1981.

Teachers in both the summer institute and the thirty-hour in-service program
participated in the curriculum outlined in this book—a sequence of activities
that did not mandate any lock-step teaching plans or approaches. Instead,
teacher choice and initiative were encouraged, for these make permanent
change in teaching much more likely to occur. When the teachers reentered
their classrooms, they used writing activities they had personally developed,
adapting them to varying student levels and needs. Monitoring through teacher
reports and classroom observations showed that, by choice, the techniques
most widely adopted were:

1   Prewriting, i.e., activities to help students discover, gather, and organize what
    to say before drafting.
2   Linking personal and formal writing, particularly through journal writing, to in-
    crease fluency and enliven the writing school requires.
3   Establishing real audiences, to motivate and to provide feedback that shows
    students the effect of their writing on others; this includes the teacher's becom-
    ing a more supportive audience, rather than just a critical one, intervening
    early in the process as well as assessing the final product.
4   Small group sharing and critiquing, to increase student responsibility, develop
    trust and sense of audience, and stimulate revision without increasing teachers'
    paper-grading load.

In most of the experiment classrooms, students wrote more frequently than
they had before, and even when not writing, were often involved in activities
leading to writing or responding to writing. In addition, the participating teachers made presentations for staff, community, school boards, and parents, and

provided awareness sessions in other schools in their districts. This helped build a climate of acceptance not only for the Writing Project, but for better methods of teaching writing in general.

To obtain pre- and post-test writing samples, we chose a writing stimulus used by the National Assessment of Educational Progress since 1969, the "Stork Expressive." We wanted a prompt that had been used nationally, that would be applicable at a variety of grade levels, and that would require a number of important writing abilities. The "Stork Expressive," in eliciting story writing, involves not just "creativity," but a range of competencies—elaboration of detail, organization, use of story conventions (beginning, presentation of a conflict or problem, resolution) and understanding of audience needs.

NAEP's primary trait scoring guide for this stimulus was used as well. Primary trait scoring provides objective, reliable evaluation of content because it focuses on a single trait in a piece of writing. Since different purposes and audiences call on different writing skills, scoring is more likely to relate to the student's actual effort if a single, relevant trait is identified, and a separate scoring guide designed for each trait and task. By focusing on a single trait, with explicit explanations of the strategies that contribute to a writer's success on that trait, the test designer can assure some objectivity for scoring—that is, scorers will tend to agree on a score. Furthermore, the interference of other factors—other values scorers may espouse, or aspects of the writing extraneous to the main trait—is minimized.

Various controls were used to assure the integrity of the data. A pilot run of the test was conducted to make sure it was workable at all grade levels. NAEP procedures and guidelines were followed in test administration and training of scorers, to provide consistency. Each essay was scored by two readers, with discrepancies reconciled by a third. Interreader reliability was checked and found to be over 90 percent. A select amount of data was hand tallied to verify computer recording and analysis. Each round of testing was confined to a four-week span, so that timetables were essentially equivalent for all classes tested.

Three groups of students were tested: (1) students in the classes of the thirty-one teachers who participated in the summer institute (group E_1); (2) students in the classes of the twenty-four control teachers (group C) in districts separate from the E_1 group; (3) students in the classes of teachers (group E_2) who participated in thirty-hour in-service programs led by the E_1 group members in their own districts. The second-level group (E_2) was measured only in the 1980–81 year since only then did their training, which came in spring 1980, affect students.

Control teachers (group C) were from separate schools, based on matching the overall characteristics of school communities. Data showing equivalency of schools took into account community type (based on NAEP classification criteria), racial-ethnic breakdown, and profiles of standardized test scores. High school matching also considered the percentage of students continuing their education after graduation. In addition, control and project teachers were matched closely according to these criteria: grade level and primary subject taught, attitude toward writing, and amount of writing assigned to students.

Student selection was controlled in a variety of ways. Classes of all grade levels and tracking levels were included. Since teachers, not students, received Project training, students were not aware that they were part of a special study (except for the fact of testing, which applied to treatment and control students alike). A group of students was given the post-test only, as a check to assure that there was no effect simply from taking the test twice.

Because of the large number of students tested (approximately 1,600 in 1979–80 and 2,450 in 1980–81), a randomly selected group of tests from each of the three groups was scored. Randomization was within three stratified groups—elementary, junior high and high school—so that the student sample would be proportional to the structure of the teacher sample. Tests were coded to prevent test readers from distinguishing between primary treatment, second-level treatment, and control teachers' students. Tables 1 and 2 show the breakdown of pre-test and post-test scores for each of the groups tested.

Table 1
Mean Writing
Scores by Grade
—1979–1980
School Year

grade level	N		pre-test		post-test	
	E_1	C	E_1	C	E_1	C
2	29	27	0.76	0.93	1.66	1.56
3	18	28	1.50	1.75	2.06	1.93
4	76	21	1.88	2.05	2.36	2.05
5	30	17	2.20	2.18	2.30	2.18
6	18	7	2.50	2.43	3.00	3.00
7	25	5	2.40	2.60	2.76	2.60
8	54	26	2.61	2.58	2.89	2.81
9	72	55	3.06	3.09	3.22	3.16
10	117	20	3.10	3.20	3.22	3.05
11	89	57	2.82	2.96	2.97	2.96
12	57	31	2.95	2.90	3.01	3.00
TOTAL	585	294				
AVERAGES			2.51	2.51	2.81*	2.64
S. D.			0.85	0.76	0.70	0.93

Pre-test P-Value = 0.228—confirms initial homogeneity.
Post-test P-Value = 0.012—confirms significance.

Scale for scores was 0 to 4.
E_1: Institute-trained group. C: Control group.

Table 2
Mean Writing
Scores by Grade
—1980–1981
School Year

grade level	N			pre-test			post-test		
	E$_1$	E$_2$	C	E$_1$	E$_2$	C	E$_1$	E$_2$	C
4	20	20	20	1.85	1.85	1.85	2.35	2.15	2.00
5	15	15	15	2.20	2.00	2.00	2.87	2.27	2.13
6	15	15	15	2.13	2.27	2.00	2.73	2.93	2.07
7	25	25	25	2.16	2.32	2.36	2.48	2.48	2.28
8	25	25	25	2.44	2.20	2.24	2.60	2.56	2.44
9	25	25	25	2.36	2.36	3.52	2.64	2.60	2.56
10	25	25	35	2.64	2.36	2.32	2.68	2.68	2.32
11	25	25	25	2.60	2.60	2.40	2.92	2.72	2.32
12	25	25	25	2.72	2.56	2.80	2.96	2.80	2.64
TOTAL	200	200							
AVERAGES			200	2.38	2.30	2.31	2.69*	2.58*	2.33
S.D.				0.57	0.53	0.55	0.68	0.58	0.56

Pre-test P-Value = 0.326—confirms initial homogeneity.
Post-test P-Value = 0.001—confirms significance.

Scale for scores was 0 to 4.
E$_1$: Institute-trained group. E$_2$: In-service-trained group.
C: Control group.

Significance figures for comparison of treatment and control post-tests were strong: .012 for post-tests in 1979–80, and better than .001 in 1980–81, for both E$_1$ and E$_2$ students. Meanwhile, pre-tests of treatment and control groups were essentially equivalent. Thus, data were significant over two years, for averages based on multiple schools, districts, grade levels, and achievement levels. The effect was essentially as strong for in-service-trained teachers' students (group E$_2$) as for the institute-trained teachers' students (group E$_1$).

Several complexities and limitations in the data need to be mentioned. First, the students in each year comprised different groups. While it would have been valuable to follow the same students for several years, the spread over six districts made this logistically impossible. Samples were scored separately by year, as well, so that averages from one year to the next aren't comparable.

Scores from one grade to the next do not reflect advances in ability, for readers adjusted the definitions of success for particular grade levels. Given the limited number of score points (5), this was necessary in order to make the testing sensitive to variations within a given grade.

Finally, as the tables indicate, post-test comparisons vary from grade to grade, and are most positive for treatment groups in earlier grades. We can speculate that the greatest growth in writing usually occurs for students of younger ages. It may also be that older students find more difficulty in general engaging with a task arbitrarily set before them and disconnected from any immediate social context—and thus more students in all the older groups may fail to give the writing their best effort, flattening all the results.

It is still striking that students of Project teachers improved on the average more than twice as much as controls, if *differences* between pre- and post-tests are compared. Another way to interpret this is that in 1980–81, 37.5 percent of primary treatment students (group E_1) increased scores one point or more on the five point scale, and 10 percent went down, while only 20.5 percent of control students (group C) went up one point and 16.5 percent went down. 34.5 percent of the in-service-trained teachers' students (group E_2) scores went up and 7 percent went down. The gain represents about one-third of the standard deviation for scores, confirming the meaningful size of the improvement.

System-Wide Development

Not every school system that holds writing project workshops uses them to promote broad-based improvement. In some districts, participants represent a small fraction of teachers. We've even seen districts sponsor writing workshops while curriculum committees are simultaneously reducing the time available for writing. But when a district *does* decide to spread new ideas more widely, the results can be gratifying.

A series of studies published in *Educational Leadership* (November, 1983) compares school districts which have sustained innovative programs with those where such programs have fizzled over a period of years. Factors crucial to success included strong administrative backing and committed teachers who served as facilitators and models for other teachers. Change was often mandated from above, but this was effective only when teachers were given adequate training and resources, plus latitude to implement the program in their own classrooms.

We've observed similar patterns. In a high school where the English department chairperson remains skeptical, project teachers may feel isolated, though they are usually free to innovate in their own classrooms. This is not necessarily a "failure" for the project. If workshops help good teaches to survive and encourage their students under less-than-ideal conditions, then the workshops have been valuable. But in a district where understanding and influential individuals—administrators or teachers or both—give consistent backing, efforts continue long after a project has completed its direct training.

The story of development in one district shows how this can happen. We've chosen Oak Park Elementary District 97 in Chicago's western suburbs as our example, though some other districts have done just as much. In November,

1981, Oak Park's Director of Reading and Language Arts, Mary Schneider, attended the NCTE national convention and participated in a workshop conducted by Donald Graves. Inspired by this experience, she returned to her district, studied more, and began to imagine possibilities for her teachers. During the 1982–83 school year, she worked with faculty in one school building, studying research on composition and helping them try new methods.

Meanwhile, junior high teachers were stirred into action by a workshop on primary trait scoring in the fall of 1982, and later by workshops with a presenter for *Stack the Deck,* a program many teachers have found useful. Then in the spring of 1983, six Oak Park teachers attended a thirty-hour in-service program given in a nearby high school district and taught by Nancy Sindelar, a graduate of IWP's previous summer institute.

These tastes and beginnings led Mary to approach her school board with a broader proposal. The board decided to send three people to the next IWP institute so the district could develop its own trainers, and in addition funded two thirty-hour in-service courses which reached fifty teachers in the early summer of 1983. While the board didn't specify how far the effort was to go, they agreed it should be districtwide and self-sustaining.

The superintendent gave the effort strong support as well. He was convinced that all district teachers should get some form of training, and he helped provide not only money but encouragement, changes in calendar, and freedom from conflicting obligations for those desiring to attend workshops. Mary feels this support was vital for the success of the program.

Illinois State Board of Education funds granted to IWP made possible another two thirty-hour workshops in October, 1983, and January, 1984. As of this writing, a fifth series is scheduled for June, 1984. Altogether, 102 out of 300 teachers in the district have participated, and those who haven't usually indicate that schedule conflicts, rather than any philosophical obstacle, have prevented them from joining in. Past participants continue to recommend the sessions to others, so Mary expects strong attendance at future workshops.

Another dimension in the Oak Park effort is the ongoing informal in-service activity. Clusters of teachers in each building meet once every six to eight weeks to share ideas, discuss successes and problems, and study together. About fifty-five teachers are involved in these groups, and the district has provided copies of Graves's *Writing: Teachers and Children at Work* for each. Mary helps run group meetings and visits classes of teachers who ask for help, either teaching a demonstration lesson, conferencing with students, or listening to kids read their writing.

During 1983–84, the district revised the language arts curriculum to emphasize writing as a process. A new text was adopted which, Mary feels, will help insecure teachers try new methods, even though she asserts a text cannot by itself ensure good teaching.

Evaluation of the effect of this program is now in progress. Teachers in the study groups are collecting their own informal pre- and post-test writing samples between the beginning and end of the year. They say that from general observation, the change in students' writing has been "astounding." The feeling is that this is natural, almost inevitable, when a positive approach to critiquing is used and when children are unafraid to take risks. An attitude survey and, for junior high students, a more elaborate questionnaire, are now being administered. Some Oak Park teachers are also part of a new IWP evaluation study that should provide additional data on student growth over the next couple of years. PTA, school board, and community groups have asked for presentations to hear about the program and its results.

Mary stresses that no one person runs this program. Teachers teach other teachers, leading formal workshops as well as informal study sessions, receiving recognition for their expertise.

Effects on Teachers

Whatever improvement we may observe in students' writing, and no matter how necessary administrative support may be, the key to change is still the classroom teacher. It is the teacher who is with students every day, who influences their thinking and attitudes, who can encourage and motivate children, who can make new methods convincing if she internalizes them—or may undermine new methods if she does not understand or trust them.

It is therefore helpful to study the various ways writing workshops affect teachers' growth. The most obvious domain of change will be professional—the discovery of new teaching methods, how they work, and why they are important. A driving force behind this, however, is teachers' learning about their own writing process and its accompanying difficulties, anxieties, and satisfactions. Chief among these satisfactions are teachers' sense of personal renewal and reconnection with colleagues.

These last effects, personal renewal and closeness with colleagues, have a double impact. They give teachers new energy to recommit themselves to important values and attend to students' needs. In addition, teachers realize it was *writing* and the sharing of writing that helped them achieve this renewal. When they see that writing can have this power, they want their students to experience it too.

These effects are clearly revealed in the comments participants write in evaluations submitted after workshops. Typical comments about professional learning from IWP participants:

• My outlook has changed completely as far as my approach to correcting a paper. I feel that I will be more a part of my students' writing and see myself as a definite instrument in their development and liking of writing. Writing has gained new importance to me, and I now see it as a multi-stage process. You have to be willing to change but it's worth it.
• The most important thing I learned was that as a teacher I must continue to fo-

cus on how I can help each individual student—that whatever I do and however I respond to the individual student I must be cognizant of how it is going to affect the student. I want to help each student and therefore I must be sure my actions are productive.
- Students will write better (and write more) if given the opportunity to write in a nonthreatening atmosphere and provided they are engaged in the topic. I now realize the artificiality of many of the topics I've given my students in the past.

Barbara Tervo, a participant in another writing project, wrote a lively narrative for the National Writing Project *Network Newsletter* which makes clear just how thorough-going the development of fresh approaches can be. We excerpt it here as one example of the development many writing project leaders have observed.

The Golden Key I obtained from the Alaska Writers Workshop was this simple notion: writing as process. With it, I've been unlocking blocked writers' doors ever since.

Day 1, A.W.W. (After Writers Workshop) I began encouraging pure unadulterated fluency via a daily fifteen-minute journal write. The motivation: "one point extra for every paper pumped out, and here's even more good news. I won't even read it if you put a star at the top of your paper." (I think someone was testing my credibility, as one day while collecting their journals I couldn't help but notice a fourth of a page full of milk-curdling profanities with a star on top. I didn't even flinch.)

The first couple of weeks I got stars enough to fill the Milky Way; but then I got smart. I begin to get very personal with those writers of unstarred papers. I was able to make appropriate references and responses to individuals' shared material, which not only reinforced *them,* but also, later on, served to provoke many more starless sheets.

At this point I have to force them to stop at the end of fifteen minutes, and most inquire incessantly, "Have you read mine yet?" In general the journals have become a way for them to share themselves, their experiences and their families with me.

Once everyone was feeling comfortable and capable of producing "anything," I very subtly (and joyfully) began to shift and have them produce "something." I began to structure their writing experiences a bit more by utilizing each of the myriad motivating ideas presented during the workshop, i.e., mapping, clustering, memories (these little guys are packed with them!), monologues, and stream-of-consciousness writing.

The kids especially enjoy the Creative Sensory Writing Exercises drawn up by Mary Ann Kendall of Kodiak. I personally enjoy being re-amazed at what impeccable observers these kids are. It's wonderful! To date, they are all prolific and *successful* writers.

So far, their writing constraints have been few. My next task will be to mold them with the realization that *writing is a process of making things clearer,* and it can be altered for different audiences. Heretofore they have been writing mainly for me and themselves. The next step will be to encourage writing for peers and the "public." One of James Moffett's writing assignments targets this approach: choose a special spot to sit and for fifteen minutes use the stream-of-consciousness technique to record everything that you observe. The next assignment will be to rewrite the piece (sweep it up, clear out any loose or disorderly sentences) so that it will be interesting and understandable to the rest of the kids. Willing participants will then share these with the rest of the class. Later we will rewrite the same piece and incorporate it into a letter to our pen pals in Florida. . . .

Phew! It seems like I've much work to do, but thanks to the Alaska Writers Workshop, at least I know where to begin.

The power of working with one's own writing in order to reach such discoveries is described again and again in IWP workshop participants' comments:

- I learned it is not easy to be a student! After spending my Monday nights here, I can understand how students might feel when asked to write. It is a difficult and frightening thing.
- Sharing one's writing with one's friends and peers is frightening yet extremely exciting.
- I really learned a great deal about the writing process, about my students' feelings and apprehensions about writing, about how to introduce the writing process to make it more interesting and more meaningful. Writing was easier to do than I expected (after all these years). . . . I understand my students' feelings when they are writing, because I had such feelings as well.

Michael Scriven, in his "Overview of the Bay Area Writing Project Evaluation," a major study funded by the Carnegie Foundation, summarized the professional development he observed among participants of writing projects:

What is it about BAWP that has made it so successful in getting attention and resources, getting recruits, maintaining their interest, generating loyalty and affection, and retaining an influence on their subsequent behavior? One could only answer with certainty after doing a planned variation study, but certain impressions persevere from our three years of investigation and interaction. In no particular order, one would want to mention as important: the treatment of teachers as extremely valuable resources and as autonomous agents; the heavy emphasis on the importance of the teachers doing more writing themselves; the stress on prewriting activities by students, and on multi-mode writing and on writing across the curriculum; the use of an eclectic but carefully selected range of experts as resources designed to broaden the classroom-bound teacher's horizons; the stress on holistic assessment; the continual updating of the program content; peer criticism (both of teachers' writing and of students' writing).

Renewal grows both out of the internal self-knowing that writing engenders, and the group relationships that develop as this knowing is shared. Participant evaluations tend to connect the two:

- In addition to sharing ideas about teaching, sharing personal writing proved to be a sure way of getting to know one another. I learned more about, and became closer to, teachers whose writing I shared than those I've known for years. If personal writing is that revealing then it's no wonder so many people see it as a threatening experience.
- I think it was the most interesting thing we have done in the district to have the experience of working on a topic with teachers from other buildings and grade levels. Never have I experienced this to such an extent. We now know some people in our district in ways we would never have before, and we have a common goal.
- I learned that writing is hard work—that writing is a way of becoming human, that learning to write is part of being educated. Writing is an indicator of how a student feels about himself, and is an indicator of whether the student wants to communicate. . . . Sharing the writing of my peers helped me to know them intimately. It also was a way of knowing something about myself. The IWP in-service program generated ideas, feelings, techniques, methods and philosophies which can be incorporated into classroom practices and attitudes toward instruction.

Participants tend to transfer a lot of the credit for this renewal to the workshop leader. Interestingly, however, they especially appreciate it when the leader is a teacher at their own level, someone who lives with the same problems they do—which, in an indirect way allows them to restore more of the achievement to themselves.

- The instructor obviously had struggled with many of our frustrations and had found ways to deal with them.
- There was a mixture of seriousness and humor, of understanding our needs as teachers and the needs of students. It helped tremendously to have the leaders from our own department because they experience our difficulties with us and it appeared we worked them through together.

Most striking is the occasional conscious realization that teachers' growth has been encouraged by the leader's congruence, not only with the group but with what is implied in the material itself:

- I especially enjoyed being a participant, not just an observer. So often we attend workshops and are told how to teach a particular subject or style, but the instructor himself or herself does not use the same techniques. Sherrill was able to conduct the sessions in a manner that was consistent with her philosophy and style.

Teachers may respond positively at the end of a workshop, but we may also want to know how deeply their actual behavior is affected. In regard to this, the Carnegie Evaluation Unit asked several important questions during its study of the Bay Area Project:

1 Following an institute or in-service program, do teachers actually change their methods in the classroom?
2 Do the effects of the training persist over long time periods?

The answer to both questions was "yes." Interviews with Bay Area Project participants in 1977–78 indicated:

Teachers receiving BAWP training (invitational and in-service) were more likely than comparison teachers to:

1 Teach writing as a process, not a product (with special attention to the prewriting phase).
2 Use a variety of techniques to teach writing (although focusing most heavily on encouraging students to write whole discourses rather than depending on exercises per se).
3 Involve students in the writing and editing process through the use of peer feedback.

National Writing Project Evaluation Portfolio, p. 96

In a survey of teachers who had participated in the Bay Area Project from one to four years previously (so that for many, the workshops were several years in the past) the Carnegie study found that:

• A majority of teachers (more than 75 percent) saw the BAWP experience as having increased their students' enjoyment and valuing of writing, and as having increased their students' confidence and overall skill in writing ability.
• A majority of teachers (more than 75 percent) saw the BAWP experiences as having an impact on increasing the frequency of their discussions about writing with fellow teachers. Only the summer invitational participants tended to report that the BAWP experience had increased their collaborative activities with other teachers, their program change activities (implementing new or revised writing programs, assisting with proficiency standards, etc.) or other professional activities related to the teaching of writing.
• A large majority of teachers (over 90 percent) indicated that the BAWP ex-

perience was of some use to them in the teaching of writing. The individuals rating the BAWP program most highly were those exposed to the summer invitational, while the less enthusiastic, but still *strongly* positive, ratings came from the individuals participating in the elementary in-services.
. . . Moreover, the effects of BAWP do not seem to diminish over time even though many teachers do not have ongoing exposure to BAWP. Teachers attending early workshops and in-services are just as enthusiastic about the program as teachers reached by BAWP more recently.

National Writing Project Evaluation Portfolio, p. 92

When development takes place not only for teachers and for the system but for the workshop leader herself, a spiral of continuing growth becomes possible. The following excerpts from a letter from one of our summer institute graduates shows how all the effects of a writing project can combine into one connected process:

February 28, 1984

Dear Steve,

. . . I wanted to share with you some of the responses I received after I led the second workshop series for our district; I want you to experience my thrill at knowing how effective the workshops are in a variety of ways.

Of course one important effect is the gradual awareness of what it means to be a student in a writing class and how student experiences can be shaped to create better writers. Here are a few representative comments (from workshop participants) on that issue:

- Students can learn from themselves and from each other . . . more from themselves and each other than an isolated teacher.
- The most important thing I learned was how it feels to be a student again specifically how different assignments and exercises affect students.
- I've learned to be less critical and more encouraging—to accept even the smallest amount of work in a helpful, caring way.
- I've learned the importance of prewriting activities to motivate students to write.

My department chairman observed that an experience like the workshop should be required of every prospective English teacher. He was most impressed by the effective way in which workshop exercises led to the realization of important concepts.

Another response is teacher awareness of the difficulty of teaching writing, especially in other subject areas. Both my workshops have drawn participants from across the curriculum, and this one included two first grade teachers from another district as well. One participant (I think he was the department chairman from business) reflected "that the teaching of writing is an even more complicated process than I had imagined . . . and worthy of the best effort of teachers on all grade levels."

One response that always delights me is summed up by one participant: "I learned to feel more positive about my own writing ability. . . ." That was also my reaction during the training workshop. I have to laugh when I share my writing in workshops and it receives raves. I blame the "sound" of my skill on my newly acquired confidence as a writer and tell the participants they sound just as skilled.

Perhaps the most striking effect of the writing workshop is the fellowship it builds. We cried together over our hurts and memories, laughed about the antics of students in classrooms, commiserated about over-bearing administrators and know-it-all parents, and ate enough food so that our journalism teacher moaned that she had gained 55 pounds in 30 hours! The smiles I saw as we gathered for celebration at the end of the workshop, the cheery goodbyes as we went our separate ways, all spoke of friendship.

Finally, there are those comments that speak of renewal—not just as teachers, but also as human beings:

- I feel renewed, motivated, and eager to share and model what I have learned.
- The program . . . is one of the few formal "courses" that I have been enrolled in that has given me what I wanted, better ways to teach students how to write and how to think.
- Groups like this are needed (by teachers) for therapy and idea sharing.
- I felt accepted and respected for my thoughts and comments.
- I . . . appreciated the opportunity to get acquainted with other teachers in my district and also the faculty from grade school.

For me this chance to help teachers feel better about themselves and their task is the most rewarding aspect of the experience. I leave the workshops on a high. Thanks for making all this possible.

I feel I also owe you a thank you for giving my teaching career a new direction.

Warmest regards,
Judy Johnstone

Perhaps we can best conclude this account not with more "proof," but with a statement of our own belief about what it is we have tried to achieve, and what we think is implicit in all of the responses we've quoted here. The statement takes the form of a speech Steve has sometimes given for his "Famous Last Words" at the end of an institute.

A Short Speech

People have remarked that a summer institute on teaching writing is a kind of conversion experience. I *do* relate it to my religion—and to my politics. Teaching writing is connected with democracy, with teaching and *enacting* respect for human beings, helping them to respect themselves—as opposed to worshipping the American Star and Hero System. That's the worst thing about television—the Star and Hero System. Teaching writing—if it's done in a good way and not just used to put kids through their paces—is about helping kids see that all of them are the heroes in this country. They grow up to be the people who make it run, keep it afloat, sustain its values, suffer its deprivations and self-destructiveness, pick up its always reviving struggle for connection, for community, for joy and creation.

So this is a sermon. People don't like sermons. I'm always careful not to give it.

(Ages of children are given in parentheses.)

1 Kenneth A. (2)
Once there was a little girl playing with another little girl. And the bees buzzed around and stung her. And she went home crying. Mommy wiped the blood off it. Then she went to bed.

2 Mark A. (2)
Once upon a time there was a little baby. And it went under the blanket, and they shut the door, and the baby cried.

3 Marilyn G. (2)
Once upon a time there was a little girl and she hurt herself. And her Mommy came here and kissed her and made her better.

4 Nancy C. (2)
Little boy cried and his Mommy went away. And then he went outside and then somebody hit him. Mommy came back and told him to get out of the road.

5 Cindy C. (2)
A baby cries. It eats. It just drinks out of Mommy's nipple. She goes to sleep. Then she wakes up. I cry, too.

6 Lucy S. (2)
The baby cried. The Mommy spanked the baby. The Mommy spanked her again. Then she cried again. Then the Mommy spanked her again. Sometimes my Mommy gives my baby a bottle. She falls asleep. Then she cries. Then my Mommy doesn't give her a spanking. She gives her cereal.

7 Keith M. (3)
A little bear messed up the house. He spilled all the garbage. He put the garbage in a window. Their Mommy and Daddy came home and looked at the floor. They tried to spank him and he ran away fast. He got a big rock and pushed it down the hill at Mommy and Daddy. They got hurt, and they went home to rest. Then he found some milk, and throwed it down on the Mommy and Daddy. And they had an idea—the Teddy Bear's idea. He had a hose up on the hill and squirt, squirt, squirt at the Mommy and Daddy. They got hurt.

221

8 Kirk W. (4)

Once there was a doggy and a little boy. The doggy was pretty silly. He ran away from the little boy and went farther and farther away. The little boy caught the doggy with his hands. He put the doggy down. The doggy ran away again. He came near a railroad track. He stepped on it and the train ran over him. But he was still alive. This was a big white bulldog and he wanted to go back to his home. When the little boy came back home he found the doggy. He was happy. His doggy was still alive.

9 Tracy H. (5)

There was a boy named Johnny Hong Kong and finally he grew up and went to school and after that all he ever did was sit all day and think. He hardly even went to the bathroom. And he thought everyday and every thought he thought up his head got bigger and bigger. One day it got so big he had to go live up in the attic with trunks and winter clothes. So his mother bought some gold fish and let them live in his head—he swallowed them—and every time he thought, a fish would eat it up and he felt much better.

10 Heidi H. (5)

Once there was a girl named Cindy. She had a brother named Mickey. They messed up the house. They dumped the chair over. They spilled some ink. Mommy spanked them. Then they spilled a puzzle over. Then her mother spanked them and put them to bed. They cried. Then it was lunch time. Then her mother let them out. They went out in the woods. They got lost. Then a lion came along. He smelled them. He ate them all up. Her mother called them in and they didn't come. They were in the lion's tummy. They didn't get out. They thought how bad they were. The mommy went out to look. She saw that lion and she saw that him ate them up. So she went closer to him. And the lion ate her up. Then the father came along and he found no one at the house; so he called out and then he went to look. And he saw the lion. And he got scared. And the lion ate him up.

11 (5)

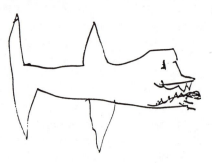

SHARK

12 (5)

IAMGOIGTOMIK
S AFTTERSCHOOL
AND WONT BE BAKTOL
5 O KLOOK
APIRIL 24HT

13 (6)

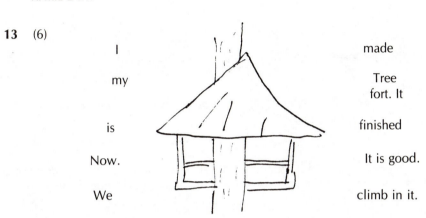

I   made

my   Tree
fort. It

is   finished

Now.   It is good.

We   climb in it.

(Note: illustration is reproduced.)

14 (6)

I got a new bike. It is good. And fast. My bike is blue
I ride my bike for a long time.
I play with my dad. I play darts with him.

15 (6)

Your moth is important too
it helps you talk
Duck's talk with
a Beke. That is wy your moth
is important.

16 (6)

One day I saw a bteefl butr fli and I sid I wil bring hr hom with me and thne
he wil lik me far avr.

17 (6)

Oenc a poen a tame
Tare was soem dolls
Taer naems aer Ann
   and Anndy

The valin is faetig
  on Ann from hrteg
  cuz Ann is a gial
Ha ha ha ha Ann is cot
She is said Anndy
Taea aer good said the
  valin.

18   (7)

It looked like teeth. It is shaped like teeth. Hail!

19   (7)

Mom I'm at Bill's house. I'm playing there. I will be back later.
Love, David.

20   (7)

At my hose I have an ofis upstars in my adick and its are printing ofis that we
print newspapers at. and we prent sports and we prent news and we even tipe
som. The end.

"ofis/BOSCHRIS/PRINTERMICHAEL/SECRETERE/CARRIE"

21   (7)

Wons thar was a sell. He was cappshrd.
But he could swim. So he puld and puld.
And he got louse. And a sharck came along.
But he was smart. So he dru a pictur
another syle. Then the sharck ayt the Rokc.

22   (7)

PETER RABBIT
Once upon a time there lived
a rabbit his name was peter. He
lived with his mother and father under the big tree. He has wiskers as
big as my little finger. Then his
mother died and his father did to.
He has blue eyes. He has long Pointed
ears and he is Pink.
    The End
    Rusty

23   (8)

  I like being eight and
nine because you get to do

stuff *exciting*. And join
clubs you want to be in.
And in brownies you fly
up to girl scouts. You are
trusted more often when you
are eight and nine years
old. you get to do things
that big people do.

24 (8)
Sunday after my hockey game I saw a guy in a red jacket and the police were
checking his pockets and his car and his coat pockets and it was exciting.

25 (8)
We went on a field trip and it was in the woods and it was called Morton Ar-
boretum and in it was insects. And we saw some ducks. And there was some
leafs that you would scratch the stem and it would smell. And there was poi-
son ivy. And there was all kinds of trees from all over the world. I thought it
was sort of fun. And then after than we went to another place that took very
fast. And after that we came home.

26 (9)
Tim do these things please.
In the morning:
Patch eye. Wash glasses.
Brush teeth. Get away from Mark.
get dressed. (practis clarenet)
make bed.

27 (9)
PAUL BUNYAN AND HIS OX
Most of you know Paul
Bunyan. He was the man
in the world. He liked
to work on roads. Did
you know he built a
bridge across the Pacific
Ocean. It only took him
one month. He started in
March and ended in Apirl.
Babe his blue ox cut the
trees. Then he hald them
down to the river Paul
Bunyan lifted them up.

Then he nailed them togetter.
He got into the muttle of
the Ocean and lifted it up.
    The
        End

28   (9)

IN THE WOODS
One day when I was walking in
the wood's I saw a great big thing.
I didn't know what it was.
So I started to walk toward it.
I saw that it was Paul Bunyan's
pipe. I knew it was his because
it was so big. Then I walked a
little bit more in the woods
And do you know what I saw
then? It was Paul Bunyan's
axe. So I walk ahead a little
bit. And then I saw Paul Bunyan
in person.
        The End

29   (10)

THE SUN
In the morning the sun is fiery red, surrounded by colors like pink, orange,
blue, and red. Hours go by. The sun is soon over head. Then once in a while
you see an eclipse. You dare not look because you know it will blind you.
Now it is over. The sun slips by with another rainbow. The world is dark, and
everyone sleeps.

30   (10)

TRY TO DIVE!
One time I went to swimming lessons. And at free time me and Sue decided to
dive off the high dive but we were both scared. Sue said if I dive off first then
she would. But I didn't believe her because last time long ago before I was in
middle prep she promised on the low bored but she didn't. But then I thought
she wouldn't be so mean. So then I did. I knew it was hard even to jump. I did
and I was so proud.

31   (10)

THE FIRST ELEPHANT
It was July 9, 423 B.C. when a little elf was swimming in Bula Bula creek.
Then all of the sudden a Bula Bula monster sprangout of the water. A Bula

Bula monster looks like a tuna can on its side with a car running over it. The little elf swam as fast as he could to shore but he was'nt fast enough The monster threw a rock at the elf and hit him in the head. The elf got so mad that he tryed to put a spell on the monster but rock took all his powers away. So he climbed up a tree. After the Bula Bula monster left he climbed doun. But without his powers he couldnt get home So he spent 180 years eating ants. After 180 years he got so big and fat you could'nt see around him. Later scientists found what happened so they colled it a elfant because it ate so many ants. Later his named was changed to an elephant.

By Craig

32 (10)

FLOWER POWER!
One dull day I sat down in our
racky rocker and started to read the News
Paper. On page 4 it said join the cools
at the Super Sonic Sack. So at 4 minutes
after 1 minute I went to the sack and I
was able to join. One Tuesday I went to
the Super Sonic Sack and we just
sat around and told jokes and riddles
and this cool kid said "Experience is a teacher,
But here's what makes me burn. He's always
teaching me things I do not care to learn.
On Wild Wednesday we went camping
to visit Flower Powered Boys!

33 (11)

CLARENCE THE CROSSEYED PRINCIPAL
One day there was a man
looking for a job. He went to school
to make a teleaphone call and he heard a
hello in the backround and it was a music
teacher a crosseyed one. He was terified
so he ran down the hall and the other prin
Mr. Peabody went out of saw him and he had
to sit in the corner with a dence cap on.
Then the music teacher started to sing and Mr.
Peabody went out of his mind.
    So then Clarence became principal
He made new rules for the school, some were
Do not walk in the halls, but run. The girls
couldn't ware long dresses and the boys had to ware
long hair. One day there was a fire alarmand

he put on a raincoat. So the town's people named
the school crosseyed school of clarenceville.

34   (11)

THE SECERET CAVE

One night when Kevin was sleeping he heard
the strangest sound. It souned like it was coming
from the Seceret Cave. So Kevin got up and
dressed and went to the Seceret Cave. When
he got to the cave there was a
bat in the doorway He was screaming. We scared him away. Then we
went in and looked around. Down
in the water hole was a young boy
He was dead. Someone had trough him
in the hole. And held him there for
a while. But who? Keven thought
Kevin went home and told his dad-
And he asked Kevin if he had touched
it. I said No. In the morning we
called the police.

35   (11)

WHAT A BLOCK!

My block is the most terrible block I've ever seen. There are at lease 25 or
30 narcartic people in my block. The cops come around there and tries to act
bad but I bet inside of them they are as scared as can be. They even had in the
papers that this block is the worst block, not in Manhattan but in New York
City. In the summer they don't do nothing except shooting, stabing, and fighting. They hang all over the stoops and when you say excuse me to them they
hear you but they just don't feel like moving. Some times they make me so
made that I feel like slaping them and stuffing a bag of garbage down their
throats. Theres only one policeman who can handle these people and we all
call him "Sunny." When he come around in his cop car the people run
around the corners, and he wont let anyone sit on the stoops. If you don't believe this story come around some time and you'll find out.

36   (12)

BASEBALL

It is summer
I am at Wrigly Feild (Home of the Cubs)
The sun is shining bright.
The ballgame is to begin right after the pledge.
Its the Cubs and the Giants yells

a fan in the crowd.
The First batter is up!
It is a realy important day for the Cubs.
I felt so good beCause I had never
been to a baseball game before.
It was real fun day for Me and I
hope to do it many times more.
(As it turned out the CUBS won
5 to 4. RON SANTO hit his 28 home-
run in the seventh inning. I yelled so
loud I had a sore throat after it.
Anyway the game was tied 4 to 4 and they
had to start extra Innings they went All the
way to the 11th inning beCause a run
was scored by AL SPANGLER
and the CUBS won. 5 to 4.
Baseball is Great.)

37   (12)

THE GARBAGE CAN
The garbage can is a neat little device.
You can throw everything in it.
The person that throws it in it gets all the credid but
really the poor tired, little, or big garbage can should
get all the credit for holding the garbage (junk). There
are green garbage cans and red ones. The Garbage's
only friend is the Garbage Man. Pretty soon Garbage
Ladies will come into being. As Patrick Henry once
said GIVE ME LIBERTY OR GIVE ME DEATH.

Yours Truly,
Your Favorite Garbage Can

38   (12)

TIME
Time is a tricky little varmit. People
get mixed up like this they say: Now
is Now and then is then so now then, then
is now and now is then so then and
now are the same. Do you follow me?
We say the Wright brothers were the first
people to Fly, but really Time was. You
can not feel time, or see it. Its Favorite
game is hide-and-seek which he plays
at night, in the day he is there and in

the night he isn't. Now then, if now is
then and then is now now and then are
then and now and then and now are now
and then, so now and then are then
and now so now and then are . . . .
. . . . NOW AND THEN!

39   (12)

   About one year ago I had a friend named David Bates. We were Pretty good
friends and we all ways went fishing to gether, and most off all We would go
sking, When
   I could not ski he tought me. So now I can ski very well. We allso would
always take a ride to Mc Donolds on are bikes, I also rember him for being
very Reasonable He just wasent the kind of kid that did what he wanted to do
   I remember one time when I was in a fight with two kid he came and
helped me a lot. There was even a time when he saved Another kids life when
he was caught under a boat

Note: 40–43 are responses to impromptu assignment: "Have you ever done anything
hateful or cruel?"

40   (14)

When I was a young tike. My little brother was in a baby stroller and I decided
to push him around. So I guess I got an Idea to push him down the stairs. And
I did. I felt bad that I had done such a thing.

41   (14)

I remember once when my brother wasn't a year old yet. He was standing up
in his playpen and I just got so jealous that I went over and smooshed his fingers on the top of the play pen. Now I feel sorry that I did that because he
couldn't do anything back.

42   (14)

One time my friend and I went fishing and he caught a big catfish. But on the
way home we got in a big fight so when I got home I took the catfish and I put
it on the road and cut it up and did burnouts on it with my bike, after he found
out, he got really red and I felt sorry for him.

43   (14)

Its vague in my memory but when ever I think about its almost as clear as if it
happened yesterday. It was when my father died. I was seven years old. It had
been a few days after his death and my family was beginning to cope with it. I
went to school and on my way home, the boys who lived down the street had
met me on the way and began to say things like "what did you do kill your

father?" Anyway it hurt me pretty bad so I wanted to get back. His mother had sort of a party for my mother and family at her house. I snuck up to his room and let all his hampsters out he had I think seven or eight. After I did it I felt good but I can't see why I did it to his hampsters and not him!

44 (14)

FAIRNESS

Once there was an old man who lived in a big city in a little apartment. He did not have any friends except for a little yellow bird that sang to him. He often let the bird out of his cage for exercise. One day the bird flew out of an open window. The old man was very sad and lonely.
He went outside searching for his bird. He looked everywhere. Days passed and he got sadder and sadder.
One bright summer morning he had to go to the store; on his way he saw a crowd of people; so he went over to see what was going on. There had been an accident. A boy and a brand new bike. The bike's wheel was all twisted and the kid was crying, but not hurt. He was scared.
The old man stepped forward and asked the boy if he could help. The old man, the boy and the bike went to the bike shop up the street—and there sitting on the counter was the old man's yellow bird!
The shop owner said the bird had flown in many days ago. Now the old man was happy.

45 (14)

THE FIVE DOLLARS

Once when I was 7, I saw my mother bag on the drawer. So I went to the drawer and look in the bag and seen a roll of money. I got five dollar out and told my boy and sister that I had got it. So we went to the store and bought lot's, and lots of candy. We eat most of the candy. Went we got home my mother was sitting on a chair she told us that she want to speak to us. We went over were she was and she ask use did we take five dollar out of her bag we said we didn't so she said OK. It was lunch time when this happen. So we went back to school and went we got home she ask us again we said no we didn't see the five dollar. Then she said that when she went to the store she asked Mrs. Heard did we bring five dollar and she said yes we did. She told use when was the rest of the money so I gave it to her. She told use to go up stairs. We went up stair and she beat use. While she was beating use my sister and brother was said they didn't take the money but she said you two went with him to spent the money. After she beat use I told her that I was going to run away. So I went out side and walked around the block and went back to the house. When I got in my mother was up stair in bed and my brother told me that my mother said I would come back home. So I did, So I did.

46 (15)

My bed distinguishes my room from any other room in my home or in any other house. Many people have single beds such as I have. Several people even have canopies over their beds, but I have a semi-canopy with long flowing white curtains which surround the head of the bed. The curtains are ruffled and at certain times of the year, artificial flowers are hung on the ruffles. My animal friends, a thirty-seven year old teddy, a black musical lamb with pink ears, and a light-gray elephant with red feet and a curled nose peer out from behind the curtains. They sit and play on a white eyelet bedspread. The lamb likes the flowered eyelet with the pink blanket showing through the holes. He also likes the maple with a fruitwood finish of which my bed is made.

My bed is the center of activity in my bedroom. On it, I may do my homework or watch television with my animal friends.

47 (15)

As I open one of the sliding doors in my room, the first unforgettable sight I see is the brown stained cherry wood on the walls. Across from the entrance there is three sun windows on the other wall is two more. My dresser and desk lay along the east wall. There is also a cozy little rug (circular shape) that covers the entire middle portion of the room. The room looks so clean homy I just like to sit in there and think of the days doings.

48 (15—same author as #46 above)

Summer school is a good idea because it provides extra learning opportunities as well as extra help. Washington High School has a plan whereby a student may take summer courses for the enjoyment of gaining knowledge or in order to make up credits for graduation. This plan seems best, because some students need extra help, while others yearn for advancement. Summer school gives one a chance to broaden his learning experiences before he enters the business-world.

Some drawbacks are presented by summer school, however. One could be working to save money for college, while broadening his experience with the business world. A job would help earn money for the future. It would also help give one an idea of life after schooling. It would help one decide on ones future occupation.

Both going to summer school and getting a job would help me.

49 (15—same author as #47 above)

I think that summer school souldent be forced to take if a person flunks a subject. I think when he or She gets in hi-school, they should realize the importance of a high school education and not to fool around and flunk. Because summer school is just another discouragement after another (flunking). If he or she still insists on flunking courses they should have their hi school education lengthened an extra year or so whatever it takes to complete it.

50 (16)

What do I feel like a nothing thats what I feel like. I can't do anything right I feel like the dimmest star of them all I feel like one that exploded and doesn't shine anymore. I always do bad in school. I get beat out of everything like Basketball or Football or baseball and everything and I don't have anyone to live up to.

51 (16)

WHAT THE PEARL MEANS TO ME

When Kino found the pearl he thought it would be the answer to all his problems. He and his family would live comfortably, the church and townspeople would accept him, but most of all his son, Coyotito, would go to school, then teach his people what he has learned. Instead of all this happiness the pearl brought evil upon them. The townspeople heard of the beautiful and priceless pearl and that horrid disease, greed, entered their hearts. They wanted to posses the pearl and they would do anything to get it. Even kill for it. Kino finally realizes the evil within the pearl when his son is killed. To rid himself of this evil he throws the pearl into the sea but he regains his soul and learns about good and evil.

52 (16)

BLESS THE BEASTS AND CHILDREN

by *Glendon Swarhout*

When Sally Z keept getting teased all the time About usiing the bath room in bed. The use to call him a sesse and he ran away and everyone came looking for him. They finely fond him. it was in the woods. it was cooled that night and everyone was shivering in the dark Cotton the leader of them He told them to listen for the radio that Sally Z took with his pillow. they fond him traping down the road.

the reason why I like this part is cause I think that its releistic and it probably would happend in real Life.

53 (16—same author as #52)

To my lovely, beautiful and gorgeous Ms. Arhok (Hope I spelled it right.)

Hello, how have you been doing. The last couple of nights I have been obsessed with you. I couldn't go to sleep trying to convince myself that you won't laugh at me if I give you this note and tell you how I feel about you. I really like you a lot. It may sound corny but when I first saw you I looked at your body and hoped you had a good personality behind it. Evidently you do. And it's killing me because I play the role of not being nervous. Whenever you're around me I get excited on the inside. (Biological Response) Well I hope you know what I'm talkin about. The main thing is, is that I would like to know you better. I mean more than the topic of school but yourself. I would tell you something that'll probably freak you out. You aren't old enough to laugh a little are you? You probably wouldn't want to be bothered with me. A lady of your stature probably has a lot of boyfriends. Give me a chance. We don't have to go together, but please don't hurt me in a way that we have to stay as we are. I want to be more. In a way I'm scared of girls I like, but since you're easy and nice to talk to you make me feel comfortable. Do you live by yourself or do you have a roomie. Why don't you let me see your place. Maybe I can have dinner with you. I know all this stuff seems sudden but you got to understand. I know I like you desperately. So give me a break baby.

Your Student

Bobby

P.S. Write back and put it into my folder. This is confidential.

54   (17)

Dear Editor,

I would like to express my feelings of regret and disappointment about the proposed busing plan to integrate schools. I regret that the schoolboard is doing such a poor job on such an important issue, by which many people may suffer; and I am disappointed with the solution they've come up with: busing.

Busing, I feel, is very disadvangageous not only because it uproots many students, but also because it will not solve the problem. In actuality the problem isn't integration but the quality of education.

The people who go to poor schools, the majority of whom are black, hispanics and other minority groups, will naturally want to be bussed to better schools. But who's to be bussed back? The people attending high quality schools won't want to give up their education for the sake of integration. Herein lies the crux of the problem, and also the answer.

Instead of spending millions of dollars busing students from low quality to high quality and visa-versa, why not spend that money to upgrade the low quality schools? I'm sure the cry for integration will be stilled if the quality education is equally available to everyone, everywhere.

Sincerely,
K. S.

COLLECTED BY:
Elaine Daniels, Lake Forest High School. (40–44, 50)
Harvey Daniels, National College of Education. (45, 51–54)

Nicholas Daniels. (11)

Wallace W. Douglas, "On Value in Children's Writing," in *Children and Writing in the Elementary School,* ed. Richard Larson (New York: Oxford University Press, 1975). (36–38, 46–49)—originally published in *English for the Junior High Years;* appears with the permission of the National Council of Teachers of English.

Lester Golub, "Stimulating and Receiving Children's Writing," in Larson. (22–23, 27–28, 31–34)—originally published in *Elementary English;* appears with the permission of the National Council of Teachers of English.

Donald Graves, University of New Hampshire. (17)

Robert Gundlach, Northwestern University. (12–16, 18–20, 24–26, 29–30)

Herb Kohl, "Teaching the Unteachable," in Larson. (35)

Evelyn Pitcher and Ernst Prelinger, *Children Tell Stories* (New York: International Universities Press, 1973). (1–10)

Steven Zemelman, Roosevelt University. (21, 39)

Bibliography

The following list of books about writing is divided into two parts. The first section has been compiled with both writing project participants and leaders in mind. It includes some of the most basic works on the theory and the everyday classroom practice of writing instruction, many of which we have frequently recommended to those asking for more information about a topic. The second list includes materials that provide further background; that are generally more detailed or more theoretical than the entries on the basic list. This second part of the bibliography also includes materials on the development, dynamics, and leadership of groups. Obviously, this larger listing will be most useful to project workshop leaders and to others who wish to broaden their background in writing pedagogy or teacher retraining. These too, however, have been selected for their practicality, and readers interested in any of the subjects covered will find texts that have important implications for the classroom. Works cited in the text of this book will of course also be included in the appropriate list below.

Participants' Bibliography

All About Letters (Urbana, Illinois: National Council of Teachers of English and the U.S. Postal Service).

Brannon, Lil, Melinda Knight and Vara Neverow-Turk, *Writers Writing* (Montclair, New Jersey: Boynton/Cook, 1982).

Cahill, Robert and Herbert Hrebic, *Stack the Deck* (Chicago: Stack the Deck, Inc., 1980).

Camp, Gerald, *Teaching Writing: Essays from the Bay Area Writing Project* (Montclair, New Jersey: Boynton/Cook, 1983).

Cooper, Charles R., ed., *The Nature and Measurement of Competency in English* (Urbana, Illinois: National Council of Teachers of English, 1981).

Cooper, Charles and Lee Odell, *Evaluating Writing* (Urbana, Illinois: National Council of Teachers of English, 1977).

Daiker, Donald A., Andrew Kerek and Max Morenberg, *The Writer's Options* (New York: Harper & Row, 1982).

Donovan, Timothy, and Ben W. McClelland, eds., *Eight Approaches to Teaching Composition* (Urbana, Illinois: National Council of Teachers of English, 1980).

Elbow, Peter, *Writing With Power* (New York: Oxford University Press, 1981).
———, *Writing Without Teachers* (New York: Oxford University Press, 1973).

Fader, Daniel, James Duggins, Tom Finn, and Elton McNeil, *The New Hooked On Books* (New York: Berkeley, 1976).

Glatthorn, Alan, *Writing in the Schools* (Reston, Virginia: National Association of Secondary School Principals, 1981).

Graves, Donald, *Writing: Teachers and Children at Work* (Exeter, New Hampshire: Heinemann Educational Books, 1983).

Hawkins, Thom, *Group Inquiry Techniques for Teaching Writing* (Urbana, Illinois: National Council of Teachers of English, 1976).

Hennings, Dorothy and Barbara Grant, *Written Expression in the Language Arts* (New York: Teachers College Press, 1981).

Hillocks, George, *Observing and Writing* (Urbana, Illinois: National Council of Teachers of English, 1975).

Johannessen, Larry R., Elizabeth A. Kahn, and Carolyn Calhoun Walter, *Designing and Sequencing Prewriting Activities* (Urbana, Illinois: National Council of Teachers of English, 1982).

Kirby, Dan, and Tom Liner, *Inside Out: Developmental Strategies for Teaching Writing* (Montclair, New Jersey: Boynton/Cook, 1981).

Klaus, Carl and Nancy Jones, eds., *Courses for Change in Writing* (Montclair, New Jersey: Boynton/Cook, 1984).

Koch, Carl and James M. Brazil, *Strategies for Teaching the Composition Process* (Urbana, Illinois: National Council of Teachers of English, 1978).

Koch, Kenneth, *Wishes, Lies and Dreams* (New York: Vintage Books, 1976).

Larson, Richard, ed., *Children and Writing in the Elementary School* (New York: Oxford University Press, 1975).

Macrorie, Ken, *Telling Writing* (New York: Hayden, 1970).

Mayher, John, Gordon Pradl, and Nancy Lester, *Learning to Write/Writing to Learn* (Montclair, New Jersey: Boynton/Cook, 1983).

Moffett, James, *Active Voice: A Writing Program Across the Curriculum* (Montclair, New Jersey: Boynton/Cook, 1981).

Moffett, James and Betty Jane Wagner, *Student-Centered Language Arts and Reading, K–13* (Boston: Houghton Mifflin, 1976).

Murray, Donald, *A Writer Teaches Writing* (Boston: Houghton Mifflin, 1968).

Myers, Miles, and James Gray, *Theory and Practice in the Teaching of Composition* (Urbana, Illinois: National Council of Teachers of English, 1983).

Ponsot, Marie and Rosemary Deen, *Beat Not the Poor Desk: Writing—What to Teach, How to Teach It, and Why* (Montclair, New Jersey: Boynton/Cook, 1982).

Tchudi, Stephen, *Teaching Writing in the Content Areas;* Elementary with Susan Tchudi; Middle School with Margie Huerta; High School with Joanne Yates (Washington, D.C.: National Education Association, 1983).

Weaver, Constance, *Grammar for Teachers: Perspectives and Definitions* (Urbana, Illinois: National Council of Teachers of English, 1979).

Wolsch, Robert A., and Lois Wolsch, *From Speaking to Writing to Reading: Relating the Arts of Communication* (New York: Teachers College Press, 1982).

Leaders' Bibliography

Bandler, Richard, and John Grinder, *Frogs into Princes* (Moab, Utah: Real People Press, 1979).

Benjamin, Alfred, *Behavior in Small Groups* (Boston: Houghton Mifflin, 1978).

Bereiter, Carl, "Development in Writing," in *Cognitive Processes in Writing,* ed. Lee W. Gregg and Erwin R. Steinberg (Hillsdale, New Jersey: Lawrence Erlbaum Associates, 1979).

Berthoff, Ann, ed., *Reclaiming the Imagination: Philosophical Perspectives for Writers and Teachers of Writing* (Montclair, New Jersey: Boynton/Cook, 1984).

Bissex, Glenda, *Gnys at Wrk: A Child Learns to Write and Read* (Cambridge, Massachusetts: Harvard University Press, 1980).

Bradford, Leland, ed., *Group Development* (San Diego: University Associates, 1978).

Britton, James, *Language and Learning* (Coral Gables, Florida: University of Miami Press, 1970).

——, *Prospect and Retrospect: Selected Essays* (Montclair, New Jersey: Boynton/Cook, 1983).

Britton, James, et al., *The Development of Writing Abilities 11–18* (New York: MacMillan, 1975).

Burling, Robbins, *English in Black and White* (New York: Holt, Rinehart and Winston, 1973).

Calkins, Lucy, *Lessons from a Child* (Exeter, New Hampshire: Heinemann Educational Books, 1983).

Cedaline, Anthony, *Job Burnout in Public Education: Symptoms, Causes, and Survival Skills* (New York: Teachers College Press, 1982).

Coles, William, *The Plural I: The Teaching of Writing* (Montclair, New Jersey: Boynton/Cook, 1978).

Cooper, Charles, and Lee Odell, *Research on Composing* (Urbana, Illinois: National Council of Teachers of English, 1978).

Daniels, Harvey, *Famous Last Words: The American Language Crisis Revisited* (Carbondale, Illinois: Southern Illinois University Press, 1983).

Dixon, John, *Growth Through English: Set in the Perspective of the Seventies* (London: Oxford University Press, 1975).

Eiben, Ray, and Al Millren, *Educational Change: A Humanistic Approach* (San Diego: University Associates, 1976).

Emig, Janet, *The Web of Meaning: Essays on Writing, Thinking, Learning, and Teaching* (Montclair, New Jersey: Boynton/Cook, 1938).

Fulwiler, Toby, and Art Young, eds., *Language Connections: Writing and Reading Across the Curriculum* (Urbana, Illinois: National Council of Teachers of English, 1982).

Gere, Anne Ruggles, and Eugene Smith, *Attitudes, Language and Change* (Urbana, Illinois: National Council of Teachers of English, 1979).

Graves, Richard, ed., *Rhetoric and Composition: A Sourcebook for Teachers and Writers* (Montclair, New Jersey: Boynton/Cook, 1984).

Gundlach, Robert, *How Children Learn to Write* (Exeter, New Hampshire: Heinemann Educational Books, to be published in 1985).

Knoblauch, C. H., and Lil Brannon, *Rhetorical Traditions and the Teaching of Writing* (Montclair, New Jersey: Boynton/Cook, 1984).

Labov, William, *Language in the Inner City: Studies in the Black English Vernacular* (Philadelphia: University of Pennsylvania Press, 1972).

Martin, Nancy, *Mostly About Writing: Selected Essays* (Montclair, New Jersey: Boynton/Cook, 1983).

Martin, Nancy, Pat D'Arcy, Bryan Newton, and Robert Parker, *Writing and Learning Across the Curriculum 11–16* (Montclair, New Jersey: Boynton/Cook, 1976).

Moffett, James, *Coming on Center* (Montclair, New Jersey: Boynton/Cook, 1982).

Moffett, James, *Teaching the Universe of Discourse* (Boston: Houghton Mifflin, 1968).

Mohr, Marian, *Revision: The Rhythm of Meaning* (Montclair, New Jersey: Boynton/Cook, 1984).

Murray Donald, *Learning by Teaching: Selected Articles on Writing and Teaching* (Montclair, New Jersey: Boynton/Cook, 1983).

National Writing Project Evaluation Portfolio (Berkeley, California: National Writing Project, 1983).

Ohmann, Richard, *English in America* (New York: Oxford University Press, 1975).

Pfeiffer, William, and John Jones, *A Handbook of Structured Experiences for Human Relations Training*, Volume I, Revised Edition (San Diego: University Associates, 1969).

Pitcher, Evelyn, and Ernst Prelinger, *Children Tell Stories* (New York: International Universities Press, 1973).

Rogers, Carl, *Freedom to Learn* (Columbus, Ohio: Charles E. Merrill, 1983).

Shaughnessy, Mina, *Errors and Expectations* (New York: Oxford University Press, 1977).

Siegel, Muffy, and Toby Olson, *Writing Talks: Views on Teaching Writing from Across the Professions* (Montclair, New Jersey: Boynton/Cook, 1983).

Taylor, Denny, *Family Literacy* (Exeter, New Hampshire: Heinemann Educational Books, 1983).

Tchudi, Steven and Susan Tchudi, *An Introduction to the Teaching of Writing* (New York: Wiley, 1981).

Thayer, Louis, ed., *Fifty Strategies for Experiential Learning: Book One* (San Diego: University Associates, 1976).

———, ed., *Fifty Strategies for Experiential Learning: Book Two* (San Diego: University Associates, 1981).

245